Henry Holman

English National Education

A sketch of the rise of public elementary schools in England

Henry Holman

English National Education
A sketch of the rise of public elementary schools in England

ISBN/EAN: 9783337097219

Printed in Europe, USA, Canada, Australia, Japan

Cover: Foto ©Suzi / pixelio.de

More available books at **www.hansebooks.com**

English National Education

A Sketch of the
Rise of Public Elementary Schools in England

By

H. HOLMAN, M.A.

Formerly Scholar of Gonville and Caius College, Cambridge
and one time
Professor of Education at the University College of Wales, Aberystwyth
Author of "An Introduction to Education" &c.

LONDON
BLACKIE & SON, LIMITED, 50 OLD BAILEY, E.C.
GLASGOW AND DUBLIN
1898

Preface

Not wealth but the power to produce wealth is the true measure of the commercial prosperity of a country. Not men but minds are the first requisites for superiority in production. Not handcraft but braincraft is the prime source of productive excellence. Not a worker but an intelligent worker is the mainstay of the industrial world. Not a machine but the creative and guiding intelligence is the greatest economizer. Mind is the great parent machine, and the great master machine. The mechanical is never the highest expression of the rational. Therefore, the best capital of a nation is the brain-power of its people.

What did Prussia do when humbled to the dust by France? Reformed her schools. What did France do when crushed by Germany? Reformed her schools. The competition of nations is a battle of minds. Not the mere fighter, but the thinker is victor to-day. It would appear that the French were not less heroic, but worse organized, in their last great war. Germany is our rival in trade because she is our superior in schools. Just as Waterloo was said to have been won in the playing-fields (and class-rooms—epigrams are always incomplete) of Eton, so the world's commerce is being won and lost in our schools.

If this be so, our country can have, in practical affairs, no higher interest, no supremer duty, and no more valuable investment than is to be found in securing an unequalled system of national education. It behoves every intelligent citizen, therefore, to know what is involved in this matter, what has been done, and what is still required. We ought to concern ourselves very seriously about what is being done to raise to its highest powers the collective reason of the nation, by developing the minds of the individuals; and whether we are most effectively cultivating, improving, and expanding the rational resources—the chief beginning and chief end of national greatness—of the kingdom.

The aim of this volume is to supply this knowledge, with

regard to our public elementary schools, so far as that is possible within the limits allowed by a small handbook. Only the main stream of development has been followed, and even that has had to be treated somewhat slightly in parts. The earlier periods have been most fully treated, because the more recent are likely to be more or less familiar to the readers, and because it is the beginnings of things which most often afford us the truest insight into their nature and value. To the reformer such knowledge is indispensable, or he may destroy what he most desires to develop; whilst even the revolutionist will best know what not to do, after his undoing, by a study of the real nature of what he means to improve out of existence. There is so preponderating an amount of the past in the present, that we can only fully know the latter through the former.

There is, therefore, an endeavour in the following pages to set forth the ideals which determined the actions of those who built up the present system of public elementary schools, and the actual steps which they took to realize their aims. The inner life of the school: its organization, methods, teachers, subjects, and scholars; the inner intentions, so far as revealed by words and deeds, of the promoters of schools; and the real results achieved, are the main topics which we seek to describe. Whether the country has been establishing a system of national education, or only a partial system of schools, and whether we are strengthening the mind or only storing the memory, are questions which have to be frequently asked whilst reading the history of its efforts. Schools, scholars, and teachers are indispensable, but, having got them, it then becomes the more important that we should have a scientific system of education—that is, a method of dealing with the mental powers, based upon a scientific knowledge of them, and designed to develop and perfect them—and that our well-trained teachers should be scientific educators. These would seem to be the standards of criticism by which to judge the value of what has already been done, and what remains to be accomplished for national education.

H. H.

WOODFORD GREEN,
April, 1898.

Contents

CHAPTER I
The Reign of the Voluntary System - - - - 9

CHAPTER II
The Reign of the Voluntary System—Continued - - 28

CHAPTER III
The Days of Doles - - - - - - - 52

CHAPTER IV
The Committee of Council on Education - - - 66

CHAPTER V
The Committee of Council on Education—Continued - 85

CHAPTER VI
A Semi-state System - - - - - - - 114

CHAPTER VII
A Semi-state System—Continued - - - - 140

CHAPTER VIII
Codes and Cram - - - - - - - 161

CHAPTER IX
The Partial Reign of Law - - - - - - 181

CHAPTER X
The Partial Reign of Law—Continued - - - 207

CHAPTER XI
Retrospect and Prospect - - - - - - 235

INDEX - - - - - - - - 252

The business of education is not, as I think, to make them perfect in any one of the sciences, but so to open and dispose their minds, as may best make them capable of any, when they shall apply themselves to it.—JOHN LOCKE.

The primary principle of education is the determination of the pupil to self-activity—the doing nothing for him which he is able to do for himself.—SIR WILLIAM HAMILTON.

In education the process of self-development should be encouraged to the fullest extent.—HERBERT SPENCER.

English National Education.

Chapter I.

The Reign of the Voluntary System.

Primary education, for the children of the working-classes, did not exist, in any general sense, till the beginning of the eighteenth century. It is true that almost all the grammar and other endowed schools, so freely founded during the sixteenth century and earlier, made provision for the education of "poor scholars". But either this had never meant much more than exhibitions, as we should now call them, for the children of those whose parents' means had become very much reduced, or it may have been intended only for a few bright and fortunate individuals, who, by some happy accident or good fortune, came under the favourable notice of those who were able to secure their admission to a school. Thus it is said that George Abbott, who afterwards became Vice-Chancellor of Oxford University and Archbishop of Canterbury, was first brought into notice because of some remarkable circumstances attending his birth. He was born in 1562, and his mother was the wife of a poor clothworker at Guildford. Before his birth, his mother dreamt that, if she could eat a jack or a pike, her child would become a great man. When taking a pail of water from the river which flowed by the house, she found therein a jack, which she forthwith cooked, and ate nearly the whole of it. The matter was noised abroad, and several persons of quality, on hearing of it, offered to stand sponsors at the child's christening. The offer was gladly accepted, and, doubtless as a result of this, the boy was afterwards sent to a Free Grammar School in the town, founded by a grocer of London, in 1553, for thirty "of the poorest men's sons" of Guildford, to be taught to read and write English, and cast accounts perfectly, so that they should be fitted for apprentices. From the grammar school he went to Balliol College, Oxford. His elder brother was also fortunate, and became Bishop of Salisbury; whilst his younger brother became a rich London merchant, Lord Mayor, and member of Parliament.

But such remarkable successes were very few and far between, and only serve to impress upon one the neglected condition and profound ignorance of the great majority. Speaking of the general condition of things at this period (the sixteenth century), with regard to the education of the children of the very poor, Mr. A. F. Leach, a writer of great authority, says: "We may approach this matter from another point of view, and ask whether it is likely that, in days when the labouring classes were still serfs, and Parliament actually petitioned the Crown against their being allowed to go to the Universities or Schools, that bishops and lords and county gentlemen would, at great expense and labour, found educational institutions for the benefit of half a dozen poor choristers? The poor who are spoken of in these old foundations are not the poor in our sense, the destitute poor, the unsuccessful among the labouring classes, but the relative poor, the poor relations of the upper classes. That occasionally bright boys were snatched up out of the ranks of the real poor and turned into clerics, to become lawyers, civil servants, bishops, is not to be doubted. But it was the middle class, whether country or town, the younger sons of the nobility and farmers, the lesser landholders, the prosperous tradesmen, who created a demand for education, and furnished the occupants of Grammar Schools."

The same writer says that of 159 schools existing at

the time of the Reformation, of which records still remain, 93 were Grammar Schools which were not free, 21 were Free Grammar Schools, 23 were Song Schools (in which boys were trained for church choirs, and received a kind of superior elementary education), and 22 were Elementary Schools. Now these last named were by no means schools for the very poor, but schools in which only reading, writing, and arithmetic were taught. In some of them only reading was taught, in others only writing, and in others only arithmetic. The class of pupils who attended such schools may be judged of by the fact that Sir Isaac Newton was sent to a village school, where he was taught reading, writing, and arithmetic; and that the great Dr. Johnson was first taught reading by a dame who kept a school for little children in Lichfield. Primary schools such as these appear to have been first established in the fourteenth century; but Mr. Herbert Spencer holds that there were elementary schools in the villages as early as the eleventh and twelfth centuries.

But most of the really primary schools which existed were entirely private in their nature, and there seems to be no evidence of any endowment or corporate control of them, except in so far as we might include the Song Schools. Indeed, the nearest approach to anything like state education was in the reign of Alfred the Great, who is said to have given one-eighth of his whole revenue to founding a school for the sons of the nobles. He is also believed to have re-established many of the old monastic and episcopal schools. It was his desire that "all the youth of England . . . should be well able to read English". He compelled every person of rank or substance, who, either from age or want of capacity, was unable to teach himself to read, to send to school either his son or a kinsman, or, if he had neither, a servant, so that at least he might be read to by some one. Thus some at least of the very poor doubtless received an education from the state in those days.

Also, inasmuch as some of the Grammar Schools were established by royal charter, and sometimes endowed from the royal exchequer, or were under some kind of public control as to their endowments, they may be said to have been semi-state institutions. And since, in some cases, little more than reading and writing, and Latin, with a little arithmetic, were taught, these were hardly more than primary schools. Few besides the clergy and those belonging to the learned professions, such as law and medicine, knew much, if anything, of Latin. Thus, Dekker, a dramatist who lived and wrote at the beginning of the seventeenth century, makes one of his characters, a man of substance, who is asked, "Can you read and write, then?" reply, "As most of your gentlemen do—my bond has been taken with my mark at it".

From the earliest times there have been schools, conducted by the clergy, in which the sons of the very poor might find a place and obtain the learning which might lead to their rising to fame and fortune. For example, it is recorded that Sampson, Abbot of St. Edmund's, a son of the people, rose to be a bishop, and became a peer of parliament, during the reign of Richard I. But such opportunities were almost wholly confined to those who were desirous of entering the church, and were thought capable of being of service to her interests. In fact, up to quite recent times, the ranks of the clergy were largely recruited from the sons of the labouring poor, in the same way as the clergy of the Roman Catholic Church are, for example, in Ireland at the present day. In former times education was, for the most part, of the church, by the church, and for the church; and it was only as the advantage, or necessity, of extending it to the laity, for the purpose of confirming and expanding the influence and authority of the church, was realized, that knowledge was more generally imparted. A very striking piece of evidence of this limitation is given us in the old law called the Benefit of Clergy, which was passed in the eleventh century. By this law a cleric could claim to be handed over from a secular to a clerical court. After a time the ability to read was considered sufficient evidence to establish the claim to this privilege, which was not finally abolished till 1706.

The Reign of the Voluntary System. 13

Two other ways in which a few of the children of the people received what may be called a semi-state education may be mentioned. The monasteries were the homes of industry as well as of knowledge. Carpenters, smiths, shoemakers, bakers, farm servants, writing clerks, and the like, were attached to monastic institutions; and these posts were naturally filled by the sons of the poor, who received more or less technical training and instruction, which would, doubtless, sometimes include something in the way of reading, writing, and arithmetic. Thus the Abbot Sampson, mentioned above, is said to have replied to one who asked him for a benefice, "Thy father was master of the schools, and at the time when I was a poor clerk he granted me freely and in charity an entrance to the school and the means of learning; now I, for the sake of God, do grant to thee what thou dost ask". The second way in which some gained an education was by going as the servant of their lord's son while he was at the university. They were known as sizars at the university, and had to perform the usual menial services of personal attendants. But they also had the opportunity of sharing in their master's education, and were able to take degrees.

Of the aims and methods of the teachers we have only partial knowledge, but such glimpses as we get of them show how meagre and limited were the aims, and how mechanical and forbidding were the methods. An old writer, who claims to set out a new and better way, in a book on the work of grammar schools published in 1612, thus describes the common way of teaching pupils how to read: "That which I take to be everywhere: to teach and hear them so oft over till they can say a lesson, and so to a new". That is to say, imitation and repetition (which is now called the look-and-say method) were the means relied upon. It is not surprising that he further tells us that it took some pupils two or three years before they could read English well, whilst others were six or seven years under instruction, and yet failed to do this. Of writing, he remarks that the best scholars wrote very ill, so that it had become a received opinion "that a good scholar can hardly be a good penman".

After leaving school they had to be taught by a scrivener before they were fit for any trade in which writing was required. The following account of the method employed is given by a schoolmaster of the day: "I have daily set them copies, so well as I could; which hath been no small toil unto me: or else I have caused some of my scholars, or some others to do it. Also I have made them now and then to write some copies; and it may be, I have corrected them for writing so badly, or guided some of their hands, or showed them how to amend their letters. This I take to be the most that is done in schools ordinarily; unless any do procure scriveners, to teach in their towns: whereof we find no small inconveniences" (he was a country schoolmaster). It will be noticed that he practically admits that he is a very poor writer, and that the help he gives his pupils is very irregular and incomplete.

When he comes to deal with the way to teach Latin translation this writer urges that the pupil should be first got to clearly understand the matter of the lesson, before he deals with the words in which it is expressed. For, says he, "it would cause all things to be gotten much more speedily, laid up more safely, and kept more surely in the memory". And he adds that the pupils are "to learn all so perfectly, as the former may be instead of a schoolmaster to the latter". That is, the learner is to get power and skill from his work, and not merely a memory story of learning. But the common method is: "I think it to be all that is done in most of our country schools; To give lectures to the several forms, or cause some scholars to do it. And therein first to read them over their lecture, then to construe them, and in the lowest forms to parse them. So when they come to say; to hear them whether they can read, say without book, construe and parse. More as I take it, is not much used, for the understanding and making use of them." In all things the chief result desired seems to have been a mere mechanical memory-storing, and it is not surprising to find a country schoolmaster complaining that "when I have taken a great deal of pains, and have made my scholars very ready in construing and parsing; yet come and examine them in those things a quarter of a year after, they will be many of them as though they had never learned them, and the best far to seek".

Another contemporary writer says: "I would have lads taught the reasons of things and the meaning of what they commit to memory. This will make them learn it with more delight and retain it with the greater steadfastness. Besides, otherwise they are unworthily dealt with, who having rational souls are only taught as parrots are. . . . It would tend to exercise and improve their judgments, and by degrees help them to understand other things."

It is worth while to notice that the idea of setting one scholar to teach another—a learned parrot to help an unlearned one—is the resource of overworked ignorance. Later on it was exalted into a great discovery, and organized as a system of immense practical value in the practical work of teaching.

The real aim of the grammar schools was to produce classical scholars. Latin was the subject which from first to last held the chief place. Latin accidence, construing, translation, composition, themes, and verses took by far the greater part of the pupils' time and energy. Greek was taught after Latin, and sometimes Hebrew was added. It is true that reading and writing were taught, but only under protest, and because of absolute necessity. Bible history and the Catechism were learnt, and the scholars were, in some cases, taken to church by the master and usher, on Sundays, and required to take notes of the sermon. Arithmetic was studied only to a very limited extent, anything further being regarded rather in the light of an extra for those who were intended for trade. Very little, if anything at all, was done in giving instruction in music. If, therefore, we leave out the classical teaching, which indeed is hardly necessary, so meagre and inefficient was it for most of the scholars, the grammar schools were the primary schools up to the end of the seventeenth century. One writer of authority goes so far as to say, that in the grammar schools, during the Middle Ages "the average acquirements were limited to reading and writing, to which, in the cathedral schools, there were added chanting, and an elementary knowledge of Latin. . . . Those who had to earn a living went to writing schools to learn good hands and accounts." But whilst this may be true of the worst of them, the best appear to have done almost, if not quite, as good work as the universities of the time.

Whilst parents controlled their children with great formality and some severity, schoolmasters managed them with the greatest severity and very little formality. Well might they have said: Thy father chastises thee with whips, but I will chastise thee with scorpions. All testimonies agree in painting the master as the slave-driver of the school. Dr. Busby, the master of Westminster School, lives in history as the champion flogger, but he only excelled amongst experts, and was by no means without rivals, even in much later times. Dr. Wooll, who immediately preceded Dr. Arnold at Rugby, was an unsparing user of the birch, and though a small man, was powerful in stripes, so much so that it was grimly suggested that the motto for the room in which the rods were kept should be, "Great Cry and Little Wool". Flogging was considered a necessary part of teaching, for the rod was the dullard's quickener. "Either learn; or depart; or in the third place be flogged", was the motto written (in Latin) on the school wall at Winchester. Not even the king's son seems to have escaped, for it is said that the tutor of James I., when he was a boy, gave him a severe whipping for disturbing him whilst at his studies.

An old writer (1612) says he "utterly dislikes that extreme severity whereby all things are done in very many schools, and the whole government maintained only by continual and terrible whipping". He urges that children be "rather trained up by all loving means of gentle encouragement, praise and fair dealing, than with buffeting and blows, or continual and cruel whipping, scorning, and reviling". It appears that some teachers always had a rod in their hands. The seals of public schools, and old prints of school life, of the time, display a birch or rod as the proper symbol of education. A lady writing to the tutor of her son, who was fifteen years of age, begs that "if the boy has not done well, he will truly belash him till he will mend". An exhortation which seems quite unnecessary, judging by the fact that the parents at Farmouth sometimes complained to the magistrates that their children were in "danger of losing their senses, lives, and limbs", because of the severity of the treatment at school. Indeed, every school reformer of the time gives very great and special attention to the evils of too great severity, and the advantages of kindness and encouragement in schools.

An amusing story is told of one of England's greatest schoolmasters, Richard Mulcaster (sixteenth century), and school punishment. He was, says the writer (probably Thomas Wateridge of the Middle Temple, in the time of James I.), "somewhat too severe, and given to insult too much over children that he taught. He being one day about whipping a boy . . . out of his insulting humour, he stood pausing a little . . . and then a merry conceit taking him, he said: 'I ask the banns of matrimony between this boy . . . of such a parish, on the one side, and Lady Birch of this parish, on the other side; and if any man can show any lawful cause why they should not be joined together, let him speak, for this is the last time of asking'. A good sturdy boy, and of a quick conceit, stood up, and said: 'Master, I forbid the banns'. The master, taking this in dudgeon, said: 'Yes, sirrah, and why so?' The boy answered: 'Because all parties are not agreed'; whereat Mulcaster, liking that witty answer, spared the one's fault and the other's presumption."

The kind of men who were the teachers of these early days is well shown by Thomas Fuller (born 1608), who says: "There is scarce any profession in the commonwealth more necessary, which is so slightly performed. The reasons whereof I conceive to be these: 'First, young scholars make this calling their refuge; yea, perchance, before they have taken any degree in the University, commence schoolmasters in the country; as if nothing else were required to set up this profession, but only a rod and a ferula. Secondly, others, who are able, use it only as a passage to better preferment; to patch the rents in their present fortune, till they can provide a new one, and betake themselves to some more gainful calling. Thirdly, they are disheartened from doing their best, with the miserable reward which in some places they receive, being masters to the children, and slaves to their parents. Fourthly, being grown rich, they grow negligent, and scorn to touch the school, but by proxy of an usher.

"Some men had as lieve be school-boys as schoolmasters—to be tied to the school, as Cooper's dictionary and Scapula's lexicon are chained to the desk therein; and though great scholars, and skilful in other arts, are bunglers in this."

John Aubrey writes: "In 1634 I was entered in Latin grammar by Mr. R. Latimer, a delicate and little person, rector of Leigh-de-la-Mere, who had an easy way of teaching; and every time we asked leave to go forth, we had a Latin word from him, which at our return we were to tell him again: which in a little while amounted to a good number of words". The schools were often in the hands of the clergyman of the parish, who frequently handed over this part of his work to an ill-paid, and worse qualified, usher. But this is hardly a matter for surprise, according to the reason which a writer at the end of the sixteenth century gives. He writes thus: "Considering the prudence and learning which is requisite in one that will teach all this, and the toil that necessarily accompanies it, together with the small encouragement that is given to such who spend themselves in this work; none will undertake this employment who are well fitted for it. . . . It cannot but be owned how slightly they are esteemed in most places with us, though in ancient times so highly honoured; how mean and sordid their salary is in many great towns, and some considerable cities, and such as is so far from encouraging a deserving person, that it is scarce sufficient to provide bread for his family, without his undertaking some cure of souls together with his school, by which he can do neither of them well." In-

The Reign of the Voluntary System. 19

deed, some of the clergy were so poor that they had to engage in manual work to obtain a decent livelihood.

It was reckoned the greatest success if the pupils were fitted for the universities; which could hardly have been a very difficult task, since boys of fifteen and even younger were admitted in those days. And yet a writer of the time says: "If all our grammar-schools were provided with masters fit for that employment (for every learned man is not qualified to make a good schoolmaster), I think it no presumption to say, that double the number that now is, might be trained up for the universities".

To find an explanation for such a condition of things as described above we must inquire into what was probably the general view of the purpose of education. Now there cannot be much doubt that, in the very early times, when learning was almost wholly in the hands of the church, schools were simply intended to train up, in such knowledge as was necessary, those who were designed for the service of the church. At first very little more than the power to read was required. It is said that, "at the period of the Reformation, the rank and file of the country clergy, who had received their education at the monasteries, could do little more than read. Herein lay one of the difficulties of the Reformation. The ignorance of many of the clergy was so great that they could not read the new offices. In the performance of their duties they reverted to memory, and preferred to say the old prayers which they knew by heart." To give learning to the laity generally was thought to be a sure means of bringing about heresy, and many and great dangers to the church and the state. It is true that some of the sons of the rich and powerful were taught in the monastic schools, but these were very few, and they were received into the schools chiefly because of their probable future position and influence in the state, factors which the church could not afford to neglect.

This idea that learning is a foe to religion seems to have been at the bottom of the church's action in opposing any great advance, even when it was forced to recognize the necessity of educating the people as a means of keeping them faithful to its doctrines. Yet the judicious Hooker wrote, in his great work on *The Laws of Ecclesiastical Polity* (1594), these notable words: "Education and instruction are the means, the one by use, the other by precept, to make our natural faculty of reason both the better and the sooner able to judge rightly between truth and error, good and evil. Theology, what is it but the science of things divine? What science can be attained unto without the help of natural discourse and reason? 'Judge you of that which I speak', saith the Apostle. In vain were it to speak anything of God, but that by reason men are able somewhat to judge of that they hear, and by discourse to discern how consonant it is to truth."

But to the laity was given some measure of technical training and instruction, for the monks and priests were skilful handicraftsmen, and to every monastery were attached carpenters, smiths, shoemakers, millers, bakers, and farm servants, who were the industrial trainers of the period.

It was the Reformation which gave the greatest of all practical helps to the progress of learning, at the beginning of the sixteenth century. The personal pleasure of the king was, by a happy chance, the means of indirectly working the public good. Henry VIII. despoiled the monasteries partly under the pretence of their neglect of education, and the promise, in the bill for the dissolution of the greater monasteries, that provision should be made to bring up the children in learning. And although he shamelessly failed to carry out this undertaking in anything like a proper manner, having founded only ten grammar schools during the thirty-five years of his reign, yet the fact that men's minds were turned to the subject, and to the necessity of providing for themselves, led to the endowment of fifty other grammar schools by private individuals. Moreover, the complete dependence on the church and the clergy was done away with, and though the religious motive was still the ruling idea in the schools, yet it was the laymen who provided funds for carrying them on, and took a large share in their management.

The struggle between the new order and the old in religion made the spread of learning a very urgent and important matter, for the new ideas had to be brought home to the people at large if they were to prevail. Henry did a very wise and successful thing in issuing a warrant permitting all his subjects to read the Bible in their own tongue, and inflicting punishment on any who hindered them. Many parents put their children to school so that they might be able to take them to a church and hear them read from the Bible that was kept there, chained to a desk. Even adults and old people took lessons in reading.

Education was still of a religious character, but from a political motive. It was desired to make the people Protestant in their religion. By the Act of Uniformity teachers had to be licensed by the bishop, and were commanded to make the church catechism the beginning and foundation of their instruction given in the schools. Bishops were ordered to make yearly visits to all schools in their dioceses, for the purpose of examining if the schools were well kept, and the teachers diligent and orthodox in their work. Curates had to call on their parishioners every six weeks to teach their children the Catechism; and churchwardens were to report whether any schoolmasters taught without a license. Thus education remained wholly under the control of the church, and its main purpose was the very practical and limited one of training up orthodox churchmen. Roman Catholic schoolmasters and teachers were imprisoned, or executed, and even some Puritan Nonconformists met with similar fates. The Canons of 1604 which renewed the command that schoolmasters must receive a license from the bishop, and accept the thirty-nine articles, also set forth that their duty was to teach the Catechism, and train their pupils with texts of Holy Scripture, and to take them to church. No mention is made in the Canons of the command given in the acts of Edward VI. and Elizabeth, that the poor should be taught to read and write. Education was thus cribbed, cabined, and confined, right up to the beginning of the eighteenth century, and even then the old laws were unrepealed, though not enforced. It is not surprising that whilst men were so intent on limiting education to the imparting of a particular kind of knowledge, they gave no attention to the idea of cultivating the powers of mind for their own sake. In fact, everything possible was done to prevent freedom of thought and mental development amongst the people. Religious controversies have thus delayed and degraded our national education.

Doubtless most of the mechanical methods employed in teaching were also due to the fact that the schools were so entirely in the hands of the church. The Jesuits, who were, without question, the best organizers and most successful practical teachers of the sixteenth and seventeenth centuries—their order being "especially for the purpose of instructing boys and ignorant persons in the Christian religion"—had laid down a cast-iron system, for which they trained their teachers, and from which they allowed not the slightest departure. Every teacher was carefully watched with a view to preventing any change in the traditional plans and methods. Lectures were given to the pupils, who were required to remember the substance of them, and to learn the rules of grammar, and parts of the classical authors, by heart. Certain boys in a class were chosen to repeat their memory tasks to the master, and then, in his presence, to hear the other boys repeat theirs, whilst the master was correcting written exercises. The end, which they definitely set before themselves and their pupils, was to strengthen and store the memory. And, as Mr. Quick has said, "originality and independence of mind, love of truth for its own sake, the power of reflecting, and of forming correct judgments, were not merely neglected—they were suppressed in the Jesuits' system". They had no principles of education, but only a system of teaching and learning; and others seem to have inherited both their poverty and their riches.

Had not teachers been so bound by tradition and

policy there was but little excuse for their professional ignorance and incapacity. Had they but attended to what Plato and Aristotle, &c., had written, they had not failed so completely. The former has said that "a good education is that which gives to the body and to the soul all the beauty and all the perfection of which they are capable", and that the soul is cultivated by acquiring knowledge, by inquiry, and by discourse. Aristotle had written, "education is to prepare the mind for instruction, as men prepare the soil before sowing seed in it". Similarly Seneca writes: "the object of education is . . . inward development"; and Quintilian, after the manner of a psychologist of to-day, says, "mental training must gradually and progressively begin in the same way in which the mental faculties of the child themselves develop". It has been well said that in the writings of Socrates, Plato, and Aristotle we see the first attempt to set forth a body of educational doctrine; we have the germs of a science of education based on psychology, ethics, and politics. Socrates has shown, for all time, the true method of stimulating and strengthening the powers of pure thought.

Still less reason was there for wrong ideals and methods. During the sixteenth and seventeenth centuries the wise and learned Erasmus wrote, in Latin, "On the first liberal education of children" (1529), and "On the order of study", wherein he, though a severe classicist, yet recommends some study of nature; condemns the barbarous severity of school discipline; and is almost psychological in directing that the memory should be trained by securing clear apprehension of facts, a correct order of these in the mind, and a careful grounding in first notions and distinctions. He analyses the character of the child, and urges that "as the body in infant years is nourished by little portions distributed at intervals, so should the mind of the child be nurtured by items of knowledge adapted to its weakness, and distributed little by little".

Sir Thomas Elyot in his book *The Governour* (1531), advises systematic kindness; careful regard to individual aptitudes; the use of object lessons in teaching; the giving less attention to the grammar and more to the meaning and spirit of Latin authors; and the use of maps when learning history. And Ludovicus Vives, a Spaniard who was the tutor of Princess Mary from 1523 to 1528, published works on education—in England—in which he urges the need of expurgated editions of the classics; the employment of observation and experiment for advancement in science; healthy sites for schools; continuity and interdependence of studies; the cultivation of self-dependence in pupils; and the teaching of Latin through the mother-tongue.

That quaint and witty book, *The Scholemaster*, by Roger Ascham, was published in 1570, and contained an admirable plan for teaching the Latin language, besides valuable advice and hints on dealing with boys. In 1581-2 Richard Mulcaster, High Master of S. Paul's School, published two books on education, in which he expounds excellent principles and methods. In most material points he is abreast of the best practical educators of to-day, and far in advance of many of the general practices in teaching. He would have "every part of the body and every power of the soul to be fined to his best"; and he holds that "the end of education is to help nature to her perfection", and that for this we must select the right materials, which are only to be known by a careful study of the nature of the child, from which we "must frame an education consonant thereto". Experiences, gained through the senses, he says, "afterwards prove our great and only grounds unto further knowledge". He would have the best masters to teach beginners; training colleges for teachers; education for girls and women as well as for boys and men; and an elementary education in reading and writing English for every one. And he gave excellent reasons for the faith which was in him, and admirable advice as to the ways and means for putting it into practice.

Florio's translation of *Montaigne's Essays* appeared in 1603. Therein are contained enlightened and sound views on education, expressed in the essays, "On Pedantry" and "Of the Institution and Education of

Children". In these he maintains that "knowledge cannot be fastened on the mind, it must become part and parcel of the mind itself", and that "to know by heart is not to know". Referring to the teaching of the time, he remarks: "we labour only at filling the memory, and leave the understanding and conscience void". The whole of youth was given up to learning to understand and use words, which is beginning, and ending, at the wrong end, for "so that our disciple be well and sufficiently stored with matter, words will follow apace, and if they will not follow gently, he shall hail them on perforce". More help from France was received when Rabelais's *Gargantua* and *Pantagruel* were done into English by Sir Thomas Urquhart, and published in 1653, in which are traced the means by which a model education can be given. Of the old learning he says: "it were better to learn nothing at all than to be taught suchlike books under suchlike schoolmasters". Like Montaigne, he holds that the training of the judgment is the first and highest purpose of education, and that this is best done through a personal study of men and things, under the guidance of a highly qualified teacher.

Above all, the great apostle of scientific education, Comenius, lived, wrote, and worked during the greater part of the seventeenth century. If to-day all our teachers really knew and carried out the principles laid down by this great man, and if our legislators appreciated his plans for a national system of schools, our country would be enjoying the benefits of an education which seems at present neither generally understood nor desired. Comenius based his principles and plans upon a real understanding of the nature of mind and the nature of knowledge—for both of which he was, as he himself acknowledges, largely indebted to the writings of Bacon. With all his limitations and exaggerations—common to reformers—his creed was immensely in advance of our practice.

It is interesting to notice that England as a nation narrowly escaped being blessed with the ideas and practical guidance of Comenius in education. At the suggestion of Samuel Hartlib—to whom Milton addressed his *Tractate on Education*—the English Parliament invited Comenius to London, in 1641, and there was a proposal to establish him as head of a college through which he might carry on his work. But troubles in Ireland, and struggles between parliament and the king, prevented any change from the policy of teaching people how to kill each other rather than how to live.

Still Englishmen, at least in particular instances, got great good from the work of Comenius. Some of his best school-books were translated into English, and appear to have been used by a good number of teachers. *The Gate of Tongues* (Janua linguarum) appeared in 1639, *A Reformation of Schools* (Prodromus pansophiae), and *The Visible World* (Orbis pictus) in 1658. The last named must have had a considerable sale, for there was a twelfth edition published in 1777, though a writer to the editor thereof complains that he had "heard it lamented by a learned gentleman in a public company, that the Orbis Pictus of Comenius is now fallen totally into disuse as a school-book, though no other comparable to it has been substituted in its place".

Milton's famous *Tractate on Education* appeared in 1644. He also is an advocate of the study of things, and the regarding of language chiefly as a means to this end. His idea of "a complete and generous education" is: that which "fits a man to perform justly, skilfully, and magnanimously all the offices both private and public of peace and war". This is at any rate a great advance on a system which is almost wholly confined to storing the mind with a knowledge of the Latin and Greek languages. John Locke, the great English philosopher and writer on mental science, was the glory of the seventeenth century so far as English writers on education are concerned. He was not only a thinker and writer on education, but also a practical teacher. Strangely enough, he is chiefly remembered, in connection with education, by his *Thoughts concerning Education* (1693), which is really a book on practical teaching, whilst the far more valuable, because psychological, works, *The Conduct of the Understanding* and *An Essay concerning Human Understanding* (1690), con-

The Reign of the Voluntary System. 27

tain an exposition of the nature and laws of the mental powers, and how practically to guide and control them. These therefore set forth the true basis, and practice, of scientific education. No writer on education, of any country, before Locke, not even Comenius, had offered anything so scientifically complete and thorough; and until Herbart's *General Pedagogy* (1806) none improved upon it.

These were, however, but as voices crying in the wilderness, for the multitude of schoolmasters either never heard, or, if they heard, paid no attention to the words of wisdom. Nevertheless forces were at work which were gradually breaking through the adamantine shell of tradition which was stunting and starving the intellectual life of the nation. The revival of learning, which began in the fifteenth century, had made men eager to know of the treasures of wisdom and beauty contained in the literatures of Rome and Greece. This in its turn led to a demand for a freer and fuller intellectual life than the church either approved or allowed, and brought about that condition of mind which, as Lecky claims, was the true cause of the Reformation. Protestantism was in a large measure the re-birth of individualism, for it came to mean that each individual was chiefly responsible for the working out of his own salvation. Hence each must at least know how to read the Bible in his mother tongue; and this was the seed from which came the fruit of education for each and all. Gradually the civil and the regal powers prevailed in school, as in state, affairs. Very few schools, before the Reformation, had lay headmasters or managers, but after that event some of the most famous, such as S. Paul's, were in the hands of the laity as to their teaching and direct management. But still the religious spirit prevailed, and the church still hindered and hampered progress, though it continued to do good work within the limits which it allowed itself.

Universal education, as an ideal, was put before the nation by some of its greatest sons. Mulcaster would have every boy and girl taught, at least, to read and write. Sir William Petty (1647) lays down the rule that "all children of above seven years old may be presented to this kind of education, none being to be excluded by reason of the poverty and unability of their parents, for hereby it hath come to pass that many are now holding the plough which might have been made fit to steer the state". Sir Thomas More, in his *Utopia*, pictures an ideal state in which "all in their childhood be instruct in good learning". John Knox proposed an elaborate system of national schools for Scotland in 1560; whilst in the next century a national system of parochial schools was actually established there.

Chapter II.

The Reign of the Voluntary System—*Continued.*

It was the eighteenth century that saw, in the founding of Charity Schools, the dawn of the days of elementary education for the children of the people, as a whole. And again it is the religious motive which underlies the work. It would seem that the Jesuits had set up, in London, a free school for the children of the poor, and forthwith a good Protestant, one William Blake, a woollen-draper, is moved to found, in 1685, the Hospital at Highgate, called the Ladies' Charity School —because he hoped that the great ladies of the land would support it—so as to "stop the mouths of the Papists". This was probably the first Charity School, called by that name, and it maintained "nearly 40 poor or fatherless children, born all at or near Highgate, Hornsey, or Hampstead", who were "decently clothed in blue, lined with yellow; constantly fed all alike with good and wholesome diet; taught to read, write, and cast accompts, and so put out to trades". It is also claimed that Bishops Patrick and Tenison founded, in 1688, a school in S. Martin's-in-the-Fields as a rival to the Jesuit school. Whilst Bishop Ken has been credited with having promoted the setting up parochial schools

The Reign of the Voluntary System.

in all the parishes of his diocese, and the establishment of village and Sunday-schools, as early as 1680.

But it is to the Society for Promoting Christian Knowledge that the greatest credit is due for the extension of education amongst the children of the poor. At the first meeting (1699) it was resolved "to further and promote that good design of erecting Catechetical schools in each parish in and about London"; and in their charter, given in 1701, they declare their object to be "promoting Christian knowledge; by erecting catechetical schools; by raising lending libraries in the several market towns of this kingdom; by distributing good books", &c. And right well did they carry out their design, for by the year 1741 they had assisted in the establishment of nearly 2000 charity schools in England and Wales, in which 40,000 children were being taught. They appointed an inspector of such schools as were in and about London and Westminster; and also proposed to establish a training institution "to prepare young persons for the arduous and responsible work of instructing children", but this project, most unfortunately, was not then carried out.

The action of the society appears to have provoked others unto good works, for Dr. White Kennet, Archdeacon of Huntingdon, in his charity sermon (1706) says of the schools then founded: "Some small country schools of Charity are maintained at the sole expense of private persons. Other schools have been built and encouraged by Corporations and the Magistrates of them. In some places, the ministers teach the children of the poor to read gratis. Several ministers pay for all the children whom their poor parents will send to school. Other ministers have applied the offertories, or collection at Communion, to this charitable purpose. In Wales, the Governors and Company of the Mine Adventures of England allow, with two several counties, £20 per annum in each for Charity-schools, to instruct the children of the miners and workmen belonging to the said Company; and £30 yearly to a minister to read prayers, preach, and catechize those children. In another county, the Lord of the Manor and Freeholders are building a Charity-school on the waste, and enclosing part thereof, which is to be given for ever for teaching the poor children of that lordship. And within other counties some numbers are taught at the expense of private persons."

Of the kind of work done, he says: "In all these schools the children are taught civility and good manners, and reading, and catechizing. In some of them the boys learn writing and arithmetic, and navigation; and the girls are taught to knit, and sew, and mark, and spin, and card, and make and mend their own clothes."

The motive for the work is, he says, that "Every Charity-school is as it were a fortress and a frontier garrison against popery. . . . We remember the time, when in a popish reign one artifice of the Jesuits was to open a Charity-grammar-school in the Savoy; to inveigle and corrupt our poorer youth. The best expedient then thought of to countermine that subtility was to open the like Charity-school in the neighbourhood, for a better education in learning and the Protestant religion. All our present Charity-schools, though not opened directly on the same view, yet will serve directly to the same purpose: to be a bulwark against popery, and a grace and defence of our reformation."

The preacher of the charity sermon in 1708, Robert Moss, D.D., says: "Where there is convenience, or stock sufficient for it, they are trained up to work. . . . Many amongst them, such as are best capable, are taught to write legibly, and cast accounts tolerably. . . . All, or most of them . . . are modestly and plainly, but neatly apparelled, or at least they wear some becoming badge of their benefactors' bounty; which serves too to distinguish them from the unnurtured crew, that lurk about the streets, either to beg or to steal. But whereinsoever they fall short, they are all sure to be very carefully instructed in the fundamentals of the Christian religion, according to that form of sound words comprised in the Church Catechism."

The Bishop of London, in the charity sermon for 1714, thus expresses the severe limitations of the teach-

The Reign of the Voluntary System. 31

ing given: "It is doubtless your intention, that these objects of your charity be so educated, as that they may hereafter become useful in inferior stations, and therefore whatever exceeds now, what may reasonably be expected to be their lot afterwards, may be too much, and ought to be avoided, lest, instead of the principles of piety, they should, by your too great indulgence, imbibe those of pride".

It will be seen from this that the design underlying the movement was by no means too generous or disinterested. As Mandeville very bluntly says, in his "Essay on Charity and Charity-schools" (1723), if they would "agree to pull off the mask, we should soon discover that whatever they pretend to, they aim at nothing so much in Charity-schools as to strengthen their party, and that the great sticklers for the Church, by educating children in the principles of religion, mean, inspiring them with a superlative veneration for the clergy of the Church of England, and a strong aversion and immortal animosity against all that dissent from it. To be assured of this, we are but to mind what divines are most admired for their Charity sermons and most fond to preach them." But, as he shrewdly adds: "The grand asserters of liberty . . . likewise speak up loudly for Charity-schools, but what they expect from them has no relation to religion or morality. They only look upon them as the proper means to destroy and disappoint the power of the priests' over the laity. Reading and writing increase knowledge, and the more men know, the better they can judge from themselves, and they imagine that, if knowledge could be rendered universal, people could not be priest-rid, which is the thing they fear the most."

But the dissenters were well able to take care of themselves, and they also had their system of charity schools. They claim, in fact, to have been the first in the field in this work. In the life of Dr. Watts, written by Rev. Thomas Milner, M.A., it is said: "The first English Charity-school was founded among the Dissenters in Gravel Lane, Southwark, in 1687, as an antidote to the school of one Poulter, a Jesuit, who instructed the children of the poor gratis". The school commenced "with 40 children, but these soon increased to 130, who were admitted without distinction of parties and denominations, and taught reading, writing, arithmetic, and the principles of religion, according to the Assembly's Catechism". In 1728 Dr. Watts wrote "An Essay towards the encouragement of Charity-schools, particularly those which are supported by Protestant Dissenters, for teaching the children of the poor to read and write; together with some apology for those schools which instruct them to write a plain hand and fit them for service, or for the meaner trades and labours of life; to which is prefixed an address to the supporters of those schools".

And whilst religious rivalry and competition were thus working to the public good, other public and private efforts were by no means wanting. Besides those mentioned in Dr. Kennet's sermon, we hear of schools founded by the City Livery Companies—the Ward schools; and successful merchants, who had risen from the ranks, and wished to make a thank-offering for their success, and to give opportunity and help to those who were as they had been, established such schools. Thus arose those free schools, over whose gates was generally set up a statuette of a charity boy (or charity girl, or both), with an inscription setting forth that Alderman —— founded this school for — poor boys, to be clothed and taught reading, writing, and arithmetic. Also we read that, in 1717, "At Winlaton, in the county of Durham, the workmen of an ironwork, who are about 400 or 500, allow one farthing and a half per shilling per week, which, together with their master's contribution, maintains their poor, and affords about £17 per annum for teaching their children to read, &c.". Individual parishes also supported their own charity school, doubtless, in many cases, doing so through becoming infected with what Mandeville calls the "enthusiastic passion for Charity-schools", which schools "are in fashion in the same manner as hooped petticoats, by caprice".

Mandeville's violent attack on charity schools deserves some notice, as it undoubtedly expresses, in a some-

The Reign of the Voluntary System.

what extreme and exaggerated form, a general feeling amongst the upper classes of that time. He argues that since drudgery, obsequiousness, and mean services are necessary for the wealth and security of a nation in which slaves are not allowed, it is better that those who are to occupy positions as laborious poor should be used to it from the very first; to give the poor knowledge is to make them discontented and rebellious, and likely to change them into rogues and vicious persons, since virtue, obedience, and honesty are most found amongst the ignorant and poor; and those who are to do the hard and dirty work must be inferiors in knowledge and understanding, for, "a servant can have no unfeigned respect for his master as soon as he has sense enough to find out that he serves a fool". And we find Bishop Butler saying, in a charity sermon preached in 1745, "Nor let people of rank flatter themselves that ignorance will keep their inferiors more dutiful and in greater subjection to them". From which we may conclude that there was much of the feudal spirit amongst the principal supporters of the schools, and that a most humiliating spirit of submission and dependence was expected from those who were taught in them. Nevertheless, since this could hardly have changed the actual conditions of the relations already existing between the rich and the poor, the new feature, viz., the giving of the elements of learning, was an open door to the greater knowledge which helped so much to bring freedom and comparative wealth and comfort to the working-classes.

Perhaps the greatest glory of the charity schools is that they admitted girls into the world of public education, from which they had been almost entirely excluded by the grammar-schools. It is suggestive to notice that charity schools flourished most at the time when beer-shops hung out painted notices inviting poor people to get drunk for a penny, dead drunk for twopence, and have clean straw for nothing.

Some of the subjects taught in these schools have been already mentioned, viz., religious knowledge, reading, writing, arithmetic, and industrial and domestic arts. But besides these Latin appears to have been taught at some of the schools. William Blake, in his most ingenious appeals to ladies of title, suggests, as a reason for subscribing: "My Lady such a one said, she would give, to bind some out, or send one or two to be poor scholars in Cambridge". And we find James Talbot, D.D., in 1811, protesting most strongly against Latin being taught in charity schools. He writes: "The teaching of Latin . . . by a vulgar error has been esteemed very necessary to the education even of the meanest children (insomuch that scarce any husbandman will venture to take his son from the school to the plough, till he has got some smattering in this language)".

The teachers were, as a rule, a sorry set, and, as might be expected, inferior even to the worst of the grammar-school teachers, the ushers, for they had as little training, *i.e.* none, and less learning. Mandeville writes of them as those who "either actually persecute with birch or else are solliciting for such a preferment. . . . Wretches of both sexes . . . that from a natural antipathy to working, have a great dislike to their present employment, and perceiving within a much stronger inclination to command than ever they felt to obey others, think themselves qualified, and wish from their hearts to be masters and mistresses of Charity-schools." This is obviously exaggerated, but there is every reason to believe that it is based upon fact. There was no proper source from which efficient teachers for such schools could be drawn. Thus we find that in a charity school for girls, at Reading, "Jane Leggatt, widow, is the present mistress; Jane Cowdrey, widow, the present assistant". Those who had had a good education naturally went to the grammar-schools, where they would obtain better salaries and more congenial surroundings.

Towards the end of the eighteenth century, however, some care was taken to secure teachers with at least some claims to previous experience. In a book on the duty of those who are employed in the public instruction of children, especially in charity schools, it is declared that, according to the orders issued by the S.P.C.K. for the management of such schools, "The master to be elected into any of them, shall be one who understands

The Reign of the Voluntary System. 35

well the grounds and principles of the Christian Religion, and likewise one who can write a good hand, and who understands the grounds of arithmetic, and that he should be one who has a good genius for teaching. In order to the further improvement of this (which is in a great measure the result of experience and observation) it has been judged advisable for any newly-elected schoolmaster to consult with several present masters of these schools concerning the best means of performing this office. And it is recommended to them to communicate to every such newly-elected master their art, and the divers methods of teaching and governing their scholars, according to the different capacities, tempers, and inclinations of the children. And moreover it will be convenient that he should have liberty on certain days to see and hear the present masters teach their scholars, and upon occasion to assist them in teaching; that he may thereby become yet more expert, and better qualified for the discharge of his duty." Though this was doubtless a counsel of perfection, which certainly produced no very general results, yet it probably fell on good ground and bore fruit in particular cases. It is interesting to notice that a schoolmistress was expected to have similar qualifications to a master, except "that part which relates to writing a good hand, and understanding arithmetic". Which speaks for itself.

The next great extension of primary education was brought about by the starting of Sunday-schools. Whilst there were Sunday-schools before Robert Raikes of Gloucester, yet so much is due to him for extending them, and inspiring others to do so, that he may rightly be regarded as the father of Sunday-schools. It was in 1781 that he first put his hand to this good work. In 1785 " The Society for the Support and Encouragement of Sunday-schools in the different counties of England" was established, and in 1803 "The Sunday School Union". The objects and methods of Sunday-schools are clearly expressed in the rules of the former, *e.g.*: "The object of the Charity shall be poor persons, of each sex and of any age; who shall be taught to read, at such times, and in such places, as the Committee by themselves or their Correspondents shall appoint. All scholars to attend public worship every Sunday, unless prevented by illness or any other sufficient cause. The religious observation of the Christian Sabbath being an essential object with the Society . . . the exercises of the scholars on that day, shall be restricted to reading the Old and New Testament, and to spelling as a preparation thereto. The Society shall provide Bibles, Testaments, and Spelling-books for the use of the scholars. The Committee shall be at liberty to order lessons on working days, where they shall think necessary."

Sunday-schools spread with remarkable rapidity. Both churchmen and dissenters were eager to avail themselves of this means of imparting religious instruction to the young and old. So much was this the case that individuals from both sides co-operated at first, but when the greater earnestness and zeal of the Nonconformists began to show practical results, then sectarian jealousy and rivalry appeared, and the work became sectional and doctrinal. Nevertheless very great good was done, unintentionally for the most part, to the cause of mental progress, for, during the next fifty years, hundreds of thousands were taught to read and write who would not otherwise have received any such instruction. There are still many living who owe all their little learning to Sunday-school teaching.

Of the educational value of the instruction given in these Sunday-schools it will be most charitable to say little. Thousands of individuals, ignorant of anything but the most meagre learning themselves, and wholly without knowledge of the end or method of imparting knowledge to others, but full of a righteous zeal to help their fellows, were let loose upon all sorts and conditions of scholars. And nothing is, as a rule, more dangerous, and often destructive, than uninformed zeal. Yet the shrewd intelligence of some of the teachers led them to the discovery of some sound practical methods, and whilst the work prospered in their hands, others were able to copy them more or less successfully. Still a high church dignitary of recent times has, probably with

The Reign of the Voluntary System. 37

justice, attributed much of the irreligion of those days to the injudicious instruction then given in the Sunday-schools. Those who have a personal knowledge of some of the Sunday-schools at the present time will readily believe that schools in which order and discipline are practically unknown, and in which bribery or bullying are the only resources of the incapable young men and women who undertake the teaching, are far more likely to corrupt than to refine the moral nature.

The closing years of the eighteenth century brought the beginning of what was wholly, till 1870, and still is largely, the English ideal of education, and system of schools, for the poor. The plan was limited, rapid, and cheap; and these qualities seized upon the sympathies of the commercially-minded, shop-keeping, practical Englishman. That it was also superficial, mechanical, barren, and often mischievous, was, for a long time, neither recognized nor suspected. A young lad named Joseph Lancaster was possessed with an enthusiasm for instructing the ignorant. At the age of fourteen he failed in an attempt to run away to Jamaica, where he hoped to teach the black slaves to read. At the age of eighteen (1798) he set up a school for the poor in London, and started with nearly a hundred pupils. In a short time he had a thousand scholars. To make it possible to give any instruction whatever to so large a number, he hit upon the plan of setting those pupils who had already mastered a step to teach it to a group of his fellow-scholars—after the manner of Robert Raikes, who having taught a prisoner to read set him to teach another—thus, as he and others thought, showing that one master could teach a thousand scholars. The greatest possible popular enthusiasm was aroused. If it were possible to teach poor children next to nothing, for next to nothing—a reasonable equation—by all means let it be done. The king, members of the royal family, nobles, and gentry, all subscribed to so pleasing a project. Lancaster was a public hero, and almost every city erected a monument to him, in the shape of a Lancasterian school. Churchmen and dissenters were at one in this matter. But there was a fatal flaw in the scheme, which was discovered by a certain whole-souled churchwoman. In the Lancasterian schools the religious instruction was given so as to "exclude everything which is peculiar to any sect or party". In brief, it was purely religious. But, said this champion of the church, "From the time that I read Mr. Joseph Lancaster's *Improvements in Education* in the first edition, I conceived an idea that there was something in his plan that was inimical to the interests of the Established Church". And she succeeded in converting to her views Dr. Bell, a clergyman who had not long since returned from India, where he had been a chaplain; and being interested in education, had likewise hit upon the plan of setting one boy to teach others. A keen and bitter controversy soon arose, and the country was divided into two parties. Pulpits, platforms, and pamphlets raged furiously every day, exalting the one and condemning the other of the two men. Nevertheless, out of this evil of bigoted party conflict came the good of school extension, with crumbs of learning for the ignorant multitude.

To rescue Lancaster from financial difficulties the Royal Lancasterian Institution was founded in 1808. This society took charge of business side of the work, but was soon obliged to entirely separate from Lancaster, because of his mismanagement of money affairs and intolerance of control. The society changed its name to "The British and Foreign School Society" in 1814. A rival society to this, "The National Society for Promoting the Education of the Poor in the Principles of the Established Church", was formed in 1811, as an outcome of the controversy referred to. This Society practically took over the work of the Society for Promoting Christian Knowledge with regard to founding and maintaining primary schools, though the latter by no means ceased its work in this direction.

Of the work done by Lancaster not much can be said in its favour as to its truly educational value, though unstinted praise is due to the whole-hearted enthusiasm and devotion with which he gave himself to a purely philanthropic and disinterested work. We owe him much for that his zeal and ingenuity led to the establishing of very many schools, to the imparting of the beggarly elements of learning to the multitude, and to providing teachers who were at least well-trained in the methods, such as they were, of conducting the work of a school. But if we are to attach any value to the ideas of the great writers on education, then the notion of children educating children is altogether monstrous and mischievous. That they can teach each other certain tricks of voice and hand does not require a Lancaster or Bell to tell us, but that they can in any sense guide and assist the development of the mind and body is, on the face of it, an absurd suggestion. As well set children to physic each other, for the fallacy is about on all-fours with a notion that one who has taken a pill is fit to be a physician. The system was a thoroughly bad one, and has clung, with disastrous effects, to our schools down to the present day. It was bound to be a mere parrot business. The monitors—those chosen to teach the others, whence the plan was called the Monitorial system—had to learn, and rehearse to the master before the morning or afternoon school work began, what they were to teach during the day. Lists of words, meanings, examples, questions, &c., were committed to memory, and afterwards drilled into the groups of pupils. And the most successful of these monitors became the best head-teachers of the time. Other head-teachers were just the odds and ends of the unemployed. Even so late as 1852 a government inspector of schools has to warn school-managers that "It is a common mistake to appoint them, or to keep them on, out of charity", without any regard to the very serious injustice, and life-long loss, to the pupils.

The idea derived from Bell and Lancaster's methods, that anyone who has learnt is able to teach, still survives in our primary schools, in which a very large proportion —something like sixty per cent—of the teachers have received little or no systematic preparation for their work. Strictly speaking, none receive such a preparation, for those who are trained begin teaching, as pupil teachers, before they have been taught how to teach, and continue for three or four years to do this before entering a training college. That is to say, after they have formed more or less rigid habits in practical teaching they are then supposed to be taught how to teach.

Dr. Bell's Madras system was, for all practical purposes, exactly similar to Lancaster's, and produced like results; and both Dr. Bell and his system deserve our thanks for the same reasons that Lancaster and his system do. The National Society took up Bell's ideas and made them almost articles of religion, so that bishops declined to have anything to do with schools unless the Madras system was entirely and exclusively followed in them. The Society's aim was a very definite one, and is thus expressed in its first report: "The sole object in view being to communicate to the poor generally, by the means of a summary mode of education, lately brought into practice, such knowledge and habits as are sufficient to guide them through life, in their proper station, especially to teach the doctrines of religion according to the principles of the Established Church, and to train them to the performance of their religious duties by early discipline". This end it pursued with energy and success. In the first four years of its life it assisted in the establishing of eighty-five schools, at a cost of about £100,000, in the spending of which there was obviously no useless extravagance, for a report of a sub-committee says that for a school "a barn furnishes no bad model, and a good one may easily be converted into a school".

An idea of the ludicrous and absurd extent to which the religious aim was pursued by the National Society may be gathered from the following examples from a book on arithmetic, prepared for the schools by the secretary of the Society:—"The children of Israel were sadly given to idolatry, notwithstanding all they knew of God. Moses was obliged to have three thousand men put to death for this grievous sin. What digits would you use to express this number?" "Of Jacob's four wives, Leah had six sons: Rachel had two: Hillah had two, and Tillah had also two. How many sons had Jacob?" Texts of scripture were used as copies for writing, reading was generally confined to the Bible, and geography teaching was almost wholly concerned with Palestine.

It was in connection with schools on Dr. Bell's system that payment by results was first suggested. Some of the teachers had become careless and unorthodox in their methods, and as a consequence Dr. Bell drew up a circular note recommending that teachers' salaries should be made to depend on the number, conduct, and improvement of their scholars.

Another hero of popular education was Samuel Wilderspin, who in 1820 opened an infants' school in Spitalfields. His interest in the subject was due to his friendship with Robert Buchanan, who had come from Robert Owen's infant school at New Lanark—the first established in Great Britain—to take charge of a school at Brewer's Green. He was entirely without experience or training when he first began his work, but with a whole-hearted devotion to the good of the little ones, and a genius for observation and discovery, he soon set himself on right lines and worked out a thoroughly sound educational method. That he was an educator, and not a mere instructor, his own words testify. He says:—" The first thing we attempt to do in an infant school is to set the children thinking, to get them to examine, compare, and judge of all those matters which their dawning intellects are capable of mastering. . . . The art of education is to follow nature, to assist and imitate her in her way of rearing men." So successful was he in his efforts that in 1824 the London Infant School Society was founded, with the object of establishing such schools as his in various parts of the country. Wilderspin then gave much of his time to lecturing and personally starting the work of new schools. The need of proper teachers thus brought about led to the formation of the Home and Colonial Infant School Society, and the starting of a training college, in 1836. In this college the principles of education which Pestalozzi pursued were taught. There was great fitness in this, for the man whose work was one of the causes of its being might well be called the English Pestalozzi. He discovered much of the true nature of the child, and employed such materials and methods in his work as are too seldom found in some of the very best infant schools of the present time.

With the founding of the Home and Colonial Training College was begun the good work of providing teachers with a definite training for their work in infants' schools. Joseph Lancaster had begun the like work for teachers of older scholars, at his school in the Borough in 1805. The National Society was for some time content with teachers drawn from the ranks of the monitors in its schools. It seems to have accepted the theory of Bell's own words, viz., "Give me four-and-twenty children to-day, and I will supply you to-morrow with as many teachers". One of the instructions for the first morning of the opening a new school was:—"The master or mistress, acting as teacher, selects the most intelligent-looking child to act as assistant". But later on the society established separate institutions for training masters and mistresses.

The Home and Colonial Training College seems to have been by far the most complete and comprehensive institution, and it is very instructive to note the kind of students it received and the subjects in which they received instruction. The committee say that "it would be desirable that a candidate should be able to read, to write a tolerable hand, to sing, should know the simple rules of arithmetic, be well acquainted with the Word of God, and possess some information in grammar, geography, and natural history". That this is little more than a pious hope is shown by the fact that during the first six weeks, out of the twenty-four which made up a full course of training, the students "are chiefly occupied in receiving instruction for their own improvement, with a view to their future training". The amount of training which those who intended to be teachers thought necessary is indicated by the rule that "the admission for short periods having been found very inconvenient to the arrangements of the institution, and attended with comparatively little benefit, the Committee do not receive teachers for less than six weeks, unless they have actually the charge of schools, and are, in consequence, unable to remain for that time". It is difficult to properly appreciate the idea that six weeks is not a short period of training, and that twenty-four weeks is a full course, unless we fully realize the meagre amount taught in the schools and the low ideal of a teacher's fitness for the task.

The desperate need for efficient teachers became the more urgent when the Factory Act of 1833 compelled a very large number of children to be taught, but made no provision of either schools or teachers. To satisfy the act coal-holes and engine-houses were turned into schoolrooms, and one of the factory hands, or his wife, made the teacher. The certificates of attendance required by the act were usually signed by the school-keeper's marks. In mining districts those who went to school at all were, as a rule, taught by miners or labourers who had lost health or been disabled. Many of the schools were taught by persons who did the work because of "old age"; "to get a bit of bread"; "to keep off the town"; or because they were unable to work, or out of employment.

With this condition of things it is worth while to contrast the fact that in Scotland, since 1696, the qualifications usually expected in a master for a parochial school were: unexceptionable character; the ability to teach his pupils to read English (which was practically a foreign language to the Gaelic-speaking Scots); a knowledge of the more common and useful branches of practical mathematics; and such classical learning as would fit him to teach Latin and the rudiments of Greek.

Some idea of the actual progress in school work made since the beginning of the eighteenth century will be obtained by the estimate that in 1818 the proportion of the population in school was 1 in every 17, whilst in 1833 it was 1 in every $11\frac{1}{4}$. Of course this includes every school of whatsoever kind. But the chief increase would be represented by the increase of poor children in the primary schools. Of these there were over thirty thousand in schools which had received a share of the government grant; and this number increased 50 per cent in the next two years. By far the greater majority of them were in Church schools.

The National Society had trained over two thousand teachers in their central schools, and had organized six hundred and fifty schools in the country, and supplied them with temporary teachers. The British and Foreign School Society had, in 1834, ninety schools in and around London, with nearly fifteen thousand pupils in them, besides over four hundred schools in the country. The National Society had about three thousand schools in union with it at this time.

The most advanced scheme for primary schools in those days was proposed in the columns of the *Quarterly Journal of Education* for March, 1833. In this it was proposed that the children of the poor should be taught reading, writing, arithmetic, geography, freehand drawing, geometry, music, religion, and morals. There should be a school in every village, conducted on the lines of the Prussian schools; parents should pay a small school fee; and attendance should be compulsory for boys up to their fourteenth year, and for girls to their thirteenth.

Worthy John Pounds, the Portsmouth cobbler, and father of Ragged Schools, deserves a tribute of gratitude for the noble work which he did. Another cobbler in Kent Street, a tinker at Hatcham, and a chimney-sweep at Windsor followed his inspiring example. Various societies were afterwards formed, and established Sunday-schools, day-schools, night-schools, and industrial classes for those neglected little ones we call street-arabs and gutter-snipes.

The voices of the great leaders of thought had, during this period, as always, given no uncertain sound as to their belief in the necessity and advantage of popular education. Adam Smith, in his *Wealth of Nations* (1776), says: "For a very small expense, the public can facilitate, can encourage, and can even impose upon almost the whole body of the people, the necessity of acquiring those most essential parts of education. The public can facilitate their acquisition, by establishing in every parish or district a little school, where children may be taught for a reward so moderate, that even a common labourer may afford it. . . . If, in those little schools [Charity schools], the books by which children are taught to read, were a little more instructive than they commonly are; and if, instead of a little smattering in Latin, which the children of the common people are sometimes taught there, and which can scarce ever be of any use to them, they were instructed in the elementary parts of geometry and mechanics; the literary education of this rank of people would, perhaps, be as complete as can be. There is scarce a common trade which does not afford some opportunities of applying to it the principles of geometry and mechanics." He insists that "The education of the common people requires, perhaps, in a civilized and commercial society, the attention of the public, more than that of people of some rank and fortune"; and he points out what great advantages to the well-being of a free state will arise from the greater intelligence and knowledge of its citizens.

Malthus, in his *Essay on Population* (1798), remarks: "We have lavished immense sums on the poor, which we have every reason to think have constantly tended to aggravate their misery. But in their education, and in the circulation of those important political truths that most nearly concern them, which are perhaps the only means in our power of really raising their condition, and of making them happier men and more peaceable subjects, we have been miserably deficient. It is surely a great national disgrace, that the education of the lower classes of the people in England should be left merely to a few Sunday-schools, supported by a subscription from individuals, who can give to the course of instruction in them any kind of bias which they please. And even the improvement of Sunday-schools (for, objectionable as they are in some points of view, and imperfect in all, I cannot but consider them as an improvement) is of very late date."

This period, so barren of worthy educational ideals in England, was yet in many respects the golden age of progress in educational theory. To the eighteenth century, and the early part of the nineteenth, belong the lives and work of such pre-eminent educationists as Rousseau, Pestalozzi, Froebel, and Herbart. And several of the writings of these men were translated into English, and had some small effect upon individual teachers during this period. The generality, however, gave no heed to such matters, but seem to have accepted the spirit if not the very words of Dr. Johnson's remark, "Education is as well known, and has long been as well known, as ever it can be". This seems to have been held, at least in so far as any general principles were concerned. So far as new tricks of training to learn were concerned, people were only too eager to receive, and credulous in trusting, them.

A very brief outline of the principal ideas held by the great thinkers just named will give some notion of what our insular ignorance and prejudices cost us, in the way of loss at the time and in the many years occupied in blundering into more reasonable and effective methods. Rousseau preached, with brilliant exaggerations and errors, the doctrine that the child has its own proper nature, which develops after the manner of plants and other animals, and that true education involves knowing and ministering to child-nature. This was in sharp conflict with the formal, rule-of-thumb ideas and methods which then prevailed, and which regarded the child as a miniature man, into whose mind was to be driven such knowledge as it was thought necessary or useful for men to have. Rousseau attacked the practical systems of his time in a very vigorous and trenchant manner. He said that education by mere words was impossible, for words can convey no real meaning apart from the knowledge which comes from experience. Hence he urged that books should be used very little, if at all. Take care of the education of the senses by experiences, he urged, and the words which express the knowledge thus gained will take care of themselves. As he himself put it: "I have no love whatever for explanations and talk. Things! Things! I shall never tire of saying that we ascribe too much importance to words. With our babbling education we make only babblers."

Pestalozzi stands out in the history of education as

both prophet and almost martyr. Though somewhat wanting in clearness and completeness of vision, his ideas were living and illuminating. He spoke as an oracle, and others have had to do much in interpreting his sayings for practical guidance. He was full of the fire of enthusiasm, of devotion, and of self-sacrifice. Though not a clear thinker himself he led others to clear thinking; and though a poor teacher, his own efforts in practical work guided and developed brilliant teachers and exceptionally successful schools. His central idea was that true education is the growth of an inward life, which the educator has to assist and guide through outward influences. The mind has the power to take in and make a part of intelligence that which is suitable, just as the body has. Therefore all education should be based upon this power of 'intuition', *i.e.* the fact that, for example, if two objects are allowed to act properly upon the senses, the mind immediately seizes upon the truths which we express by such words as: longer, shorter, lighter, heavier, larger, smaller, warmer, colder, &c. The teacher's duty is to present experiences to the learner in such ways, and order, that he gains the clearest, most complete, and most accurate knowledge about his surroundings. Thus the mind is trained to do its proper work, viz., thinking, and its fullest strength and skill therein are brought out. Instruction—the be-all and end-all of English methods—is not education, but a means of education. In all things the beginnings must be with the simplest elements, and progress must be step by step according to the order of the development of the child's powers of mind. It is this plan of basing practical education upon the idea of an organic development, and orderly growth, of the mental powers, which is the chief glory of Pestalozzi, for he was the first definitely to apply it to teaching in any clear and systematic way. Language must be connected with the knowledge gained through experience, not used as though it were a means of giving the elements of real knowledge.

Froebel is without doubt the mystic amongst educationists; and yet, so close is paradox to practical simplicity, he is the high-priest of the infants' schools, where clearness and what one may call the purity of distilled simplicity are absolutely indispensable. He expounds the idea of Pestalozzi that education must have its beginnings in the native power of mind to know, and to think. Hence he says that man "must develop from within, self-active and free, in accordance with the eternal law [of his being]. This is the problem and the aim of all education in instruction and training; there can be and should be no other" (*Education of Man*, published in 1826). Therefore, " the purpose of teaching is to bring ever more out of man rather than to put more and more into him". He sought to realize this practically by making use of the abundant activity of little children, through so organizing their play that they should systematically observe, and think about, the objects they played with. He invented a course of what are called occupations, in which are found most of the ordinary games of children. During all their play they were, under the teacher's guidance, to be using their senses in an orderly manner, and making judgments about their experiences, and expressing these in simple language. Thus the elements of learning were acquired, in the most natural and effective way, without any sense of effort or constraint. These great principles Froebel both thought out, and worked out, for he was an enthusiastic and successful school-teacher as well as a philosopher.

The first strictly scientific educationist was Herbart. Others before him had seen deep down into the chief elements of the real nature of the human being in general, and the child in particular; but it was left to Herbart to be the first to study scientifically the mental nature of man, and to apply the knowledge thus obtained to the working out of a science of education. He stands in the first rank of the German psychologists of his time, and was the introducer of more exact methods into the study of the subject. His great work for education was to show how the mind organizes the materials presented to it by the processes of apperception, *i.e.* the binding up of particular ideas and judgments into general wholes, and these into those organised systems which constitute

The Reign of the Voluntary System. 49

the great unity which we call mind. This revealed the true basis of method in education, viz., the arousing of interest (the sympathetic activity of mind), and the presenting of the right materials (experiences) in the right order. He urged that every side of the human nature should be thus exercised and developed through the interest in the physical, the rational, the artistic, the domestic, the social, and the religious. We should first train the young to understand intelligently and thoroughly by the method of discovery (analysis), and then impart a wealth of knowledge through demonstration and exposition (synthesis). Above all, the aim of the educator should be to form good moral character through the intellectual and social discipline of the school.

Not only was there such a wealth of sound theory, but national school systems were in existence which were based on broad and generous ideas, and were more or less successfully carrying out the purposes for which they were established. Prussia had set up a supreme council of education in 1787, because, as the decree says, "it is of extreme importance to us that in our lands everywhere, through suitable instruction of the youth, good men and useful citizens be educated for every rank". In 1794 an education law was passed, by which schools and universities were declared to be state institutions, and all public schools and institutions for education placed under state superintendence. Religion, education, and medicine were put into the hands of a section of the ministry of the interior in 1808, whilst in 1817 a separate ministry for each of these was formed, and in 1819 there was a very thorough and complete scheme of education for every province in the kingdom. Even so early as 1717 the principle of compulsory attendance at school was adopted. And this was, later, enforced by fines, sale of goods, or imprisonment. Holland was put under a national system in 1814. Every province was divided into educational districts, and a school inspector appointed to each of these districts. The governments of the towns and provinces were charged with the cost of maintaining the schools, for which they had to provide in the local budgets. In one of our own colonies we may be said to have set ourselves a good example, which we of course did not follow. Upper Canada passed an Elementary School Law in 1816, which provided for the spending of five thousand pounds each year in support of schools to be established. These schools were to be managed by trustees elected by the inhabitants of the localities where the institutions were set up.

England seemed to be capable of legislating for other countries only. As far back as 1537 the Irish Parliament, acting under the English Privy Council, had founded parochial schools—for the purpose of changing Irishmen into Englishmen, if that were possible. Many other steps were afterwards taken, through statutes and money grants, &c., to further the work of giving the Irish an English education and making them Protestants. Finally, an Irish Board of Education was created in 1831, which took entire charge of elementary education in Ireland. The duties of this Board were: to give grants for building schools, to the extent of two-thirds of their cost; to pay small gratuities as supplements to teachers' salaries; to publish schoolbooks, and sell them at half-price to schools under its regulations; to supply, at prime cost, all kinds of school requisites; to establish a model school for the training of teachers; and to maintain a system of inspection of the schools. Because of the decay of parochial schools in Scotland, in consequence of the decrease in the value of money, so seriously affecting the fixed payments of the teachers that properly qualified men would not accept such posts—the salary often being "below the gains of a day labourer"—the famous Act of 1803 was passed, which ordained: "That, in terms of the Act of 1696, a school be established, and a schoolmaster appointed in every parish, the salary of the schoolmaster not to be under three hundred marks (£16, 13s. 4d.), nor above four hundred (£22, 4s. 5d.)", besides a dwelling-house, "to consist of not more than two apartments", and a piece of ground for a garden "to contain not less than one-fourth of a Scots acre". The lowest and highest salary was changed to become £25, 13s. 3d. and £34, 4s. 4d., respectively, in 1828. The excellent work done by these schools, from their earliest foundation, is shown by the constant stream of day labourers' sons which they sent to the Scotch universities.

By far the worthiest and completest idea of a school system was that of the New England States. At the convention held in 1821 at Massachusetts, Mr. Webster made a noble declaration of the true purpose and end of a school system. He said: "For the purpose of public instruction, we hold every man subject to taxation in proportion to his property, and we look not to the question whether he himself have or have not children to be benefited by the education for which he pays; we regard it as a wise and liberal system of police, by which property, and life, and the peace of society are secured. We seek to prevent, in some measure, the extension of the penal code, by inspiring a salutary and conservative principle of virtue and of knowledge in an early age. We hope to excite a feeling of respectability and a sense of character, by enlarging the capacities and increasing the sphere of intellectual enjoyment. . . . Knowing that our government rests directly upon the public will, that we may preserve it we endeavour to give a safe and proper direction to the public will. We do not, indeed, expect all men to be philosophers or statesmen; but we confidently trust . . . that by the diffusion of general knowledge, and good and virtuous sentiments, the political fabric may be secure, as well against open violence and overthrow, as against the slow but sure undermining of licentiousness." And this was largely realized in a compulsory and general system of schools.

Notwithstanding all this precept and example, England had, so far, been content to be without a national ideal and system. Now there was to be an awakening, but one so full of distorted views, unworthy aims, and party conflict, that it was for a time almost a greater reproach than the absence of desire and effort.

Chapter III.

The Days of Doles.

The work of charity schools in the education of the children of the poor soon began to be the leaven which leavened the whole lump. The small amount of learning in reading, writing, and casting accounts, which had been given to some of the workers, must have proved most valuable and helpful to them when the repeal in 1824–5, of the old statutes forbidding combinations amongst workmen made the forming of trade-unions possible. And not only must the knowledge of the fortunate ones have proved very valuable to the interests of the workers in general, but it must have forcibly impressed upon them the urgent necessity of every workman possessing the ability to read and write. The more so since the world of workers had begun to be disturbed and agitated at the beginning of the present century by the introduction of machinery, which displaced hand work and caused much passing dislocation of industry and consequent distress amongst the workers. Further, men's minds were being exercised with thoughts of an utopia of equal work and equal wealth, as suggested by Robert Owen's ideas, so opposed to their actual condition of pinching poverty, that they became discontented, and determined to improve their lot in life.

Added to this social and industrial discontent, political ferment began to appear in an aggressive form amongst the working-classes. The Corn-laws pressed most heavily and cruelly upon them, and they broke out into riots. This condition of threatening unrest was eagerly seized upon by politicians, who easily persuaded the people that a reform of parliamentary representation would prove a complete remedy for all their ills. But we have nothing to do with these matters, except to notice that their effect must have been to make men eager to possess every means of getting such knowledge as would be likely to prove useful to them in gaining their ends. And not only did the workers themselves thus desire knowledge, but the wiser leaders of thought and action saw that education was a condition of sound progress. For who would be likely to be more ready to obey laws than those who were instructed enough to understand them, and to have some intelligent part and lot in the making of them.

'Hence we find a common movement amongst the workers themselves, and the friends of the poor, to provide every possible means of spreading the elements of learning amongst the masses. From 1820 to 1835 the years were most fruitful in the founding of mechanics' institutes, reading-rooms, education societies, and lectures. Cheap literature was made to take its share in spreading knowledge, by means of such publications as the *Penny Magazine, Penny Papers for the People, Poor Man's Guardian, Penny Cyclopædia, Library of Entertaining Knowledge*, &c. Two of the most important and valuable societies were "The Society for the Diffusion of Useful Knowledge" and the "Central Education Society", which were founded and conducted by many of the very ablest men of the time. Amongst the workers such societies as "The British Association for Promoting Co-operative Knowledge", and the "London Working Men's Association to Procure a Cheap and Honest Press", did modest but meritorious and valuable work in furthering the desires and opportunities for obtaining knowledge.

But even these efforts of self-help and self-improvement were viewed with suspicion, and met with direct and indirect opposition from many. The views of such found expression, for example, through writers in *Blackwood's Magazine*, in which it is said that mechanics' institutes would be used to form the labouring classes into a disaffected and ungovernable faction; that the only education fit for poor people was a religious one, which "renders them patient, humble, and moral, and relieves the hardship of their present lot by the prospect of a bright eternity"; and that the founding of the London University was "the creation of a God-excluding seminary", and "the worst sentiments in politics and religion would pervade it". There seems indeed to have been a general opinion amongst the rich that knowledge amongst the poor would mean infidelity and atheism in religion, combined with lawlessness and efforts to confiscate the wealth of others.

But the nation as a whole, through its parliament, was awakened to a sense of its responsibility and opportunity with regard to education, chiefly through the almost heroic efforts of one man, viz. Lord Brougham. It is true that he was not the first worker in this field, but he was the first to make real progress in the matter. In 1807 Mr. Whitbread had introduced a "Parochial Schools Bill", which was to give power to overseers, with the consent of the vestry, to raise money for establishing and supporting parochial schools. The bill, in a modified form, was passed by the Commons, but thrown out by the Lords. The chief arguments used against it were: the enormous and incalculable expense which it would involve; the difficulty of getting school-teachers; and the danger to religion if education were taken out of the hands of the clergy. As a specimen of what was actually said in the Commons, the following by Mr. Davies Giddy is worthy of notice:—However specious in theory the project might be, of giving education to the labouring classes of the poor, it would, in effect, be found to be prejudicial to their morals and happiness; it would teach them to despise their lot in life, instead of making them good servants in agriculture, and other laborious employments to which their rank in society has destined them; instead of teaching them subordination, it would render them factious and refractory, as was evident in the manufacturing counties; it would enable them to read seditious pamphlets, vicious books, and publications against Christianity; it would render them insolent to their superiors; and in a few years, the result would be that the legislature would find it necessary to direct the strong arm of power towards them, and to furnish the executive magistrates with much more vigorous laws than were now in force. On the other hand, Earl Stanhope, in the Lords, objected to what he must call the abominable principle, that no part of the population of this country ought to receive education unless in the tenets of the Established Church. Was it reasonable or just to say that the children of Catholics, Presbyterians, Quakers, and all the other innumerable sects of dissenters from the Established Church in this country, were to be debarred all sources of public education, supported by public benevolence, unless they were to become converts to our established religion? Would he [the Archbishop of Canterbury] contend, that because the Catholic religion was the established one in Canada, no poor Protestant should be educated unless he was allowed to be brought up a Catholic? . . . He could not see that its purpose had anything to do with sects of religion. It was merely to teach its objects spelling, reading, writing, and arithmetic for purposes useful in life; and in a manufacturing country like this, when so much of excellence in production depended on a clear understanding and some degree of mathematical and mechanical knowledge, which it was impossible to attain without first receiving the rudiments and foundations this bill proposed, the superiority of workmen with some education over those who had none, must be sensibly felt by all the great manufacturers in the country.

It is a significant fact that on the same day as Mr. Whitbread presented his bill, the Commons "resolved, that a sum, not exceeding £23,270, Irish currency, be granted to His Majesty, for defraying the charge of the Incorporated Society in Dublin for promoting English Protestant Schools in Ireland" during the current year. So easy was it found to do the good to others that they would not do unto themselves.

It was in 1816 that Brougham began his great work for popular education, by moving for, and obtaining, the appointment of a select committee of the Commons to inquire into the educational condition of London, Westminster, and Southwark. In discussing the granting of this committee Canning uttered the notable saying that he supported it because he was "satisfied that the foundation of good order in society was good morals, and that the foundation of good morals was education". Amidst quite general approval the committee soon set to work, and under Brougham's guidance it did its work in a very thorough way, and gave a very wide interpretation to its instructions. In dealing with the charity schools it was found that very gross neglect, misapplication, and often worse faults, were committed in the carrying on of the charitable trusts for educational purposes. When presenting the report of the committee to the Commons Brougham stated that there were in London 120,000 children wholly without means of education. The small proportion of those who received some sort of education were, for the most part, attending such schools as those described in the previous chapter.

Because of the neglect and abuses connected with charitable bequests for furthering education, Brougham, on behalf of the committee, recommended the appointment of a parliamentary commission to inquire into the administration of such funds in England and Wales, as a preliminary to legislation on education. He confidently asserted that, for a system of national education, "a very small part of the expense would ultimately rest with the public", if all the charitable funds were properly used. A bill for this purpose passed the Commons in 1818. But it met with a most determined opposition in the Lords, and was so changed by amendments that Brougham declared it would make the work of a commission of very little, if any, practical value. No compulsory powers were given it; many charities were exempted from its operations; and its opponents were appointed commissioners. Doubtless this was due to the fact that the select committee had called upon some of the dons of Oxford, the masters of Winchester and Eton, and the like, to reveal their means and methods. Great ill-feeling towards Brougham resulted from this, largely prompted by class prejudices and selfish interests and fears. He was regarded with feelings of personal hatred by many, and Tories generally declared they would not permit such a man to come to their houses, even to weed the garden. Nevertheless the commission which pursued its inquiries, and made reports, from 1819 to 1837, did a work which was far-reaching, and valuable beyond calculation. Perhaps the greatest tribute to its labours was the permanent establishment of the Charity Commissioners, which put an end to the grosser abuses, and did much to bring about a more wholesome condition of things.

Following up the work of the Select Committee, Brougham introduced, on June 28th, 1820, a "Bill for better promoting the means of education for His Majesty's subjects in England and Wales". This bill proposed to place the power of initiative in the hands of the members of the Quarter Sessions, who might proceed according to their own finding, or on the representation of the justices of the peace, the clergyman of the parish, or five resident householders. The money for building the schools was to come, in the first place, from the county treasurer, but, finally, from the Receiver General of the land tax. Whatever else was required in the way of money was to be levied by the parish officers every half-year. The vestry was to appoint the schoolmaster, who was required to be a communicant of the Church of England, and to have a certificate of character from a clergyman. He was to be approved by the clergyman of the parish, who had also the power to dismiss him. School fees and the course of teaching were to be fixed by the clergy, and they had the right to visit and examine the schools. The Bible alone was to be taught, and no form of worship allowed except the Lord's Prayer, in the day-school; but every child must attend church or chapel on Sunday, and a school meeting was to be held on Sunday evenings, when the Catechism and liturgy were to be taught.

Although the excellent features of imperial grant and local rates, and the exclusion of denominational teaching in the day-schools, must have appealed to many, the idea of giving the complete control to the Church roused the greatest possible indignation and resentment amongst all classes of Nonconformists. The bill was so generally and strongly opposed that it had to be withdrawn; and Brougham was afterwards almost as much distrusted by his friends as disliked by his opponents.

Failures such as these were, however, but the beginnings of success. Public opinion had been effectively aroused, private generosity and effort stimulated, and further serious neglect and abuse made almost impossible. Petitions were sent to the Commons by various public bodies, and there was a general movement, both in thought and effort, towards some system of national education. For example, a petition was sent from the inhabitants of Epping and Harlow, praying that something might be done to rescue the young from the temptations to crime to which ignorance and poverty exposed them. Statistics were quoted to show how closely connected ignorance and criminality were. The Unitarian congregation of Green-gate, Salford, also petitioned, pointing out that there seemed to be ample funds already existing in charitable endowments; and should these prove insufficient, they would cheerfully pay their share of any necessary rate.

It would indeed have been surprising if, when the life of the nation was feverish in the struggles for freedom from political, social, and religious servitude, an endeavour to secure intellectual liberty and development had been absent. But the first direct efforts taken for freedom of thought consisted in the agitation for doing away with the tax on knowledge, viz. the stamp duty of fourpence on every copy of a newspaper. Through the opportunity offered by the papers by working-men for working-men which sprang up during this period many must have found themselves to be possessed of powers of expression and argument unsuspected by either themselves or their friends. And all must have been aroused to a recognition of what was possible to them, when opportunity and means were offered. On such good ground as this it was that societies like the Central Society of Education cast their seeds of learning and self-help.

The passing of the Reform Bill in 1832, and the assembling of the reformed Commons—containing an overwhelming majority of reformers—in 1833, opened the flood-gates of legislative reforms. The reform of most vital importance to the national life and prosperity was, as it were, surreptitiously introduced by a back door. On 17th August, 1833, in the Report of the Committee of Supply, an item of "£20,000 for the purposes of education" was set down. In support of this vote Lord John Russell and Lord Althorp pointed out that it was only carrying out a suggestion made in the report of the Select Committee (1818), in which it was said that "several parishes would maintain schools if, in the first instance, they could be assisted with money to build the school-house". Hume opposed the vote on the grounds that the amount was quite inadequate for a system of national education; and that without such a system no grants should be given, for they would only have the effect of drying up private bounty. Cobbett, strange to say, was a root-and-branch objector to the grant. He said: "Take two men, one that can plough and make hurdles, and be a good shepherd, and one that can plough and read", and the former "was the best man". To which a correspondent to *The Poor Man's Guardian* very pertinently replied: " I consider if Mr. Cobbett had acted fairly, he would have taken two men, both of whom could plough, make hurdles, and be a good shepherd, and then have shown that the one that could not read was the best man. . . . If reading is such an injury to the working-man, why does Mr. Cobbett continue to inflict further injury by writing articles week after week in *The Poor Man's Guardian*, which is chiefly circulated amongst working-men?" Cobbett also argued that with the great increase of education, in the Bell and Lancaster schools, during the last thirty-five years, morals had greatly declined and crimes multiplied by seven. "If all were to be scholars," said he, "it would be necessary for the whole population to shut up their mouths, and determine to eat no more."

The voting of this money attracted practically no notice. It was merely chronicled as an item of parliamentary news. Thus the *Poor Man's Guardian* for August 24 has, under "Parliamentary Doings", the note: "an opposition was made to the grant for education, on the ground of its being too small. It was, however, eventually agreed to." Other papers also confined themselves to brief statements of fact. Only the *Quarterly Journal of Education* (published by the Society for the Diffusion of Useful Knowledge) gives some general remarks on the topic, when publishing the conditions on which the grants were to be given. The writer points out that there was no measure to make public instruction a branch of our polity, but merely a recognition of the positive expediency of voting public money for public education. There was no special department of government to control the outlay, and therefore this work had been handed over to The National Schools Society and the British and Foreign Schools Society. But the principles of neither of these societies were such as were proper for a system of universal instruction. Whilst the terms of the latter society were, "as was well known, of a more comprehensive nature than those of the other society"; yet, since the former "is the more wealthy and influential, it is probable that it will be enabled to secure much the larger portion of the grant: the superior zeal of the other society (for nobody can doubt that it really is more zealous in the diffusion of education) will hardly be able, we think, to make up for its inferiority in wealth and other means of influence". It is rightly remarked that "the parliamentary grant may increase the number of schools, but it will not tend, in the slightest degree, to improve teachers; and, of course, can exercise no really beneficial influence on national instruction".

The grants were paid by the Treasury on the following conditions:—

1. The money was to be spent on new school-houses only, which were not to include dwellings for teachers or attendants.

2. At least half of the total cost for the building was to be raised by private subscriptions. This money was to be received, expended, and accounted for before the receipt of any public money.

3. All appeals for grant were to be sent through The National Schools Society or the British and Foreign Schools Society. These were to report to, and satisfy, the Treasury Board as to the need for a grant, and as to

the reasonable expectation of the permanent support of the school to be built.

4. The managers of schools built by the aid of such grants were to be bound to submit their accounts to audit, and make periodical reports on the state of the school and the number of children educated therein.

5. In giving grants, preference would be shown to large towns and cities; and due inquiry would be made as to the charitable funds available for public education already existing, in judging of the needs of the place.

The reasonable expectation of permanent support for a school took the form of a promise from the societies that they would raise ten shillings per head for every child for whom accommodation was provided in a school assisted by a government grant. The whole grant was divided between the two societies, according to the amount of subscriptions which they could guarantee.

The unreasonable and unnecessary principle of helping most those who are most able to help themselves (see conditions 3 and 5) has continued to vitiate the grants up to the present, and seems likely to continue to do so. The conditions are as limited, from the point of view of a generous and statesmanlike policy, as the funds are meagre. And yet they represent the best that the nation was prepared to do for itself, at a time when it had just risen to the moral and material magnificence of voting twenty millions of pounds for negro emancipation.

For six years the sum of £20,000 was administered by the Treasury through the two schools societies. It is hardly surprising to find that the money was practically wasted. The officials charged with the duty of granting it had no real knowledge or qualifications for their work. Hence no care was taken to insist on good school buildings, and their proper maintenance, or on the employment of efficient teachers. There was only rather more money to be spent, in many cases by those who had already shown how negligent, and worse, they could be in the control of public funds. In a few years the school buildings were falling into ruins, and formed but more bad homes for more bad schools.

Here we have a glaring example of the greatest weakness and most mischievous element in the so-called education system, viz. the absence of expert technical knowledge in those who constituted the court of final appeal. The result of this has always been that the wrong lines have constantly been taken, and persisted in till an overwhelming opposition has been set up. All sorts of *a priori* theories have been thrust upon the schools by politicians and permanent officials, without rhyme or reason other than the uniformed promptings of philanthropy, officiousness, or party tactics. Of these evils we shall have abundant instances in following the history of events from this time.

The unsatisfactory results obtained from the government grant soon led to further parliamentary action. On 3rd June, 1834, Mr. Roebuck moved for a committee to inquire into "the means of establishing a system of National Education". In the discussion which followed, the education given to the poor was declared to be as deficient in quality as in quantity, and to consist mainly in the teaching of words which conveyed no real ideas, or such dim and doubtful ones as to be of no real benefit. The need of training efficient teachers was insisted upon; and, finally, the appointment of "a select committee to inquire into the state of education of the people in England and Wales, and into the application of the grant made last session for the erection of school-houses, and to consider the expediency of further grants in aid of education" was passed.

This committee occupied two years in receiving evidence, but made no definite suggestions for further action. It served, however, to show that the desire for education was such that parents would send their children to church schools, where no others were available, even though they were dissenters and strongly objected to their children being compelled to learn the doctrines of the Established Church and attend Church services. The only places where teachers could get even a pretence of training were the Model Schools of the National School Society, and the British and Foreign School Society. At the latter's school in the Borough Road, three months appear to have been the usual limit of time given to the process. During this time, the secretary informed the committee, "our object is to keep them incessantly employed from five in the morning until nine or ten at night". It of course followed that many suffered in health through overwork. How hurried the whole business must have been is evident when we consider that the student had to acquire the little knowledge of the different subjects which he was to impart; to learn how to impart it; and to practise himself in the working of a school. The secretary said that each student was "put to superintend the lowest division in the school, the children learning their letters; and he goes from grade to grade up to that of superintendent of the school, so that no part of the school business is omitted".

Suggestions were put forward by the witnesses called before the committee as to the desirability of combining industrial training with learning, as was done in the charity schools; and the advantage of including drawing and singing amongst the subjects taught, as means of training the senses and giving pleasure. The old fears of a national system of education were re-stated again and again:—the inevitable result of school rates would be the destruction of voluntary subscriptions; some two millions of pounds would have to be provided if every parish were compelled to have a school; and a national system would mean "placing in the hands of the government, that is, of the ministers of the day, the means of dictating opinions and principles to the people". The only immediately practical result of the work of the committee seems to have been the appropriating, in 1835, of £10,000 for the establishment of a Normal School under the control and management of the government. But this sum was never used for the purpose for which it was originally intended.

In June, 1838, Mr. Wyse, the Chairman of Committees for the Central Society of Education, presented petitions in favour of a national system of education, to the House of Commons, and moved, "An address to Her Majesty, that she will be graciously pleased to appoint a Board of Commissioners of Education in England, with a view, especially, of providing for the wise, equitable, and efficient application of sums granted, or to be granted, for the advancement of education by Parliament, and for the immediate establishment of schools for the education of teachers in accord with the intention already expressed by the Legislature ". In support of his motion he said that of two millions of children between the ages of seven and fourteen years, in England and Wales, one-half was wholly uneducated. In England the proportion of educated children to the whole population was 1 in 14; in New York 1 in 3; in Switzerland 1 in 7; in Prussia 1 in 6; in Holland 1 in 9; in Belguim 1 in 11; in Austria 1 in 12; in France 1 in 16; in Russia (omitting serfs) 1 in 6. Of those regarded as receiving education, in England, more than half received it in Sunday-schools, where it was of the most inadequate and superficial kind. Whilst every country in Europe except England had its board of education, in this country the work of looking after this important matter was handed over to a government department, which could not possibly manage it effectively. He proposed, therefore, that a central board of education should be established, to be composed of fair proportions of representatives of the different parties and feelings prevalent in the country; and that with this board there should be combined a system of local bodies, or boards, to give efficiency to the general scheme and to control abuses as they arose. The central board would be able to acquire such extensive information as would enable them to act with enlightened views; while the local boards would supply the valuable elements of individual interest, personal knowledge, and prompt control.

Lord John Russell, on the part of the ministry, said that the principle on which the Treasury acted in distributing the grant was, that it was their duty, not to give half of the grant to each of the two schools societies, but so to administer it that the greatest amount of education should be obtained. Hence the society which raised the greatest amount of voluntary subscriptions received the largest share of the grant. This had given the following results: in 1833 the number of scholars whose education had been assisted by the grant was 30,356, and these were in places the population of which amounted to over a million. In 1834 the number of children was over forty thousand, out of a population of nearly two millions; whilst in 1835 the scholars were over forty-five thousand, from a population of just above one and a half millions. So long as the rule of giving grant in proportion to voluntary subscriptions held, it was evident that a large portion of the country, including the poorest classes, would be left without education. He would suggest that they might give grants to increase the salaries of teachers, since it was found that the best of them soon left a profession in which they got only forty or fifty pounds a year.

Mr. Colquhoun said that the Treasury had never attempted to regulate the system of education. Their duty had been confined to the distribution of the grant which was annually voted. Of the £100,000 granted during the last five years, the National Society had received £70,000, and had raised £220,000 by voluntary subscriptions. With this money they had built over seven hundred additional schools, providing accommodation for 130,000 more children. The British and Foreign Schools Society had received £30,000, and had, he presumed, added proportionately to their schools and scholars.

Other speakers urged the absolute necessity of inspecting the schools aided by the government grant, and the wholesome effect which this was likely to exercise. One member declared that the grant should be £200,000, and ought not to be entrusted to two irresponsible bodies; and another pointed out the folly of so arranging matters that those who were least able to help themselves, and therefore required the most assistance, found it impossible to get any aid at all. When put to the vote the motion was lost, there being 70 ayes and 74 noes.

This continued impotence of parliament to provide a national remedy for what every single member of both houses admitted to be a national disgrace and danger, is probably one of the most striking features in the whole of its history. The only thing that kept the government from making the mass of the people human, was the determination of some to keep them from being made anything less than divine.

Chapter IV.

The Committee of Council on Education.

We shall now have to deal with the subject of national education whilst it is the shuttlecock of religious, political, and philanthropic parties. The forces and factions which have from then till now busied themselves with the matter, sadly to its hurt, began to take definite form and action at this point. The State was at last definitely represented by a committee of the Privy Council. The actions of this authority were in many instances keenly resented and resisted by the Church party, who continued to assert their exclusive right to the control of education. The monopoly thus claimed and exercised, in a large measure, by the Church, aroused the jealousy and just resentment of the Dissenters, who soon realized the power they possessed among the working-classes, and were not slow to make use of it. Besides these there were the purely political and social forces making for education, and though largely opposed to the sectarian rivalries, yet constrained to make use of the religious organizations as the best practical means for obtaining some kind of progress. And there was the earnest and enlightened party which founded "The Central Society of Education", and which was disinterestedly concerned only to establish a sound system of national education for its own sake. Decidedly this party represented the best intellect, the most advanced knowledge, and the most generous and statesmanlike views on the subject in the country at that time. They were called "secularists", because they wished to separate the teaching of secular and religious subjects, and they were accused of desiring, and aiming

The Committee of Council on Education. 67

at, the downfall of religious faith. Nothing was more untrue of them, as a party, or unworthy of their accusers.

It is fair to say that the thought, energy, time, and money which ought to have been given to the advance of education were mainly consumed in a game of party checkmate. Whilst all parties should have been united in building up the national culture, they were engaged in breaking down or preventing party privileges in the control of the work. It is a sorry story to read, this account of a struggle in which nearly all were for their parties, and only a faithful few were for the state. It is not as though there had been no solution of the religious difficulty. Able men of all parties suggested practicable schemes which met all reasonable demands, and there were systems at work, in Ireland and elsewhere, which showed that such plans were actually satisfying reasonable people. But there is nothing so ignorant as ignorance. Ever since then the country has been engaged in regaining from the sects powers and duties which ought never to have been separated from the State, as both sound theory and actual practice seem to have abundantly and conclusively demonstrated during the last twenty-eight years.

The twelfth of February, 1839, was a day somewhat memorable in the history of elementary education, for it was the birthday of our Education Department, and the beginning of a real governmental control of popular instruction. Lord John Russell, after indulging in a general review of education, and denying the claim of the Church of England to the complete control of the matter, announced the intentions of the ministry with regard thereto. He said that, since a board of education would not be likely to possess the confidence of the Church, he thought it better that the government should form that body—call it a board, or committee, or what you will—not from any one religious body or sect, or from members of various sects, but from the official servants of the crown, who must always depend upon the confidence of that House, and who must look to them to decide whether or not the system which they recommended was such as should be supported. He had, therefore, by Her Majesty's command, proposed that the President of the Council, and other Privy Councillors, being not more than five persons, should form a board, who should consider in what manner the grants of money made by that House from time to time should be distributed. He also hoped that the annual grant would be increased to £30,000. Two of the duties proposed for this committee were to establish a good normal school, which should give religious instruction, general education, moral training, and cultivate habits of industry through the learning of some trade or profession; and to superintend the compilation of a superior class of school-books. It might grant gratuities to teachers, and in various other ways promote the great cause of education. He thought it would also be possible, with the co-operation of the guardians of the union, to make some advances in the establishing of infants' schools. He was not prepared to introduce a bill, nor did he think that the plan proposed was the best which could be adopted, but it was the most practicable in the present state of the country.

Considerable and general surprise, and some irritation on the part of the Tories, was expressed by members of the House, on hearing the above statement. One Tory member said that he felt much satisfaction that the noble lord proposed to do so little mischief on this occasion; but another declared that the scheme appeared to him to be full of the most alarming mischiefs. Of course Mr. Wyse was highly delighted to hear of such a promising outlook. For, as he said, bad teachers and bad methods; a very limited circle of subjects, and those taught in the worst manner—from a wretched supply of ill-written books in many cases—in the worst situations, and under the most unfavourable physical and moral circumstances; such were the leading characteristics of all schools as shown by inquiries lately made, either in or out of that House, upon the subject. The two schools societies had never had a regular body of inspectors, and up to that hour no inspection existed on the part of the government, that is, the first of all securities for the proper application of these educational funds had not yet been established. They had hitherto been taking account not of good schools but of good school-houses.

During the adjourned debate, four months later, Lord Stanley led the opposition. He objected to giving the control of education to a body so composed, and so constituted, as to be decidedly and exclusively political in its character, and necessarily fluctuating and uncertain in its composition; a body in which there was no element of a defined or fixed principle of action; and into which, from its constitution and composition, it was impossible that it could so happen that a single individual could be admitted of those who were by the laws of the country entitled to superintend the moral education, and to direct the spiritual instruction, of the people. He found it laid down by a Chief Justice in a case so early as the 11th of Henry IV., in the old French of those times:—" La doctrine et information des enfants est chose espirituel". Chief Justice Holt had confirmed this when he said: "Without doubt, schoolmasters are, in a great measure, intrusted with the instruction of youth in principles, and, therefore, it is necessary that they should be of sound doctrine; and in order thereto subject to the regulation of the ordinary" (The King v. Hill, 1701). If the control of religious instruction were given to laymen, the foundations of faith would be destroyed, and general scepticism and national infidelity introduced.

The church party directed all their force against the government proposal to establish a normal school at Kneller Hall, because chaplains were to be appointed for the different denominations, provided that there was a certain number of scholars of each sect in the school. In the debate in the House of Lords, the Bishop of Chichester said that such a plan would lead to evil, for the idea that it did not matter to which religious party one belonged would give rise to the notion that any religion or no religion would do. To establish the school would be to deal the heaviest blow that had as yet been struck at the religion of the country. Lord Brougham protested very strongly against the claim that the education of the country belonged exclusively to the Church, and that the Church should control the teaching, or that the people should not be instructed. It could not be admitted that it was right or just to tax dissenters to pay for the religious education of churchmen; or that only the religious instruction of churchmen should be paid for out of the public funds. To which the bishop replied that he had never made any such proposition as that which the noble and learned lord had demolished with such vigorous blows.

The result of the strong agitation carried on by the church party was that Lord John Russell felt compelled to tell the Commons that it was not the intention of the government to persist in the proposal to found the normal school. The money set apart for this object would be divided between the two schools societies. At the same time he felt bound to observe that he was by no means satisfied in leaving the matter as it was, and giving the control of education to two voluntary societies, who might have very imperfect and defective plans of education, which might be open to the most serious objections.

But the position was one of real difficulty for the government. The original mistake of giving grants only through the societies—instead of doing national work by governmental machinery—had seemed to imply the admission of the Church's claims and created something like vested interests. And now, when the public conscience recognized the need of public instruction, and demanded that it should be supplied, the government found that it had armed what would otherwise have been but a feeble foe to the nationalization of education. All, therefore, that was obtained from parliament was the vote for £30,000 and the constitution of an education department—the Committee having been already constituted by an Order in Council dated April 10, 1839. In the same year that this sum was voted for the education of some three millions of children, £70,000 was voted for building royal stables.

It is surely a very significant fact that Lord Stanley,

who led the opposition in the Commons, had himself been the leading official concerned in the institution of the Board of Commissioners of National Education in Ireland in 1831. This board not only took over the entire management of the education of the poor, because the government was of opinion that no private society, deriving its income from "private sources, and only made the channel of the munificence of the Legislature without being subject to any direct responsibility, could adequately and satisfactorily accomplish the end proposed"; but it dealt firmly with the question of religious instruction, laying down rules and regulations as to the time and manner for it, and actually compiling a book of "Scripture extracts" to be read in schools, during the hours given to ordinary literary instruction. It issued a series of official school-books, and sold them to schools at reduced prices; and established a training college and normal school; appointed inspectors to visit and report on the schools; and made grants for school-buildings, and for increasing teachers' salaries.

We must, therefore, look deeper for the reasons of the intense feeling and opposition which the plans of the government aroused amongst churchmen throughout the country. There were still those who, like the Bishop of Durham, heartily wished that some form of religious instruction, which might be used in all schools, could be agreed upon, while catechisms and all peculiar doctrines were taught only on the Sabbath-day. But, as Dr. Overton points out in his book on *The Anglican Revival*, it was just at this period that the rise of this movement was at its height, and it can hardly be doubted that the re-awakening of the Church to renewed thought and action was the chief cause of the vigour and perseverance with which her claims were pressed. The theory of the Church as an institution of divine origin, with divinely-appointed powers, authority, and duties, constantly maintained and renewed through an order of priests in apostolical succession, was being urged upon the minds and lives of churchmen. The divine rights of the Church were not only before and superior to the rights of the State, but they would not allow of any admixture of secular, or dissenting, authority or control in what churchmen deemed the sphere of the Church. No one outside the line of priestly apostolical succession could effectively undertake the Church's work. And it was considered that the religious instruction of the people was the right and duty of the Church.

The general character of the claims of the High Church party is shown by the words of its leader. Keble boldly declared that England "as a Christian nation was a part of Christ's Church, and bound in all her legislation and policy by the fundamental laws of that Church". How much less, therefore, could it be admitted that the State should take under its entire charge the control of what Archdeacon Denison calls the "parish school—the nursery of the parish church". Bishop Blomfield (London), the able and vigorous champion of church schools, declined to admit the claim for religious equality, and said, during a debate in the House of Lords, that if every sect was to have the same privileges as the Established Church, it might as well abdicate its functions. The duty of the bishops, as rulers of the Church, was to protest against any system not connected with it, or which by implication might throw discredit on it, or raise dissenting sects to a level with it.

Such views of the relation of Church and State were by no means a theory special to the clergy. They had a real place in the intellectual and religious life of the nation taken as a whole. That the State should profess, and cause to be taught, at least the Christian faith was, practically, held by all intelligent and worthy men. Speeches by members of the House of Commons, throughout the discussions on education, almost invariably assert or assume this. Perhaps its finest and most forcible expression, on behalf of laymen, came from Mr. Gladstone, some twenty years later, in his work *The State in its Relation with the Church*. In this his aim was to prove that every state must have a conscience, and, therefore, must profess a state religion. The Church of England was, therefore, the authorized exponent of the religious views of the state, and a guide to the nation in religious matters.

The two great barriers to the success of this theory were: the growth of religious dissent, and political utilitarianism. Dissenters were reasonably enough jealous of the privileges and prerogatives which churchmen enjoyed, and with regard to which they had equal rights as citizens. Macaulay was easily able to show, in his criticism of Mr. Gladstone's theory, that it was impossible for any state to have the kind of transcendental conscience which was assumed. It could not pledge itself beforehand, as such a conscience would require, to do only certain things under any circumstances whatsoever. But this view, as a general conviction, has only been evolved through the stress of political necessities, and the development of intellectual freedom and culture. Besides, the possession of a national conscience, though vital to a worthy national life, is quite a different matter from the profession of a religious creed, which must always mean a political house divided against itself in religious affairs. It is quite possible for the truly moral to be the sternest opponents of the intensely religious—in a sectarian sense. The whole history of the education movement is, indeed, an account of the gradual triumph of the purely political and moral theory over the church-and-state and denominational religious theory.

In the preface to a published sermon, preached in February, 1838, Bishop Blomfield writes: "no system of education can be forced upon the people at large which shall not be in conformity with the principles of the Church of England, and worked by its instrumentality. It will be our own fault if it be otherwise." In the sermon itself he frankly declares: "We assert that *this* [the imparting of the rudiments of knowledge] is not to be the main and primary, much less the sole, object of our endeavours, in educating the youth of this country, of whatever class they may be".

Whilst one can appreciate the devotion to conscientious belief which animated churchmen, and for which they made considerable sacrifices of time, effort, and money; yet one cannot but feel that it is more than regrettable that they did not more clearly and effectively recognize the very serious national loss—moral, spiritual, and material—which was involved in delaying and lessening the instruction of the masses. They themselves admitted that the more the intelligence and knowledge of the people were increased, the more easily and fully would they be able to receive religious instruction. But they were determined to capture the schools for the Church, at all costs. And they practically succeeded, for the time being. Not only did they compel the ministry to give up the plan for a normal school, but, in the House of Lords, they carried an address to the Queen, praying that no steps might be taken to give effect to the other plans put forth until the Upper House had considered them. The address was taken by the peers in procession to Buckingham Palace. The Queen replied that, whilst she regretted such an address at such a time, "You may be assured that, deeply sensible of the duties imposed upon me, and more especially of that which binds me to the support of the Established Church, I shall always use the powers vested in me by the Constitution for the fulfilment of that sacred obligation. It is with a deep sense of that duty that I have thought it right to appoint a Committee of my Privy Council to superintend the distribution of the grants voted by the House of Commons for public education. Of the proceedings of the Committee annual reports will be laid before Parliament, so that the House of Lords will be enabled to exercise its judgment on them; and I trust that the funds placed at my disposal will be found to have been strictly applied to the objects for which they were granted, with due respect to the rights of conscience, and with a faithful attention to the security of the Established Church." Whilst, however, soothing their lordships' fears, the reply indicated that the ministry was firm in its purpose.

Four days after this reply was given, the second reading of a bill by Lord Brougham was taken. In drawing attention to the neglected state of education, and the poor quality of the little which was given, Lord Brougham mentions the following incident: A schoolmaster was

The Committee of Council on Education. 75

asked if he understood Greek. Yes, was the reply. Latin? Yes. Geography? Yes. Then one of the examiners observed: "Aye, we have *multum in parvo* here!" Upon which the teacher, seeing that notes of his answers were being made, added: "Yes, and you may put down *multum in parvo* too".

Lord Brougham put forward what he considered the chief points of his bill. First: there was to be no compulsion. He was persuaded that if the people of England were now for education, compulsion would set them against it. Second: no attempt was to be made to ensure the universal adoption of any one kind of schooling or mode of instruction; because, in different places different sorts of instruction were required. For instance, one kind of instruction was required in the manufacturing districts, and another in the agricultural districts. Third: those who contributed towards the expenses of the schools should have a considerable share in their management. People would be more likely to send their own children, and to get others to send theirs, under such conditions. Fourth: a central board was to be established, which, under due restrictions, should have the check and control over the local management of the ratepayers. Fifth, and sixth: this board should maintain communication between the Church, or the government (as might be provided), and the schools. Its special duty would be to collect from all parts the lights and improvements which experience would produce, and to diffuse these generally throughout the country.

Every parish, or place, might summon a meeting of the ratepayers, to consider the need for schools, and a majority of such persons had the right to communicate with the central board, for the purpose of establishing a school. This central board was to consist of two great officers of state, who would be responsible to, and removable by, parliament, and three irremovable commissioners, to be appointed by the crown, or by statute, as might therefore be decided. They were to be removable only through an address to both houses of parliament. The central board would thus be connected with, and dependent upon, the executive government. No act of this board, involving the payment of money, would be valid unless agreed to by a majority of its members, one of whom must be a minister of state. And this rule was also to apply in the distribution of school patronage, and the appointment of inspectors, secretaries, and clerks.

The first duty of the board would be the distribution of the government grant; but it was also to control the decisions of the local ratepayers so as to protect minorities, *e.g.* it might allow a minority to establish a voluntary school, even where the majority were in favour of a rate-aided school. It was not to be lawful for it to sanction the establishment of any school in which it was not part and parcel of the regulations that the Scriptures—the Authorized Version—should be taught; but there was always to be provision made for the withdrawing of the children of any parents who objected to such instruction. With such a provision the board might sanction the teaching of the Catechism, liturgy, and articles of the Church.

The persons to whom he proposed to give the power of voting at school meetings were those who had been members for three years of a mechanics' institute. And he would go a little further and say that the right of voting at the choice of a school committee should also extend to every person who should possess the certificate, from a schoolmaster, of his due attendance at any of the public schools.

Against these plans the Bishop of Chichester objected, because they did not provide for the *ex officio* rights of the clergy. On the contrary, as the ratepayers were to elect the committee of management, the chairman might be a shopkeeper or clerk of the parish, and the clergyman might sit as one of the committee. Such a change as this, in country parishes, could never be tolerated. Besides which, the inspectors and the central board would take the conduct of the schools very largely out of the hands of the clergy. What the clergy required was to be the sole superintendents of the Christian doctrines and lessons taught in the schools; to select the books; to visit frequently the classes; to try and examine the children, especially in their Catechism and religious progress; and to counsel and aid the masters. That the Church was discharging the duty she undertook was shown in her diocesan and local boards, already formed, or in process of formation; the steps being taken to establish a college for the more effectual training of masters; and the night-schools, which the clergy had formed, to continue the work of instructing those who left the day-schools at so early an age.

This bill represented the high-water mark of what was considered to be in any way practicable, even by the most advanced advocates of national education. It was very far short of what even its author thought desirable, having been drafted so as to catch, if possible, the consent of the more enlightened of the religious parties, by offering a generous compromise. But both Churchmen and Dissenters feared and distrusted it; and it shared the common fate of such attempts.

The bishop's fear that inspectors would take the control of the schools out of the hands of the clergy was shared very generally by the clergy, and so intense was their objection to admitting them to the schools that they refused no less than half the total grants offered, rather than submit to the inspection which was insisted on by the minutes of the council for 1839. The Rev. Dr. Biber, the biographer of Bishop Blomfield, declares that Archdeacon Sinclair (then secretary of the National Society) protected, and saved, "the church, through the medium of the committee of the National Society, from the insidious machinations of the secretary of the Committee of Council, who, in his subordinate position, had assumed to himself large and irresponsible powers, as *quasi* minister of public instruction". The National Society and the Committee of Council, however, negotiated; and finally, what has been called a concordat was entered into, and found expression in the minute regarding the appointment of inspectors. The agitation, doubtless, also gave rise to the very urgent instructions to inspectors against interfering with, or, unless requested, even making suggestions about, the control and conduct of schools.

We have set out at considerable length the attitude and actions of the Church party, because of the overwhelming influence which it then exercised, and also because of the necessity of clearly understanding the nature of the influence which has always been, and still is, a determining factor, of the first importance, in any and every change in our system of national education. At that time the Tories claimed, and the Whigs admitted, both in words and deeds, that the country as a whole was with the Church party. Of their high-minded and conscientious motives, as a party, no fair-minded critic can doubt; but of the wisdom of their policy some of the most able of their own body have spoken in terms of strong condemnation, and subsequent events have shown how mistaken and short-sighted was much that they did, even from their own point of view.

One element of the opposition which the government plans met with, viz. that of the working-classes, deserves special notice. At this time of the uprising of democracy the masses were like dry tinder to a living spark with regard to the influence both of the dreamers and the doers in religion and politics. Not a few of them were equally prepared to make a riot for, or to worship as a person of the deity, the lunatic Thom; they believed that Robert Owen would lead them to a socialistic land flowing with the milk of riches and the honey of laziness; and they were convinced that Chartism was to bring the millennium of the poor. But so frequently were they deluded, deceived, defeated, and betrayed—as dense ignorance stimulated by brute force was bound to be when exploited, as it sometimes was, by self-seeking and unprincipled men—that they at last became sullen and suspicious of all outside their own ranks who pretended to be their friends and helpers. As Mr. Rose points out in his *Rise of Democracy*, the people were soured by their disappointments and hopeless of help coming from above them socially. He records how, "alike spurning and despairing of any help from the government, Lovett proposed (in his book on *Chartism*) that the people should educate themselves (politically) by a vast voluntary effort. The subscription of a penny a week by everyone who had signed the national petition for the Charter would, he affirmed, yield a fund sufficient to establish 80 district halls and 710 circulating libraries, besides maintaining four paid Chartist lecturers and distributing 20,000 political tracts."

A very practical exhibition of this feeling was given in Burnley, in 1847. At a public meeting held to consider the government proposals for the extension of education, a vote adverse to its plans was carried by a majority in the proportion of 150 to 1. A manifesto put forward by the working-men declared that the government plan was designed to give knowledge that "it may be so engrafted into the minds of your children, that they will always be passive slaves, and submissively obedient to the powers that be". A working-man writing on the subject says: "I have carefully read over the Minutes of the Council, and I cannot help thinking that the 'scheme' is deeply laid, that the 'thin edge of the wedge' is intended to be introduced; and if the Government once introduce it, there will not be wanting those who will drive it forward. The hopes of salary, emolument, and pension, I fear, will cause a whole host of expectants to be a sort of tools that will train the youthful minds to believe in that doctrine so useful to those who fatten on the industry of others—the doctrine of passive obedience and non-resistance. And the 'scheme' of granting 'certificates' is such that not only the whole of the 'pupil-teachers', &c., will be put completely in the power of the Government, but also their families; the fact is, they will all be bound to their good behaviour towards all Her Majesty's subjects, but more especially to the 'parochial clergymen' and 'managers of schools'."

This fear of the workmen with respect to the dictation and cultivation of opinions in secular matters had its counterpart in the fears of the Dissenters that the government plans were designed to foster and further the religious dogmas of the Church of England; whilst Churchmen themselves believed that there was, in the schemes of the Whig governments, an insidious attempt to promote secularism in education. It is not surprising that men having such fears made common cause against the efforts of the Whigs, and that these efforts were unsuccessful. The policy of the Church, conducted by men of commanding ability, position, and influence, was managed with consummate diplomacy, and made use of the fears and wishes of the Dissenters and working-classes in such a way as to safeguard her powers and privileges from the activities and ambitions of the followers of democracy and dissent, and to secure still further opportunities for extending her own influence and dominion.

Now that we have reviewed the conditions and forces which were the determining influences in the progress of popular education, we can return once more to the chain of events which make up its history. In 1841 Mr. Gillon moved, in the Commons, that grants of money be made to Mechanics' Institutes, for the encouragement of art instruction, other than that given in schools of design. He drew attention to the fact that the estimates included a sum of £30,000 for the education of emancipated negroes, and yet only £40,000 was given for education in England. Sir Robert Peel supported the motion, on the grounds that foreign countries, especially Prussia, were in advance of us in art instruction, and, therefore, our industries would be likely to suffer; also, such work as was done in Mechanics' Institutes was good for the health and morals of the working-classes. Mr. Labouchere said that the government were willing and anxious to promote such education, and thought that they could best do so by establishing normal schools for teachers, publishing elementary text-books, and collecting works of art adapted to the study of design. The matter might very well be left in the hands of the government. It was so left.

The following year a somewhat important agitation took place. Mr. Hullah had started some demonstration classes in theoretical and vocal music for teachers in Exeter Hall, and they had become so popular that others were allowed to join the classes, until at last the whole building was required to accommodate the pupils, amounting to no less than 3300, taught by Mr. Hullah

The Committee of Council on Education.

and others. Besides these students it was estimated that there were 50,000 children in London alone who were being taught vocal music by teachers who had been trained in these classes. The fees were very small, being only 8 to 10 shillings to mechanics, 15 to teachers, and 30 to other persons, for the course of sixty lessons. The success was such as to create an enthusiasm for learning in the pupils, and they managed to get petitions presented to parliament praying that grants might be given for establishing classes in writing, arithmetic, and linear drawing, and erecting a building in which they might be given. Lord Wharncliffe (President of the Privy Council), in the Lords, and Sir R. Peel (Prime Minister) in the Commons, presented the petitions, and expressed themselves as being warmly in favour of them, except as to a grant for building. But the matter was again and again postponed, for further consideration, and finally no grant was given. The incident is, however, important, in that it is the first occasion on which the principle of grants for teaching, as well as for buildings, was approved by both Houses.

At the beginning of 1843 Lord Ashley moved, in the Commons, "that an humble address be presented to Her Majesty, praying that Her Majesty will be graciously pleased to take into her instant and serious consideration the best means of diffusing the benefits and blessings of a moral and religious education among the working-classes of her people". This motion was grounded upon the evidence of the truly terrible condition of the children of the working-classes, brought to light by the work of the select committee on the education of the poorer classes in England and Wales, appointed in 1838. Both political parties heartily sympathized with this motion, and Sir J. Graham announced that he was prepared to introduce, on behalf of the government, for immediate discussion, a bill which would attempt to remedy some of the evils mentioned. The bill was to provide for the compulsory education of children in workhouses, and those employed in woollen, flax, silk, and cotton manufactories. Children between 8 and 13 years of age were not to work more than $6\frac{1}{2}$

hours per day, and were to attend school for at least 3 hours. Government loans were to be made for the erection of schools, which were to be maintained out of the poor-rates. Thus far the bill, though limited in its scope, was thorough, effective, and even advanced in its principles. But the management clauses formed the fatal bone of contention. These provided that the majority of the trustee managers should always be churchmen; the headmaster was to be a churchman, and his appointment subject to the approval of the bishop; and the right of inspection was to be reserved to the clerical trustees and the committee of council. There was to be a conscience clause, but this was but a poor palliation of the fact that where the children would be nearly all Dissenters the managers would be nearly all Churchmen.

A violent agitation against the bill took place throughout the country. More adverse petitions were presented regarding it than had ever been previously known in parliament. As a result the government introduced several changes when the bill was in committee. But this availed nothing, and the government had to admit defeat, and withdraw the bill. The ministry had avowedly fought for the pre-eminence of the Church influence in a State scheme, and had been ignominiously worsted. The Dissenters were elated with their victory, and the knowledge that they had so much influence in the country. But this triumph was, in a large measure, unfortunate, in that it led them to adopt an aggressive attitude towards both the Church party and the committee of council. They now fought for their own hand in the same way as the Church party did, and combined with the latter and others to resist the exercise of control by the State authority; and thus they became real obstructionists to national progress in education. How far this feeling went is best shown by the action of the Congregational Union, which decided, in 1843, not to accept any aid whatever from the government; and was of opinion that government interference in education could not be sanctioned "without establishing principles and precedents dangerous to civil and religious liberty, inconsistent with the rights of industry, and superseding the duties of parents and of churches". They had the courage of their convictions, and by 1859 they had raised £180,000 for school buildings; established the Homerton Training College; and had about 400 schools wholly supported by subscriptions and school pence.

Three months after Sir J. Graham's bill, Mr. Roebuck brought forward a motion that any bill passed should exclude any attempt to teach peculiar religious opinions, because it would give rise to sectarian jealousy and conflict, and so hinder and defeat the spread of education. National education consisted, he held, in the endeavour to impart that knowledge to children which might enable them to do their duty in that station of life in which Providence placed them, and to consult their own happiness consistently with that of others; and also in the endeavour, whilst they gave the knowledge which taught children to know what was right, to give that knowledge which would enable them to follow it. The State should leave the teaching of religion to the pastors of the various sects, and confine itself to secular instruction. Of course such a motion suffered a heavy defeat.

The following month Mr. Hume moved for leave to bring in a bill for the establishment of schools to promote a sound education for the rising generation of the United Kingdom, at the public expense, without wounding the feelings or injuring the rights of any sect or class of the community, but confining the business of the schoolmaster to the secular and moral training of the children, and leaving all religious instruction to religious teachers distinct from the school; to the end that general instruction, and a spirit of Christian brotherhood and good-will may be disseminated amongst all classes and denominations. He proposed this separation of religious and secular instruction because the endeavour to combine them had defeated every previous attempt to found a system of national education. He did not wish to prevent the diffusion of religious instruction, far from it, but he wished to promote secular education for all. This would be all in favour of the spread of religious influences. That the country was keenly interested in the subject of education was shown by the fact that 25,705 petitions, signed by 4,389,496 persons, had been presented concerning Sir J. Graham's bill—more than ninety per cent of the petitioners being against the bill. Mr. Hume's bill was on much the same lines as Lord Brougham's, except as to religious instruction, and the fact that the providing of schools for each district was a compulsory duty. The bill was counted out.

Mr. Ewart, in 1845, moved "that a statement be made on the part of the government, of the condition and prospect of such educational establishments as were supported wholly or partially by a vote of this House"; and "that it is expedient that schools for the training of masters be more extensively promoted". In reply to which Sir R. Peel pointed out that the reports of the inspectors of schools were annually laid upon the table, and promised that a statement should also be made when the vote for the education estimates was taken. Mr. Ewart brought forward the same resolutions the following year, but nothing further came of them.

When laying the Minutes of the Committee of Council, for 1847, upon the table in the House of Lords, Lord Lansdowne said that whilst any bill for the extension of education on a large and comprehensive plan would meet serious if not overwhelming difficulty, from religious parties and those who object to any state interference, yet the government hoped to do something to still further advance the work of education, by means of certain proposals which he was about to submit. They proposed to increase the number of inspectors, who even then would be unable to pay a visit to every school in the course of a year; to give to qualified teachers in good schools the right of taking apprentices (pupil-teachers), for whose training they (the head-teachers) would receive a special grant; to send such of these pupil-teachers as proved themselves capable to training colleges, by means of Queen's scholarships, and to receive the others into the government revenue departments; to give small old-age pensions to teachers (men and women) who had served for not less than fifteen years in approved schools, and gratuities to specially-recommended teachers; and to provide apparatus for the learning of trades, with workshops in towns and fields in the country. These proposals met with general approval.

Chapter V.

The Committee of Council on Education—
Continued.

That the State authority must prevail amongst parties at strife with each other and with the central authority is obvious. So long as the great religious bodies were ready and eager to accept grants of money from the state they were bound to submit to the conditions attached to them; and it was only a question of how little control, direct and indirect, the central authority would be content with, and how much the voluntary managers would yield of power rather than refuse the grants. A kind of double, and contradictory, process seems now to go on. In response to agitations the government and the department—a government within the government, in a very real sense—continue to grant concessions to religious denominations with respect to the control of the schools; whilst, at the same time, they are gradually securing more and more power over them in their own hands. How this came about will be easily seen. Without any ulterior or party aims the department was bound to require certain guarantees, checks, and powers in order to satisfy parliament that the money voted was faithfully and effectively used. The final result was that the central authority managed the schools, substantially, through the local voluntary managers. That this was so, in fact though not in theory, can hardly be denied when one considers the detailed regulations laid down by the code; the fact that the inspectors of the central authority were the judges as to whether these conditions had been properly fulfilled, and that the grants were wholly dependent upon their decisions. As time went on these conditions became more detailed and rigorous, and the margin of liberty left to the local managers grew less and less, but always sufficient to allow of their perpetuating the miserable minimums of education and the petty economies which are the most costly of wastings instead of pressing forward to those generously wise maximums which are the cheapest economies.

Professor Lecky has said: " Education in its simplest form, which is one of the first and highest of all human interests, is a matter in which government initiation and direction are imperatively required, for uninstructed people will never demand it, and to appreciate education is itself a consequence of education ". There seems not to have been even a dim and doubtful idea of this truth lurking remotely behind the efforts of the Committee of Council. Initiation was left entirely to localities, and even if the most neglected districts did demand help, they were sent empty away unless they came already half-filled. Instead of being regarded as the most profitable national investment for increasing the productive capacity of the country, and as a cheap insurance against many social and political dangers, the grant seemed rather to be regarded as somewhat of the nature of a necessary bribe to the "lower orders", an undeserved benevolence to the poor, and a bulwark of religion and morality against the barbarism and crime which undoubtedly existed amongst the very poor. And this was the result of the report of the Committee on the Education of the Poorer Classes, issued in 1838, which said, " that the kind of education given to the children of the working-classes is lamentably deficient; that it extends (bad as it is) to but a small proportion of those who ought to receive it; and that, without some strenuous and persevering efforts being made on the part of the government, the greatest evils to all classes may follow from this neglect". The principle of political fears now supplements the principle of religious fears. People

The Committee of Council on Education. 87

seem to have realized the force of Paley's dictum: "To send an uneducated child into the world is injurious to the rest of mankind; it is little better than to turn out a mad dog or a wild beast into the streets". Contrast this miserable motive with the Prussian principle: It is my duty towards myself to develop to the utmost the powers with which I am endowed; it is my duty towards my neighbour to help him to develop his; we can best help each other through the state; the state therefore establishes a complete system of education, making the lowest kind imperative for all and the highest accessible to all.

In sketching the history of events it will be observed that we rely almost wholly upon the volumes of *Hansard*, and the Minutes and Reports of the Committee of Council. These must always be the main and most reliable sources of the history of our public elementary schools. Within the limits at our disposal it would be quite impossible to trace the workings of the external forces in any detail; besides which they may be said to have all reached their culmination and final expression in the House of Commons, or in the House of Lords.

The Committee of Council had been up and doing whilst parliament and the sects had been wrangling. Except that it could not directly do what the country and parliament had said should not be done, the Committee was a law unto itself with regard to the regulations which it drew up, and enforced upon those who accepted the aid of the government grant. By the aid of truly remarkable diplomacy and tact, it managed to constantly enlarge the borders of its work and influence, and to gain many a march upon the Church party. In short the real legislators on education were the lords of the Privy Council, and right well they did their work, considering the conditions and limitations under which they were compelled to do it.

An order in council, dated 3rd June, 1839, recommended that the £10,000 voted in 1835 for establishing a normal school, should be equally divided between the two schools societies; whilst the remainder of the money for the two preceding years, and the whole of that for

the current year, should be chiefly applied in aid of
school buildings, and, in particular cases, for the support
of schools. Several important and valuable modifications were made in the conditions upon which the grants
were to be given. These appeared in detail in the
minutes of the council for September 24 of the same
year, and as they express a new policy it will be well to
transcribe them in full.

"The following regulations will govern the appro-
priation of the sum entrusted to the superintendence of
the Committee for the present year.

"1. Every application for a grant to be made in the
form of a memorial addressed 'To the Right Honourable
the Lords of the Committee of Council on Education'.

"2. The committee will consider the memorials, according to the dates at which they have been or shall
be received.

"3. The right of inspection will be required by the
committee in all cases; inspectors, authorized by Her
Majesty in Council, will be appointed from time to time
to visit schools to be henceforth aided by public money:
the inspectors will not interfere with the religious instruction, or discipline, or management of the school, it
being their object to collect facts and information, and
to report the result of their inspections to the committee
of council.

"4. Before any application for aid shall be entertained,
the committee will require to be satisfied, by reference
either to the inspectors or to the National or British
and Foreign School Society, or, if the school be in
Scotland, to some competent authority there:—

"1st. That the case is deserving of assistance.
"2nd. That there are no charitable or other funds or
endowments which might supersede the necessity of a grant.
"3rd. That the site of the school-house has been
obtained with a good legal tenure; and that,
by conveyance to trustees, it has been duly
secured for the education of the children of the
poor.

"4th. That it is reasonable to expect that the school will be efficiently and permanently supported.

"5. The Committee will require that every building, on behalf of which any application is entertained, shall be of substantial erection, and that in the plans thereof not less than six square feet be provided for each child.

"6. All recipients of grants will be required to bind themselves to submit to any audit of their building account, and to furnish any reports of their schools, which the committee of council may require.

"7. The committee will require that the certificate hereto annexed [declaring that all these conditions have been, or will be, fulfilled] shall be signed by the applicants, and presented to the committee, before their lordships will authorize the payment of any grant which may be made to a school.

"8. In all ordinary cases the grants will be made in aid of the erection of school-houses (exclusive of residence for master or assistant) upon the following further conditions:—

"1st. That for every 10s. to be granted by the committee, the means of educating one child (at least) shall be provided.
"2nd. That the amount of private subscription shall be received, expended, and accounted for before their lordships will authorize the payment of the grant.

"9. In every application for aid to the erection of a school-house in England or Wales, it must be stated whether the school is in connection with the National Society or British and Foreign School Society; and if the said school be not in connection with either of these societies, the committee will not entertain the case, unless some special circumstances be exhibited to induce their lordships to treat the case as special."

The applications already received, on the date of the above, numbered 307, for schools to accommodate

50,302 scholars, the amount of grant asked for being £48,590.

To those applying for grants a circular was sent asking for replies to a long list of questions, which were to give details as to the site, its tenure, size, surroundings, and drainage; the trustees, their names and professions; the building, its foundation, materials, and dimensions; the windows, their number, size, frame material, and openings; the roof, its size, material, manner of construction, and drainage; the floor, its material, and height above the ground; the ventilation; and the playground. Also full information was asked for as to the district which the school supplied, its boundaries and population; the endowments or charitable funds for the education of the children of the poor which existed in the district; the other schools, and the number of pupils attending them; the grounds for regarding the case as deserving of assistance; the probable amount of annual subscriptions, donations, collections, fees, and other sources of income; the cost of site and building; the amount already subscribed; and the extent of the expected deficiency in the funds for the erection of the school-house. Very full information was given as to the manner of answering the questions, and some specimen replies were appended.

To establish a claim to be treated as a "special case", it had to be shown that there was great deficiency of education for the poorer classes in the district, and that, in spite of vigorous efforts by the inhabitants to obtain funds, there was indispensable need of further assistance. Or it might be that the loss of a generous patron, or a local disaster, might temporarily impoverish a school and make it a case for special treatment. If the school were not connected with either of the two societies, the objections to such connection had to be stated, and information supplied as to the religious instruction given, and attendance at church or chapel, and whether the parents were at liberty to withdraw their children from any peculiar religious instruction, or from attendance at church or chapel to which they objected, without suffering any disadvantage therefrom. In addition to

The Committee of Council on Education. 91

this the questions described above had to be answered, with additional ones dealing with the teachers, school-books, and methods of instruction.

A second order in Council, dated 10th August, 1840, dealt with the appointing of inspectors of schools in connection with the National Society of the Church of England. The archbishops were to have the right to recommend persons for such posts, and a right of veto in every such appointment. The instructions for these officers with regard to religious teaching were to be drawn up by the archbishops, and the general instructions given them by the committee of council were to be communicated to the archbishops before being finally sanctioned. Duplicate copies of the reports made by the inspectors were to be sent to the archbishop of the province, and the bishop of the diocese, in which the districts reported on were situated. The order further recommended that the grants of money should be in proportion to the number of children educated, and the amount of private subscriptions. But the committee was to have the power of making exceptions in certain cases, the grounds of which were to be stated in the annual returns to parliament.

We may mention here that in 1843, as the result of a sharp passage-at-arms between the committee of the British and Foreign School Society and the Committee of Council, concerning the somewhat searching and adverse report by the inspector appointed to visit British schools, Lord Wharncliffe promised that "no inspector for your schools will be appointed without the full concurrence of your committee". This concession had been preceded by a promise of an annual grant of £750 towards the maintenance of the Borough Road normal school.

In the instructions to inspectors, issued during the same month as the foregoing, the attitude of non-interference was strongly emphasized, and the inspectors were plainly told that they were not to offer any advice or information unless it were invited, nor were they to press any suggestion when disinclination to accept it was shown. They were to visit schools not in receipt of government grant if they were asked to do so, and so far as time and opportunity served. Besides visiting and inspecting schools, and examining the scholars, they were to conduct inquiries with regard to the ordinary and special cases for which grants were asked, and to inquire into the state of elementary education in particular districts. A special note was to be made of the fact "that no plan of education ought to be encouraged in which intellectual instruction is not subordinate to the regulation of the thoughts and habits of the children by the doctrines and precepts of revealed religion". And they were to inquire, with special care, how far the pupils at Church schools were having the doctrines and principles of the church instilled into their minds; if proper, sufficient, and convenient church accommodation was provided for them, and their attendance and behaviour at church satisfactory; whether they profited duly by such attendance; what was the practice as to opening and closing of the school with prayer and psalmody; and what religious instruction was given daily.

A very helpful minute was drawn up, for the guidance of school promoters, as to the plans and cost of school buildings. Full details, and plans and specifications for various kinds of schools, were given, as well as many pieces of excellent, though sometimes quaint and curious, advice. For example, it was suggested that a schoolroom would make an excellent place for the parochial or village library, and that the master might well be secretary to the local benefit society. The meetings of the society could be held in the schoolroom in the evening, which would be preferable to the tavern; whilst the money usually expended at the tavern, to repay the landlord for the use of his rooms, would be far more than sufficient to remunerate the schoolmaster secretary. The plans proposed rooms for the master—though no grant was given in aid of them—consisting of a sitting-room, bed-room, and a kitchen. If the numbers increased, a scullery was to be added. When the number of boys and girls exceeded 100, two bed-rooms were allowed, and all the rooms were to be larger. Why this increase

The Committee of Council on Education. 93

was thus regulated it is hard to tell. If the master had a family, common decency would seem to require a good deal more; whilst if he were a bachelor he would riot in luxury with two bed-rooms—notwithstanding that "the arrangements for the dwelling of the master are limited to the strictest simplicity".

Exact directions were given as to the arrangements of desks, teachers, and classes, and the different methods of conducting the teaching of a school. Holland was constantly held up as a model to be imitated, and glowing descriptions of the admirable discipline and methods in Dutch schools were given—"all corporeal punishment and every kind of degrading chastisement being by law banished from them". The salaries given in these schools, viz. £75 yearly for the ordinary duties of head-master of a school with 1000 day-scholars and 150 evening-scholars, and £8, 6s. 8d. for instructing pupil-teachers in the evening, in addition to a house; £33, 6s. 8d., £25, and £10 for senior and junior assistants; and £5, 16s. 8d., £6, £5, £4, 3s. 4d., £3, 6s. 8d., and £2, 10s. for senior and junior pupil-teachers were considered as good guides for salaries in England, since the cost of living was about the same.

The method of turning dwelling-houses into school-houses is described, and the National Society's instruction that the "form of a room should be oblong: a barn furnishes no bad model, and a good one may be easily converted into a school-room", is quoted with apparent approval. Indeed, a plan is given of a contractor's workshop, which was also required as a chapel, and whose form "was exceedingly inconvenient", but which was turned into a school-room by the poor-law commissioners, even "though too small a space is allotted to the teacher between each class", in a room where 400 children were taught at one time. No surprise, therefore, is felt when an inspector reports "the infant-school secured a Treasury grant, by the aid of which an old building, then used as a rag warehouse, was converted into a school. The site is nearly an acre, the situation low and damp, and the building out of repair." Plans, and full instructions for building an orphan house or school of industry, and a normal school, with apartments for residential students; forms for conveyance of sites, apprenticing of pupil-teachers, and building contracts; and a copy of an act to facilitate the conveyance of sites for school-rooms (1836) were also included in the minutes for 1839-40. And, finally, there is the "report of Mr. Seymour Tremenheere on the state of elementary education in the mining district of South Wales", which shows that in Wales elementary instruction was in as bad a state of neglect as in England.

From all this it seems clear that there was a determination to have real work done in return for the money spent, since the grant was to be in proportion to the number of children taught; to make a real endeavour to raise the quality, as well as increase the quantity, of the work, through the examination, reports, and suggestions of the inspectors, and by supplying the fullest possible practical information and guidance; and to enlarge the opportunities of school promoters by allowing them to deal directly with the committee of council, by showing that no really deserving case whatever would be refused help, and also by giving grants for the building of normal schools (training colleges).

During the year 1841 the committee gave the following grants for training colleges:—£5000 to the British and Foreign School Society for the Borough Road College, for building; £2500 for the Church Training College at Chester, for building; and £1000 to the Battersea Training College, towards expenses previously incurred. These grants were given on conditions similar to those made for schools with regard to subscriptions, expenditure, and inspection; besides which an account of the number of students and scholars, together with the general plan of the school and the regulations to be adopted, had to be submitted.

In the same year good work was done through the holding of classes, under the sanction of the committee, in Exeter Hall, for the purpose of demonstrating improved methods of instruction. The secretary and other officers of the committee, and Mr. Hullah, were the demonstrators. The classes were self-supporting, mainly owing to the profits arising from the concerts given by the musical students, in addition to the fees and donations. They were attended mostly by teachers—from 300 to 400 of them—and included singing according to the method of Wilhelm, writing on the method of Mulhauser, arithmetic after the method of Pestalozzi, besides popular classes on chemistry and other subjects. The committee, as well as the Houses of Parliament, was petitioned by the students attending them for a grant to assist and develop the work. But no grant was given.

Another interesting fact is recorded in the minutes for 1841-42, viz. that the Leicester Archidiaconal Board of Education petitioned the committee for a grant to assist them in forming a summer training-school for teachers in the district, who were to attend at a school in Leicester during the harvest time, and receive instruction in school subjects and the methods of teaching them—especially in that of singing as taught by Mr. Hullah. In the petition mention is made of the very great good that had been effected in the schools by an organizing master appointed by the board, one-half of whose salary was paid by the National Society. No reply is recorded. The idea and institution of holiday courses for teachers is obviously not so new as it is sometimes thought to be.

Further progress was effected in the following year. The committee determined to give grants towards the providing or enlarging of houses for schoolmasters and schoolmistresses, and towards the supply of furniture and apparatus for school-rooms. But this was somewhat discounted by their resolve to limit grants for training colleges to building expenses only, and by requiring that all applications shall be sent through one of the two schools societies. To secure these grants a long series of questions, on the same lines as those proposed to promoters of schools, had to be answered. More inspectors were to be appointed, as the two already at work, one in church schools and the other in those connected with the British and Foreign School Society, were found to be quite inadequate for the work. It was hoped that a sufficient number would be appointed to allow of two visits a year to schools receiving government grant. And special attention was drawn to the readiness of the committee to consider the question of giving larger grants to poor and populous districts.

A minute by the secretary, dated 2nd December, 1843, suggested that the country shall be divided into five inspectorial districts—viz. northern, midland, eastern, western (including Wales), and southern. The schools in each district were to be visited twice in a year. In reporting on them, the inspector was to write such remarks and recommendations as he might wish to be conveyed to the trustees or committee of the school, for their information and as suggestions for the improvement of the school, in separate memoranda, which were to be submitted to the Lord President, and, if approved, communicated officially to the school authorities. As the number of schools in a district increased, it was suggested that sub-inspectors should be appointed, at lower salaries, to be employed in the examination of the inferior order of schools, and likewise in the organization of schools. The visits of the inspectors were to be after the manner of the visits of inspection as carried out at the present time. It was recommended that five additional inspectors be appointed, one of whom was to be inspector of normal schools. These should have enjoyed an university education, and be men of extensive acquirements and good manners. They ought to be well paid, because of the importance of their duties, and in order to encourage them to remain in the service. It was frankly admitted that few of them would possess, when they entered on the discharge of their duties, the peculiar knowledge, tact, and skill which the business of inspection required, and which could only be gradually acquired.

The minutes for 1844 declare the readiness of the committee to instruct their own architect to prepare, gratuitously, a pencil sketch, if none of the plans already drawn up seems to meet a special case. To enable this to be done the necessary information must be supplied by the applicants. They also include a copy of "An act to afford further facilities for the conveyance and endowment of sites for schools" (1841), and "An act to secure the terms on which grants are made by Her Majesty out of the parliamentary grant for the education of the poor; and to explain the act of the fifth year of the reign of Her present Majesty for the conveyance of sites for schools" (1844).

With regard to the grant for school furniture and apparatus, the inspectors were directed to assure themselves that every effort had been made, and had failed, to secure the necessary funds, before they recommended that such grants be given. For the supply of sets of three or four parallel desks to schools which had none, or to replace desks affixed to the walls, the committee would contribute two-thirds of the cost. No grants were to be given for books, but aid would be given to facilitate the universal introduction of the black-board and easel; the black-board ruled for writing or arithmetic lessons; suitable maps; the reading-frame; and other mechanical contrivances. For such things sums ranging from £5 to £20 would be given, on condition that half as much was raised by subscriptions. But such grants were to be made only in those cases in which the apparatus would be appreciated, and used with skill; and in which the funds, though gathered by zealous trustees, and applied by an intelligent industrious master, were inadequate to maintain the efficiency of the school without further aid to enable the trustees to adopt improvements in its management. The inspector had to audit the account at his next visit, and at every subsequent visit to inspect the schedule and to see if the apparatus was in good repair. A schedule of the items of apparatus for which grants would be given, their prices, and by whom supplied, was drawn up. It will be seen that this is practically the same as the "Aid Grant" now given.

Two special functions were laid upon the inspectors this year. They were to inquire into the means which existed for the maintenance of schools, and the mode in which the income was expended, with a view to considering how the income might be increased, or made more effective by judicious economy or improved arrangements. It seems that the income was usually derived from the children's pence—the children of farmers and shopkeepers paying higher fees, remaining longer at school, and receiving more advanced instruction; and a voluntary rate among owners and occupiers, in proportion to the parochial assessment. Sometimes there was a voluntary arrangement by which owners and occupiers contributed according to the number of children attending school from cottages on their respective lands; or an arrangement by which each employer of labour always contributed a sum equal to the school pence of the families employed by him. In the latter case the attendance at school of the children of all labourers was rendered compulsory at certain ages on the parents, the proprietor paying the charge to the school except when the children were withdrawn for labour, when the charge was borne by the occupier. The possibilities with regard to the use of small endowments were to be investigated.

The other special duty was to inquire into the use which had been made of grants given by the Treasury for school buildings, and discover how far those who had received such money had effectively carried out the conditions laid down. They were to offer their services in the matters of inspection, examination, and advice, and, if these were accepted, to visit the schools in the same spirit as those under the Committee of Council. It was known that most of the school buildings were badly constructed, and some closed and in ruins; that many trust-deeds were invalid; and that practically nothing had been done to improve the teaching given in the schools.

A long minute on methods of teaching reading, writing, and vocal music was drawn up and published by direction of the committee. This is chiefly remarkable as an evidence of the earnestness with which the problem was being attacked, and as showing how much technical knowledge was possessed by those in command. Whilst there is much sound advice for making the best of the prevailing bad methods, there is no really scientific grasp of the subject, though Pestalozzi, the Socratic method, analysis, and synthesis, and Miss Edgeworth are invoked. The strange statement is made that from

The Committee of Council on Education. 99

the most elementary knowledge to the highest speculations one method is universally applicable. This consists first, in carefully examining the constituent parts of any object before us, *i.e.* in *analysing* it; secondly, in classifying and separately considering these component parts. Thirdly, in reconstructing the object which has been analysed by the educator, *i.e.* in operating by synthesis. Such is the work of the teacher in elementary schools.

The teacher is therefore to do all the thinking, and the children have merely to learn the trick of putting things together again. But this is the very essence of the mechanical. If there be one thing that the true educator does, it is to guide and aid, so far only as is really necessary, the process of analysis—the truest and best, because the first step in mental development. The synthesis will take care of itself if the analysis be well done. Yet the minute deserves praise if for nothing more than that it attempted the impossible task of finding a good principle for bad practice. Besides this, much good and sound general advice, and many moral maxims, are introduced. Of the method of teaching vocal music it is said that it is such as to enable a monitor of ordinary skill, with the aid of previous instruction, to conduct a class through the whole course. Surely no truer test of the really mechanical could be desired. But then the method of teaching was avowedly based upon the pupils' powers of imitation. Manuals for teachers, and primers for pupils, on the subjects discussed, had been prepared under the sanction of the committee. The secretary and Mr. Hullah had been directed by the committee to proceed to Paris and examine in detail the teaching of vocal music by Wilhelm's method, in primary schools, before drawing up the manual on the subject. This seems to have been the first instance of this kind of work, which has quite lately been re-introduced as a new department, viz. Special Inquiries and Reports.

The man whose mind and heart were the mainspring of all this movement and improvement deserves to live in the annals of national education as its most faithful promoter and defender. This man, Sir J. P. Kay-

Shuttleworth—his family name of Kay he changed to Kay-Shuttleworth on his marriage—would have shone in any sphere, but he was, in a large measure, the saviour of his country with regard to primary instruction. He was able, discreet, diplomatic, yet energetic, enthusiastic, and self-sacrificing, just when these qualities were needed to make the man of the hour. The times were critical, the man was sufficient. He was a member of a brilliant family, and was born at Rochdale in 1804. One of his brothers became a Lord-Justice of Appeal, and the other a Q.C. As a youth he served in a bank, but this did not satisfy either his powers or his desires, and at the age of twenty-one he went to Edinburgh to study medicine. At the university he had a distinguished career as a student. He proved himself an impressive speaker, and in his second session was made senior president of a medical society. He took his M.D. in 1827, and forthwith began work in a poor and populous district in Manchester, as medical officer to the Ancoats and Ardwick Dispensary—established mainly through his own influence and exertions. He did devoted work during the cholera epidemic of 1832, and so got to know more fully and truly the dreadful conditions under which the poor lived.

His writings on subjects connected with the lives of the poor, and the measures needed to remedy the evils and dangers of their surroundings, brought him under the notice of the government, and he was appointed an assistant poor-law commissioner in 1835. As such he worked in Norfolk and Suffolk, Middlesex and Surrey, at different times, and became deeply interested in the training of pauper children, about which he wrote some exceptionally valuable reports.

In 1839 he became the first secretary of the Committee of Council for Education, a post for which he was probably by far the best qualified man in the country. He brought a scientifically-trained mind to bear upon the work; his medical knowledge was of direct and firstrate value in dealing with schools; he had studied carefully the writings and works of the most famous teacher of the time, viz. De Fellenberg; he had visited and studied schools in Holland, France, Prussia, and Switzerland; and his whole soul was consumed with the desire to advance the work of elementary instruction amongst the poor. He lacked only one thing, but that the most vital, namely, the saving grace of actual training, by a life experience and disciplined thought, in the practical work of teaching. Had he but been through a technical course to prepare him for educational work, as he had for medical work, he would have been almost ideally qualified. Nevertheless there is but very little to regret with respect to the work he did, considering the conditions under which he had to do it, and there is very much for which to be devoutly thankful. Through his knowledge, work, and influence the teaching in the schools began to be touched with the spirit of true education; teachers began to be enthusiastic; and the public almost became enlightened.

Meantime some good work was being done by the two religious societies, and others. They had been up and doing, and the extra money given by the government had been met by increasing sums from voluntary subscribers. Under the stimulating influence of the visits of inspectors, and their reports, which made public both the good deeds of the worthy, and the misdeeds and neglect of the unworthy, a more lively sense of responsibility and duty was aroused amongst those who had, or affected to have, an interest in national education. Such knowledge as the inspectors gained simply by seeing things better done in one school than another, was passed on and bore fruit in many of the weaker schools. Buildings, apparatus, teachers, and methods were all gradually improved in this way. Many were willing and even anxious to learn, and had only sinned because no light of knowledge had been thrown upon the darkness of their ignorant zeal.

After the defeat of Sir James Graham's proposals on behalf of the government, in 1843, churchmen had made an effort to meet the needs which all admitted. Over one hundred and fifty thousand pounds were collected, as a special fund for providing more schools, and in other ways extending the work of elementary instruction.

Diocesan boards of education were established, and did much good work in securing local, and more permanent efforts on behalf of the work. The National Society established two training colleges at Chelsea (S. Mark's for men, and Whitelands for women), and also took over the one at Battersea—which had been established, supported, managed, and presided over as teacher and friend, by Dr. Kay. The diocesan boards at Chester and Salisbury also founded training colleges. To the clergy individually also great praise is due. Under the awakening which the High Church party had aroused, parishes which for years had had serviceless churches, once more came under the influence of the energy and devotion of earnest and educated men. With their coming often appeared the parish school beside the parish church; and the former was not only sometimes mainly dependent upon the parson for its pecuniary support, but also for a good deal of the actual teaching done within its walls.

We read in the reports of inspectors such remarks as: "The clergyman and his lady give great attention to the school, taking themselves an active part in the instruction". "The girls' school is principally supported by the vicar." "The school is chiefly supported by the munificent contributions of the incumbent." "The clergyman makes great sacrifices for its support." "The preferment of Mr. —— is £135 a year, and his whole income considerably less than £300. He has a wife and three children, and he finds it necessary to contribute £20 a year to the support of his school." Allowing for the natural bias of clerical inspectors towards clerical managers, and church management, still the constant testimony to the financial and practical help which the clergy gave to their schools remains as an abiding monument to their devotion and self-sacrifice.

The British and Foreign Schools Society likewise had increased the number of its schools, and had put up a much larger and more convenient building for the students in training at their Borough Road normal and model schools. The Home and Colonial college was still doing its good work; and the various religious denominations were taking an active part in spreading education.

The inner life of the school, which, after all, is the true test of the value of everything that was done by all parties and persons combined, had improved, but not greatly. The number of teachers who had received some training in the way of organizing and managing a school, and in the methods of instruction, was being constantly added to, and this was so much to the good. But their original qualifications were, in many cases, so unsuitable, and the period of training so utterly insufficient, that most of them were merely provided with the little knowledge which is so dangerous. It is a frequent complaint, made by the inspectors, that teachers are far too satisfied with themselves, and their ignorance, to listen to advice or suggestions from others.

The students at the Battersea training college were not, in the first instance, representative of the ordinary type of teachers, since the majority of them were the pupil-teachers from the Norwood School of Industry, only a few being accepted on the recommendation of private patrons. But those who were entered at the college in 1845 were fairly typical. Of these 83 students, 4 had been schoolmasters; 11, assistants in schools; 8, clerks, chiefly writers in attorneys' offices; 6, shopkeepers and shopmen; 4, schoolboys; 5, printers; 9, unskilled workmen in connection with manufactures; 5, skilled manufacturing workmen; 3, shoemakers; 1, tailor; 1, gardener; 2, farm labourers; 1, factory overlooker; 2, companions; and 1 had been sent by the Dublin Society of Fine Arts. The following general description is given by the Principal:—"They are commonly selected from a humble sphere. They are the sons of small tradesmen, of bailiffs, of servants, or of superior mechanics. Few have received any education, except that given in a common parochial school. They read and write very imperfectly; are unable to indite a letter correctly; and are seldom skilful even in the first four rules of arithmetic. . . . All their conceptions are vague and confused, even when they are not also very limited or erroneous."

Dr. Kay had high and generous ideals with regard to the work at Battersea, when he himself was carrying it on, and was paying a large part of the cost from his private purse. He laid it down that the main object of a normal school is the formation of the character of the schoolmaster. Eighteen months was regarded as the shortest time in which anything worthy of the name of training could be effected, and it was the usual rule that a student must be eighteen years of age on entering the college. The first month of training was, under any circumstances, to be regarded as probationary—a very necessary and valuable precaution with respect to such very raw material as came for training. The subjects of instruction were so taught to the students as to be models to them for their own teaching in schools; and the best methods of the day were employed. Thus, arithmetic was taught on Pestalozzian principles; reading according to the phonic method; writing on the Mulhauser system; drawing after the plan of M. Dupuis; and vocal music by the Wilhelm method:—a very wise and helpful way of fitting the students for practical teaching. The subjects which occupied the students' time were religious instruction and services, geography, reading, etymology, grammar, composition, history, arithmetic, pure mathematics, mensuration, mechanics, natural philosophy (science), Pestalozzi, teaching in village schools, garden work, and music. Later on languages were added.

There was a very definite idea in the minds of the promoters of these colleges that the schoolmaster was not to be educated above his station. Thus we find that Dr. Kay declares that "in the training school, habits should be formed consistent with the modesty of his future life"; whilst Rev. Derwent Coleridge, principal of the Chelsea college, holds that "the object being to produce schoolmasters for the poor, the endeavour must be on the one hand to raise the students morally and intellectually to a certain standard, while, on the other hand, we train them in lowly service". The former was, at Chelsea, striven after by a distinctly generous syllabus of studies, comparatively speaking, and the latter, by the performance of menial household duties, and farm-labourers' and gardeners' work. There was another object connected with farm and garden work, namely, to enable the students to get a practical knowledge of, and sympathy with, such industries, so that they might take an interest in training children in country schools for their probable life-work.

Schoolmistresses were, in most respects, sadly wanting in early preparation for their work. The committee of the Home and Colonial College complain that the candidates "come from a class whose education is in general so exceedingly deficient". Of two hundred applicants for admission, none of them possessed enough knowledge of arithmetic, grammar, or geography to be of any practical value to them. Their social positions are thus described: 88 were unemployed; 32 in business; 26 engaged in millinery, needlework, &c.; 15 in service; and 39 engaged in teaching. Their course of training appears to have been by far the most thorough and complete from the purely professional point of view. And be it recorded to his honour, in those days of ignorant rule-of-thumb, the inspector of normal schools writes:—
"Mr. Dunning (the training-master) has prepared himself for his duties by a careful study of the works of Dugald Stewart, Abercrombie, and others, masters of the science of mental philosophy, and invaluable guides to a teacher, by the insight they afford him into the operations of the human mind, and the phenomena of our moral and physical nature. It is by having a due regard to these, and by pursuing a course in conformity with them, that education will be most satisfactorily conducted." About a hundred students were trained every year; but this was due to the lamentable fact that twenty weeks was the period of training; although this was sometimes extended, or increased by a subsequent additional period. And such was the demand for these trained mistresses that, "for want of funds and fit persons", the college authorities were unable to supply "one half of those patrons, &c., who have applied to them".

They were also constrained to complain of the low salaries offered. They say, "it is to be regretted that in this wealthy country so low a rate of payment as £25 or £30 per annum should be deemed an adequate return for the discharge of duties so difficult and so full of responsibility". They very justly urge that: "When it is considered that the teacher of an elementary school is expected to possess ability and acquirements; to present, in his appearance, manners and conduct, an example to those around him, and to command, by the weight of his character, and by superior intelligence, the respect and deference of the parents, often ignorant and neglectful, whose children he has under his charge, it must be confessed that the remuneration falls far short of the value expected to be received. Nor, in estimating these services, should the wear and tear of the body and mind, which must attend their energetic and faithful performance, the difficulties and discouragements often incident to them, the confinement, the declining health, the anxiety for the future, be overlooked, as they too frequently seem to be." The inspector for the southern counties, speaking of "the scanty salaries that are offered", says that "as soon as it is felt by the owners of property in this country that the wages of one who is fit to teach the children of the poor ought not to fall below those paid to a humble mechanic, this blot on the face of our social condition will be got rid of".

Nevertheless the forward tendency was being felt along the main lines. The pupil-teachers were an advance upon the monitors, in that they were permanent, and received more or less training—before, between, or after school hours—at the hands of teachers who had themselves been more or less trained. The better ideas as to classifying pupils, arranging lessons, and putting knowledge before the learners in a more orderly and connected form, all served to make the work of the school more effective. And the fact that the teachers themselves knew more about the subjects which they taught was a great advantage. Still there was a large preponderance of the old style both in men and methods. Even in the schools aided by the government grants only about a fourth of the teachers had been through a training-college course, and as many more had attended for a short period at some school where they might receive some slight training. There was, therefore, still a large number of the untrained and untaught in them.

Of these untrained teachers an inspector says: "The spelling is frequently incorrect; 'believe' and 'receive' are as great puzzles to them as to the children. Timetables are badly arranged, and little observed; and in some cases unknown. Language is provincial and ungrammatical. There is also a species of scholastic 'slang' used by them in the nomenclature of their classes: 'Them's the Bibles,—them the Testamenters,—them the a-b-abbers,—and them the alphabetters', was the literal description of her school, given to me by a middle-aged mistress, whose heart was more full of kindness than her head of learning." At one school in Yorkshire he asked why arithmetic was not taught. "Because I know nothing about it", was the honest reply. The partially-trained teachers seem to have suffered very much from the results of little knowledge: "They not only rest upon it as it were for themselves, but they obtrude it upon others as a distinction and a superiority. They are often persons whom vanity, or misfortune, or inability to succeed in other trades, or caprice, or the mistaken kindness of their friends, or what is called 'accident', have placed in the deeply responsible situation of teachers. . . . In this class the most obvious defect, as it is the greatest hindrance, is self-conceit." Of the head-teacher of a school with over a hundred pupils, in the Midland counties, the inspector remarks: "The master of this school was a farm-labourer, whose education has not qualified him for the duties which have been intrusted to him". The inspector of the northern district writes: "In two places, during summer, I found the master in his shirt-sleeves; of course in those places children's jackets were dispensed with". But a high tribute of praise is given to the excellent character and work of the trained teachers.

The monitorial system is adversely criticised by the inspectors, but all plead for its practical necessity and usefulness. One writes that the monitors must have knowledge, skill in teaching, patience and kindness in the discipline of their classes, self-respect, and the respect of their pupils because of their character and conduct. They will be worse than useless whilst they, "as may sometimes be seen, beat and box their pupils; or, as on other occasions, drag them up for punishment to the master's desk, and in divers ways betray a want of knowledge and self-command utterly at variance with order and good discipline". Another urges: a teacher should comprehend that "the teaching of the children of his school by other children is an expedient which he is justified in using only in so far as he is unable to teach them himself". And he very justly points out that the skill and judgment required to secure interested attention, the adaptation of instruction to the individual minds of the pupil, and the moral control which means so much, cannot be expected from teachers of the tender age of eleven years. From them only an acquaintance with mechanical expedients, and restraint from juvenile tyranny, can be expected. Whilst admitting these objections, he points out that "the monitors are, in reality, the principal and the most important agents in elementary instruction in its existing state". Another states that after duly considering, and allowing the force of objections against the system, he still retains "the opinion that its introduction into the primary schools of this country is absolutely essential to their proper efficiency as educational means".

But the importance of improving such instruments of instruction was generally acknowledged, and it was due to Dr. Kay's enthusiastic desire for progress that an experiment in this direction was tried. Whilst working as poor-law commissioner in Norfolk, in 1837, he heard of a case in which a boy had carried on the whole work of a pauper school during the illness of the head-master. His own account is: "The master fell seriously ill; William Rush (the head boy in the school), unbidden, though a boy of only thirteen years of age, took charge of the scholars. The master of the workhouse found the school in its usual order. The whole discipline and routine of the garden, workshop, and class instruction went on unbroken." Dr. Kay recommended that he should thenceforth be regarded as the apprenticed assistant of the schoolmaster. Regarding the affair, as giving a valuable hint, he proposed the introduction of the same plan in the organization of other workhouse schools. The system spread, and though all these teachers were not apprenticed, they were all to be retained in the school for a series of years, and were known as pupil-teachers. Dr. Kay distinctly says that this arrangement was already working before he visited Holland, where he found a system in which the chief features were similar, and which confirmed him in his views of its value.

Doubtless a good deal was gained in mechanical completeness and expertness by the continued practice and precepts which these pupil-teachers obtained, but it hardly strikes one as a cure for their real inefficiency, viz. the inability to estimate the powers of their pupils, and adapt themselves to their needs. To make ignorance a more permanent factor does not change it into knowledge. At the best, the pupil-teacher system is but a glorified form of the monitorial. Its origin and basis is the remarkable individual success of an impromptu monitor. The very age of this boy seems to have settled what was the proper age at which all boys were fit to become pupil-teachers. But the most interesting fact about the introduction of the pupil-teacher system is that it was held to be justified by the example and success of its working in Holland; and this doctrine was preached twenty years after the Dutch authorities had awarded a prize, open to public competition, to an essay condemning the whole plan of monitorial instruction upon which the system was based, root and branch, as being unsound in every point that bears upon true education. The pupil-teacher system was also regarded as unsatisfactory, after fifteen years' trial, and it was continued only as a supplement to the normal-school course. It was recognized that it produced only routine teaching, and arrested the progress of improvement by perpetuating the methods, whether good, bad, or indifferent, learnt in a certain school. But England is the country in which dead systems of education live.

How the monitors actually did their work is well shown by one of the inspectors, who writes: "On entering a large school, I requested that the instruction of the children might go on according to its accustomed course, that I might judge of the means daily called into operation before I proceeded to inquire into the results. Astonished to find that some time elapsed before the machinery could be put in motion, I proceeded to inquire into the cause, and found that the monitors were in the act of placing the finger of each individual boy upon the first word of the lesson to be read. This accomplished, and the monitor having read one word of the lesson and the boys simultaneously after him; each boy advanced his finger one word, and the process was repeated." Could anything be more mechanical? And yet the pupil-teacher would go through the same kind of training; and by far the larger part of the teachers in schools consisted of monitors and pupil-teachers, or young men and women who were spending a few weeks in acquiring sufficient practical knowledge to take posts as head-teachers. Will it be believed that identically the same kind of work is done in our schools to-day by trained certificated teachers?

Great progress was, however, made during this period in the number and extent of the subjects taught in the schools. Of nearly twelve thousand children in the schools inspected in the Midland counties, about one-third could read simple narratives, one-fifth were able to read the Scriptures with ease, and about one-half had not got beyond letters and monosyllables. Writing on slates was done by nearly all, and writing on paper by about one-third. Some teachers seem to have thought that ordinary copies were too commonplace, and so took extracts from a letter-writer, with such beginnings as "My lovely Emma", "My dear charmer". The introduction of the Mulhauser method of teaching writing greatly helped to spread the accomplishment. In the first circular of instructions to inspectors on inspecting schools they are directed to report whether the children write with chalk on the wall or on a board, on slates or on paper; and whether they do so imperfectly, fairly well, or with ease and skill.

In arithmetic more than one-half were under instruction. Of the whole number over one-third had not got beyond the simple rules, one-tenth did compound rules, and nearly four hundred had reached the rule-of-three. Just over two thousand children, in fifty schools (out of 250 in the Midlands), learnt geography; eleven hundred, in thirty-one schools, learnt history; one thousand children, in thirty-five schools, learnt grammar; and nearly four hundred children, in twelve schools, learnt etymology. Singing was taught, on Mr. Hullah's (Wilhelm) method, in twenty-two schools, to nearly one thousand pupils. But some subjects, and more advanced work in a subject, are regarded as extras, for which higher fees—3d. or 4d. a week—are paid, and the fortunate pupils have Master —— or Miss —— written on their books, instead of plain John or Mary; and were addressed as Miss ——, Master ——. Religious instruction was invariable and extensive.

One inspector complains that the results of the teaching are very mechanical, and that there is "a want of general intelligence and everyday knowledge—a lack of aptitude and vivacity of thought—a paucity of ideas, and a corresponding poverty of diction". Another remarks that middle-aged men spell, write, and reckon badly, because "some of their instruction was almost entirely given and obtained by rote, whilst the mechanical part has passed away from want of practice". And this is not felt to be strange when one reads that a teacher objected to his children who learnt grammar being tried as to their ability to pick out the nouns and verbs in a sentence, because his way of teaching was to make them learn by heart page after page of Lennie or Murray. But the work in infants' schools is highly praised for its intelligence and sympathy, and it is regretted that in going from these to the schools for older children, so much is changed and so much is lost. It is wisely suggested that young teachers in the latter schools might gain much by visits to the infants' school, to observe the methods of teaching and management. In them object-lessons had an important place in the work, and much was done to cultivate the intelligence of the little ones.

Physical exercises and recreation were not forgotten, and the inspectors inquired what amusements and games the children had; whether they had any and what gymnastic apparatus; if the children were trained in walking, marching, and physical exercises methodically; and how often, and for what time, intervals of recreation occurred daily. He was also to report whether the monitors and pupil-teachers had acquaintance with elementary movements, or more complex combinations, and were capable of conducting a class under exercise. In the specimen plans of schools sent out by the Committee of Council such things as parallel bars, swings, &c., are marked on the playgrounds.

Industrial training is recognized, and reports have to be made as to how many children learn to sew, knit, plait straw, keep the garden-border free from weeds, sweep the school-floors, &c. It is to be noted whether there is a cabinet in the school stored with natural objects which the children are likely soon to meet with in their rambles or visits to friends; if there be a cabinet of domestic utensils or implements of industry, of a small size, the uses of which may be explained to the children; and if the children are exercised in examining and describing in very simple and familiar terms the properties of those natural objects by which they are surrounded. This last, with the inquiries as to the teaching of reading, constitute the soundest, if not the only, pieces of truly educational suggestions, as to methods, in the whole record of the minutes, instructions, and report, so far. With regard to the reading, the inspector is to inquire if the head-teacher has been instructed in the method of making the children familiar with letters: by showing them the figure of a natural object having a monosyllabic name; by analysing this word into its constituent sounds; and by showing the children the sign of each sound, beginning with the vowel sound, and then combining them into the word by the phonic method.

The Committee of Council on Education. 113

It is difficult to reconcile a method of this kind with the following suggestion, made by one of the inspectors in his official report, on the method of teaching reading. "The monitor reads one word, which is then clearly pronounced by the first child, then repeated by the whole class, and so to the end of a sentence. This should not be done more than twice or thrice; it is then better to read over the sentence, explaining it familiarly, and questioning the children. When they know the words and understand the sentence, they may read it round the class, word by word, without the assistance of the monitor; they may then be called upon to read the sentence separately." But what else could be expected when the ablest and most capable of the inspectors remarks: "What we appear to want now, is the free action of thought upon education, and that public interest which is the result of such action—the collision of system with system, and method with method. This suits the character of social and political relations among us, and the regimen of public opinion. Nothing could be worse than to stretch education again upon the rack of a system, or to put it in an iron boot. I am very far, however, from believing that which I advocate to be the best system. I have compared it, of course, with all others that I know of, and give it the preference; but I am of opinion that we are as yet in the infancy of our knowledge and experience in such matters, and that something a great deal better will soon be devised. Meanwhile, the bringing of this forward will contribute to that end, because it will open up again the question of organization, agitate it, and provoke the discussion of it on *new principles.*"

What a strange ignoring is here of all that had been written and done concerning education and instruction, as well as of what was being done in the schools of Holland and Prussia at that very time! But the argument that it is of the nature of the English genius to thus hammer out success from its failures—due to self-satisfied ignorance concerning other people's knowledge—is used at the present time to excuse, if not to justify, the many and mischievous anomalies which still exist in our so-called national education. Whilst, however, it may be satisfactory to our insular self-complacency to reflect that, in spite of all, we have managed to effect something that is good, it would perhaps be more creditable to our sanity if we had done much less that has proved so disastrously wrong, and more that we might reasonably be proud of. What is the peculiar value of such rediscovery, at such tremendous cost, of elementary truths, it is somewhat difficult to see, even on the principle that bought wit is better than taught wit; still less does it appear the height of reason to behave, so to say, after the manner of the ostrich, and, sticking one's head in the barren sands of one's own ignorance, to exclaim: "There is no knowledge". This is indeed ploughing the sands.

One question inspectors were asked was: "Are the walls lined with a broad belt of black-board, or prepared with mastic, painted black, for lessons in chalk-drawing and writing?" Linear drawing was sometimes a subject of instruction; and land-surveying was not infrequently taught.

All these things must have made for righteousness in school affairs, for the knowledge of the best often makes good things done; and still oftener the fact that neglect and misdoing are known and noted tends to correct them. Without doubt the quality of the work done in the schools, the suitability of the building and apparatus, and the qualifications of the teachers, were all steadily improving; whilst the number of children coming under the influence of the improved conditions was rapidly increasing.

Chapter VI.

A Semi-state System.

Slowly but surely the strong hand of the central authority was laid upon the schools, until they were completely and firmly within its grasp. First the staff came within its power. The pupil-teacher system was introduced and maintained by the Committee of Council. The salaries of the pupil-teachers were paid from London by post-office orders. Head-teachers were also made largely dependent upon the Department by numerous supplements to their stipends, paid directly by the central authority, and promises of state pensions were made to them. Thus teachers were almost entirely civil servants, and so regarded themselves. Even their hours of labour were, practically, fixed; their qualifications were minutely regulated; they had to be approved from year to year; and all under the authority and power of the Committee of Council. School buildings were already partly supplied by the government, and now the provision of school furniture, apparatus, and books was undertaken in part by the same authority. And this was followed by a still more comprehensive act of State, viz. the provision of a maintenance fund, through the annual grants. To secure this certain items of knowledge were required from the scholars, and thus the school curriculum was, practically, dictated by the central power. Public rights were recognized by the pressing for a conscience clause — not insisted upon, however, as yet — in trust deeds. Thus almost all was provided by the government, and almost all was regulated by it.

But though there was advance there was no true internal and natural development, and it would be mere pretence to attempt to show anything like an organic evolution in the matter. The crude machinery was made a little less rough, the poverty-stricken meagreness was somewhat redeemed, and product as well as process was insisted on; yet the whole was as innocent of the true spirit of education as ever. The way for better things was being made; but the makers knew not the better things.

A new and far-reaching change in the relations between the Committee of Council and the schools was made in 1846. In a minute dated Aug. 25, it is stated that their lordships have had under consideration the question of the inspection of schools, and have come to the conclusion that it was highly expedient that every school should be visited at least once in each year; but that the number of inspectors was insufficient for this, and allowed of only one visit in two years. They therefore resolved to appoint three new inspectors at once, though this would not provide for an annual visit to every school. Next, they have also considered the many representations made to them as to the advantages which would arise if the pupil-teacher system were general, since the monitors left at a very early age. And it has been resolved that annual grants may be made towards the stipends of apprentices in elementary schools, if certain conditions as to the qualifications of the schoolmaster, the efficiency of instruction in the school, and the local contributions are fulfilled. Indentures are to be prepared, declaring the duties of such apprentices, and the instruction they are to receive. Periods are to be fixed for their examination by inspectors, and the conditions of dismissal determined. The stipends are to increase in each year. Such masters as were deemed qualified to have charge of the instruction and training of pupil-teachers were to be rewarded for their extra work by receiving annual grants in aid of their stipends, according to the number of apprentices trained by each master.

Further, it was resolved that regulations should be drawn up to provide, in certain cases, retiring pensions for schoolmasters and schoolmistresses who had served a certain number of years. In addition to these pensions, teachers were to be encouraged by small gratuities, to be annually distributed to those whose skill and success in teaching led the inspector to recommend them as deserving of such encouragement.

Four months later a minute appeared setting out in detail the exact conditions on which these grants, pensions, and gratuities would be administered. The managers were to make application to their lordships, requesting that one or more of the most proficient scholars might be apprenticed. Then the inspector was to report on the qualifications of the teacher; the organization, discipline, and furnishing of the school; and the

A Semi-state System. 117

probability that the permanent financial support of the school was such as to justify the granting of the request. If everything was satisfactory, the candidate, who must be at least thirteen years of age and not subject to any incapacitating infirmity, had to pass a qualifying examination. This test was nearly up to the level of the fifth standard requirements of the present time, and included besides an examination in religious knowledge (for Church people), and the teaching of a junior class before the inspector. In each succeeding year a more difficult syllabus of work was to be studied and examined on. The period of apprenticeship lasted five years, and if all the examinations were passed a certificate was given, declaring that the apprenticeship was successfully completed. If any apprentice showed superior merit the period of service might be shortened, or, if the later examinations were passed in the earlier years, then the higher salaries would be given earlier.

If the head-teachers were not sufficiently well qualified to have pupil-teachers under their charge, they might, in small country schools, and for a few years to come, have monitors who were to be retained, under an agreement with the parents, to the age of seventeen, and receive a small stipend, with extra daily instruction. These were to be called stipendiary monitors, and their appointment was subject to the same general conditions as were required in the case of pupil-teachers. They also had to be thirteen years of age, to pass a qualifying examination, and more advanced examinations in each succeeding year. Both pupil-teachers and stipendiary monitors had to present, at the close of each year, certificates of good conduct from the managers; of punctuality, diligence, obedience, and attention to duties, from the head-teacher; and of attention to religious duties, from the parish clergyman or the managers (in the case of dissenters).

Pupil-teachers' salaries commenced at ten pounds per year, and rose by yearly increases of two pounds ten shillings. The salaries of stipendiary monitors began at five pounds, and rose at the same rate as the pupil-teachers'. The head-teachers were to receive, if the character and progress of the pupil-teachers were satisfactory, five pounds for one, nine for two, and twelve for three, and three for each additional one, per annum; and, on the like conditions two pounds ten shillings for one, four pounds for two, six for three, and thirty shillings for each additional stipendiary monitor, each year. If the boys were skilfully trained by the master in the culture of a garden, or in some mechanical arts suitable to a school of industry; or the girls instructed by the mistress in cutting out clothes, cooking, baking, or washing, as well as in the more usual arts of sewing and knitting; an additional gratuity, proportioned to the degree of skill and care displayed, was to be given, on the inspector certifying that the pupil-teachers were thereby in a satisfactory course of training for the management of a school of industry. The pupil-teachers and stipendiary monitors were to receive instruction from the head-teacher during one hour and a half at least, on five days in the week, either before or after the usual school hours.

Not content with thus providing junior teachers for schools, the Committee of Council took steps to supply well-qualified head-teachers, in the following manner. Those pupil-teachers who had successfully completed their apprenticeships were to be allowed to enter for a public competitive examination, to be conducted by the inspector and the principal of a normal school in a certain district. The most successful and best qualified of the candidates were to receive the offer of exhibitions worth twenty or twenty-five pounds, to one of the normal schools under inspection, whilst to others might be offered an opportunity of entering the public service. Those who accepted the exhibitions were to be called "Queen's Scholars", and the colleges at which they were trained were to receive grants of twenty pounds at the end of the first year, twenty-five the second, and thirty the third, if the student obtained a favourable report as to his practical powers as a teacher, and also successfully passed certain annual examinations.

In the case of any such teachers being appointed as head of a school under inspection, their lordships would grant, in aid of salary, fifteen or twenty pounds to those who had received one year of training, and five pounds additional for a second and third year of training. This was to be on condition that the trustees and managers provided a house rent-free, and a further salary, equal at least to twice the amount of the grant; that they annually certified that his character, conduct, and attention to his duties were satisfactory; and that the inspector reported that his school was efficient in its organization, discipline, and instruction. Schoolmistresses were to receive two-thirds of the sums given for schoolmasters.

In an answer, dated 17th December, 1847, to a letter of inquiries from the Wesleyan body respecting the providing one-half of the master's salary by subscription, the justification for the grant in aid is given, viz. "to sustain the principle that the school of the poor is not to owe its support generally to their own unaided sacrifices for the education of their children. . . . Their lordships will be ready to extend that aid from the public funds, which the poverty of the applicants alone prevents them from contributing from the wages of their labour."

This almost paternal anxiety about the teachers' salaries was doubtless the outcome of the complaints of inspectors and others as to the low salaries given, and the consequent want of qualification and fitness in the candidates for the position of teacher. The inspectors had been instructed, two years before, to inquire, in the case of a proposed new school, as to the probable amount of the teacher's stipend, which "ought to be such as will enable a well-qualified schoolmaster to live in comfort and respectability, if he devote his whole time to the duties of his vocation; and will therefore be a subject of special inquiry to the inspector". It may be, therefore, that no less a person than Her Majesty the Queen, through the august persons of her privy councillors, is the author of the idea of "the living wage".

As to pensions, it was announced "that a retiring pension may be granted" to masters and mistresses who, after not less than fifteen years' service in a normal or elementary school—during seven at least of which it was under inspection, should be rendered incapable by age or infirmity of continuing to teach a school efficiently. Applicants for such pensions were to produce a report from the inspector, and from the managers, as to their character and conduct, and the manner in which they had educated their pupils. The amount of pension was to be determined by the nature of these reports, but in no case was it to exceed two-thirds of the average amount of the total income of the applicant during the period that the school was under inspection. Certificated teachers who worked in training colleges were, later, included in the scheme.

In 1853 the senior inspector prepared a very elaborate list of apparatus for the teaching of experimental science in elementary and training schools. He recommended that the makers should be permitted to exhibit specimen cabinets of apparatus in the Museum of Practical Geology. Included in the list is a set of diagrams published by the Working-man's Association, and declared to be excellently adapted to the purposes of popular instruction.

It was at first thought that the various favours were only intended for trained teachers, but the secretary wrote letters explaining that only the grants in aid of salary were limited to such, and that opportunity would be offered to untrained teachers to obtain certificates by examination, which would entitle them to this privilege as well. The Wesleyans also were greatly disturbed by the idea that such advantages were dependent upon the report of inspectors who were churchmen, and straightway proceeded to organize a petition from all their members praying that the Committee of Council should be abolished, and education left entirely free from governmental interference. Their outraged feelings were soothed by a reassuring and spontaneous letter from the secretary, and their support obtained by a promise from their lordships that in future they would not recommend any inspector for appointment as inspector of Wesleyan schools without previously consulting the Wesleyan Education Committee. A promise

A Semi-state System. 121

was also given to the Roman Catholics that minutes would be prepared providing for grants to their schools. It was further resolved that no clergyman or minister could receive any grant as a teacher, since this would cause the grant to become an indirect means of supporting religious sects. And the proof of "special circumstances" was abolished, in the case of schools, not in connection with either of the schools societies, for which grants were requested.

Another minute stating that "the committee will require as an indispensable condition, that an inspector acting under their authority shall be enabled to visit every school to which any grant shall in future be made", was issued on July 10, 1847, together with a resolution which states that no certificate of the religious knowledge of pupil-teachers or monitors will be required from the managers of schools who object, on religious grounds, to make a report concerning the religious state of their schools. This latter obviously enlarged the borders of the committee's influence and work.

During the same month instructions to inspectors were issued directing them to point out to managers, teachers, and scholars, the advantages which the government placed within their reach; and to indicate, after the examination of a school, those scholars who appeared to be intellectually best qualified to become pupil-teachers. Only in exceptional cases might scholars from one school become pupil-teachers in another. Teachers' houses must be provided with, at least, a parlour, kitchen, scullery, and two bedrooms (three where school-building grants were given). No scholar over the age of sixteen was to be eligible for apprenticeship. Those trained teachers who had not got a certificate, but who desired to pass the qualifying examination, were to take them when they were being held at the colleges where they had been trained. Untrained teachers were to be examined at convenient centres. The subjects were to be the same as for pupil-teachers at the end of their fifth year, but the candidates for certificates were to show a higher range of acquirement, and greater accuracy and facility in them.

A decidedly interesting minute, entitled "Brief practical suggestions on the mode of organizing and conducting day-schools of industry, model farm-schools, and normal schools, as part of a system of education for the coloured races of the British Colonies", appeared on January 6, 1847, and was accompanied by a circular of exhortation and reflections on the benefits derived from education.

While providing in a large measure for the staffing of schools, the Committee of Council soon after pushed their policy of state supply still further. In a minute dated 18th December, 1847, their lordships express their readiness to give grants for school-books and maps. These are to be selected from schedules prepared by the committee, from such books and maps as have received the most extensive sanction from public opinion. The grant is to be at the rate of two shillings for every scholar in schools without pupil-teachers, and two-and-sixpence in those with pupil-teachers, on condition that two-thirds of the cost is met by subscriptions. The grants might be renewed after three years on condition that four-fifths of the value was subscribed. The books and maps might be sold to teachers and scholars only, at the same prices at which the managers obtained them, viz. two-thirds of the reduced prices, which averaged just over one-half of the ordinary published prices. In an explanatory circular the managers are strongly recommended to provide every scholar in the first class with a satchel, and to allow each to take home, daily, a reading-lesson book, and two other text-books, to prepare the lessons of the succeeding day. Later (in 1851), normal and training schools, under inspection, were included under this minute.

This was indeed a wholesome and helpful act. Of all things most required to further the real work in the schools, good and appropriate books were most urgently needed. The Bible was still, in too many cases, almost the only reading-book; and was, of course, for teaching purposes, an inadequate text-book, because of the absence of any grading as to language and subject-matter. Books on all school subjects, as well as some on teaching, were included, and a very large choice was offered.

The most striking and conclusive evidence of the way in which the grants aided most those who needed it least, and left either without any help, or with the most shallow pretence of help, just those districts which needed it most, is given by the grants for school-books. The parishes of Shoreditch and Shadwell, with a total population of over thirty-seven thousand inhabitants, received *nothing*. Kensington, with a population of thirty thousand, received over two thousand pounds. Four poor parishes in London, with very large populations, obtained twelve pounds and eightpence amongst them, whilst four rich parishes obtained just upon four thousand pounds between them.

On the same day as the foregoing minute appeared, there also appeared one dealing with grants to Roman Catholic schools. Applications were to be made through the Roman Catholic Poor School Committee. Only the secular instruction in such schools was to be reported upon, and inspectors for them were not to be appointed without the previous concurrence of the above-mentioned Committee. No teacher in holy orders could share in any grant, except in the case of training and model schools, at their lordships' discretion.

A great deal of correspondence took place during 1847 concerning the management clauses required by the committee to be inserted in the deeds of trust, as a condition of receiving grants. These were designed to secure that the lay element should be represented in the government of church schools, through a local committee which was to be appointed; and to prevent many abuses which had arisen through absentee parsons, and others, being sole managers and refusing to allow the resident clergyman to interfere with the management of the school. The great point of objection urged by the clergy was that whilst the final decision regarding the religious and moral instruction in the schools was to be in the hands of the clergyman of the parish and the bishop of the diocese, the right of deciding what were religious and moral instruction was taken out of their hands and placed in that of certain arbitrators. Another was that the making compulsory, in certain cases, the election of a committee by the subscribers to the school. In the end their lordships made several modifications to meet the views of the Church party, the Catholics, and others.

In June, 1848, appeared the first list of those who had successfully passed the examinations for the "Certificates of Merit" issued by the committee. Instructions were issued, previous to the examination, informing the inspectors that from 800 to 1000 schoolmasters would be assembled for the examinations. A delightfully paternal exhortation is given to the inspectors, urging upon them the serious importance of the occasion, and of their behaviour thereupon. They are not to be "betrayed into impatience by fatigue, or even by misconduct of the candidates. On the contrary, by cheerfulness, affability, anxiety to consult the convenience of all, and such sympathy with their success as is consistent with the impartial discharge of your duties, it is hoped that you will leave on their minds the most grateful personal impressions." The unsuccessful ones are to be comforted with the information that even their failure will be useful to them, and no disgrace; and cheered by the knowledge that subsequent success will raise them to a position of dignity and comfort, or their present failure may be the passport to some office in the various departments of the public service. The certificates not only officially certified that a teacher had passed for the Higher, Middle, or Lower Certificate, in the first, second, or third division, but gave an estimate of the attainments in each of the subjects, and of the practical ability shown in teaching a class. Of those who took the first examination 332 were successful. Two broadsheets were issued by the committee, one setting forth the conditions under which pupil-teachers were appointed, their salaries, and the syllabus of subjects for the annual examinations; and the other stating the conditions under which augmentations of teachers' salaries would be granted, and the subjects for the certificate examinations. These were to be hung in a conspicuous situation upon the inner walls of the school-room so that they might be read by scholars, parents, and visitors.

Such was the effect of this bold advertisement, and the tempting promise of salary and promotion, that no less than 817 pupil-teachers were added, in seven months, to the 1243 who had been admitted since 1846. Their lordships were, in consequence, obliged to be more rigorous in excluding candidates, either on account of their poor qualifications or the poor conditions of the schoolrooms in which they would have to work. Also in cases where more than one pupil-teacher to every fifty scholars had already been appointed, any fresh candidate had to pass an unequivocally good examination. And all pupil-teachers were to give evidence, in the improvement of their classes, of having zealously and efficiently done their duty as teachers, or to lose their stipend if there was any gross neglect. Inspectors were directed to inquire very particularly as to the moral character and conduct of pupil-teachers.

As the result of a memorial, and subsequent correspondence, addressed to their lordships on November 14, 1851, by Sir Moses Montefiore, on behalf of the London Committee of the British Jews, schools for Jews were admitted to a share in the education grant, subject to the conditions already in force.

Still another onward and upward movement was made in this year, by a letter from the Lord President to Rev. Henry Hughes of Gordon Street, Gordon Square, stating that "evening schools for young persons between the ages of 12 and 17 among the respectable and well-conducted portion of the labouring class . . . would be admissible to receive grants for the purchase of books and maps at reduced prices". Further, that certificated teachers, engaged by the managers of an elementary school under inspection, would receive the usual grant in aid of salary if employed either morning or afternoon in the day-school and during the evening in the night-school. But under no circumstances ought a teacher to be employed to teach during the morning, noon, and night of the same day. For "six hours of such daily labour, with another hour and a half devoted to pupil-teachers, and the time needed for private study, form a task which few constitutions, even of the strongest kind, can continue to fulfil without suffering. To add to this routine of labour the charge of an evening-school can end only in exhausting or driving away the teacher." Pupil-teachers might not be employed in evening-schools.

One or two rather curious incidents are recorded in the course of the correspondence now being referred to. It appears that pupil-teachers—some in their fifth year, and some who had completed their apprenticeship—intending to take the Queen's scholarship examination, had been invited to reside for a time in the colleges to which they hoped to go, so that they might be coached for the examination. Their lordships very much disapproved of the practice, since it gave some competitors an advantage, irrespective of merit, and also favoured the idea of cramming, as against regular and equable study at home. Those who interrupted their apprenticeship in such a way were to be disqualified for holding a scholarship. One of those who were fortunate in securing a scholarship accepted an appointment as headmaster of a school during the first year of his training, and was on the point of leaving the college, when "my lords" objected to this, as against the whole spirit and purpose of their system, and informed him that if he left the college he would not be allowed to have a pupil-teacher under him, neither would he receive any grant in aid of his salary. He changed his plans.

But perhaps the most striking letter is that of a candidate at the scholarship examination, who writes to say that he has been more than surprised to find that he is not amongst the successful ones. He fails to understand this, since "without being guilty of egotism, I think I can confidently say that all the questions proposed to me were correctly answered, save those in mathematics, and one or two in history". Further: "I find, however, the names of some who have succeeded, although they did not fill up three papers to my number; and again, I find that there is one candidate included in the list whom I had the honour frequently at his examination of putting right in orthography. I do not name these things from any feelings of resentment; only, I think it rather too bad to confer honours upon those who are inferior to myself. After all, may I ask, Have not my papers been overlooked? May I trouble you to let me know something about the matter at your earliest convenience." This ingenuous and ingenious objector—a head-master—was suspended for three years from the benefits of the grants in aid of salary.

Not only were teachers provided for the schools, but their qualifications were looked after, and, in the year 1851, an advance in their qualifications was insisted on. Pupil-teachers were not to be admissible to be examined for certificates of merit, or to receive the augmentation grants which depended upon them, unless they had resided for one year in a training college, or had served three years as head or assistant in a school under inspection; and after the year 1852 no candidate (not having been a pupil-teacher or a student in a training college under inspection) could be admitted to the certificate examination unless he was twenty-two years of age, and his school had been inspected and favourably reported upon by an inspector. The promise to pupil-teachers of employment in the public service was withdrawn in 1852. It was also required that an assistant teacher should be up to the standard of attainments expected from pupil-teachers in their fifth year, and, unless he offered some special subject for examination, the inspector might require him to pass an oral or written examination in any, or all, of the subjects prescribed for a fifth-year pupil-teacher. Pupil-teachers were specially warned that their apprenticeship was not regarded as a sufficient training for a post as head-teacher.

During the same year, ragged schools were admitted to a partial share in the grants. They might receive grants for pupil-teachers, though these would not be sanctioned with the same readiness as in common schools; for the purchase of books and maps; for the erection or hire (one-half the rent) of workshops, and for the purchase of tools; and, where master workmen (not being otherwise remunerated as teachers at the public expense) were retained, a fee for the average number of children under each such master's instruction, at a rate not exceeding ten shillings per annum for each scholar. No grant in aid of the master's salary was to be given unless he obtained a certificate of merit. In an early letter on this subject considerable doubt was expressed as to the advisability of allowing pupil-teachers in such schools, since such "institutions, by the offer of food and of gratuitous instruction, affect injuriously such schools as recognize the responsibility of parents to pay for the education of their children, and they tend in the same degree to weaken the sense of this responsibility in the labouring class. . . . The position of the pupil-teacher is a public one, and my lords think that it should be understood, as it is formally declared, to be a prize for the children of independent parents who make sacrifices to educate them properly." Truly a strange doctrine in the face of the fact that the system had its origin in a pauper school. But then this letter is signed R. R. W. Lingen, whilst others had been signed J. P. Kay-Shuttleworth.

In 1853 the minute of 1847 granting schoolmasters' associations orders for the purchase of books and maps for the libraries of their associations was extended, as a means to increasing their professional knowledge. The application was to come through, and with the recommendation of, an inspector, and accompanied by a copy of the rules of the association and a list of its officers and members. No grant was to be claimed in respect of any member whose subscription was unpaid, or who was not in a school under inspection. For every ten shillings of grant a like amount was to be raised by the applicants. The books and maps were not, by any means, to become the property of an individual member.

All this has gradually led up to the necessity of practically recognizing that the State must undertake the duty of permanently maintaining all the machinery which it has been at such trouble to establish. Hence on April 2, 1853, appeared the great revolutionary minute, introducing the principle of contributions from the public purse towards the annual expenses incurred in the

A Semi-state System.

support of schools. The minute was headed: Annual Grants, and was said to be a minute as to grants for the support of schools in the agricultural districts and in unincorporated towns (not containing more than 5000 inhabitants) in England and Wales. Under this minute any school under inspection might secure annual grants, at the following rate per scholar:—

No. of Scholars.	Boys' Schools.	Girls' Schools.
Under 50	6s.	5s.
Above 50, but under 100	5s.	4s.
Above 100	4s.	3s.

To claim such grants the school must have an income of fourteen shillings in subscriptions for every boy, and twelve for every girl. Before a scholar could count for the grant, he or she must have attended one hundred and ninety-two days in the year, and there must have been paid for his or her education not less than one penny, or more than fourpence, per week. The school must be under a certificated teacher, to whose salary, and that of an assistant, at least seven-tenths of the whole income (including the grant) of the school should be applied. If the school contained more than one hundred and twenty scholars, then a part of this seven-tenths of income might be used to pay additional pupil-teachers or assistants. "Half-timers" were to count for the grant; and registers and school accounts were to be kept as the Committee of Council should direct. Finally, three-fourths of the children were to pass such an annual examination as should be prescribed. The exclusion of incorporated towns was due to the fact that a bill to deal with these was to be submitted to the House of Commons. It was, and was thrown out; and large towns thus lost the capitation grant for nearly three years. One additional inspector, and five assistant inspectors (co-ordinates, not subordinates as at present —they are now called second inspectors for a district) were appointed in view of the increase of work which annual examinations would cause.

This was indeed a far-reaching act. At last the education of the people is very definitely, though by no means wholly, in the hands of the government. At least they are going to provide, more or less effectively, for the doing of the work; though the initiation and control of this work is left in the hands of private individuals, acting under certain limitations and obligations imposed by the Committee of Council. The worst that individuals can now do is to hinder the extension of the work by declining to open new schools in which these aids may act; or retard the improvement of the schools by regarding the minimum requirements of the government as the maximum of their aims and endeavours. The great merits of this measure were that it decidedly encouraged local efforts, and very much increased the guarantees of efficiency in the work of the schools. A supplementary minute still further encouraged local efforts by conveying an offer to grant one-half of the outlay for putting up and furnishing school buildings, provided that such grant did not exceed the rate of six shillings per square foot of area in the school and class-rooms if the plans included a teacher's house, or four shillings if they did not—another instance of the consideration shown towards teachers. In connection with this it may be noticed that care was taken to prevent teachers' salaries from being reduced because of the grants in aid. A schoolmistress had complained that, when she received the grant in aid of her salary, her managers had discontinued an allowance of sixteen pounds per annum previously paid for playing the organ. So their lordships issued a circular letter pointing out that such proceedings violated the conditions on which the augmentations of salary were given.

In a circular explanatory of the minute relating to annual grants, issued to inspectors, "my lords" very wisely say that schools which have not hitherto been regarded as suitable to receive grants may under the new conditions become eligible, since annual grants may supply just that lack of means which had hitherto made it impracticable to put the school in an efficient condition as to premises and apparatus. Inspectors are, therefore, to report whether a school which is at the time below the requirements is yet in the hands of persons who lack neither the intelligence nor the wish, but

A Semi-state System.

only the means, gradually to improve it. Only in regard to the number of those scholars for whom the grant is claimed will the income of the school be estimated. The grant will be refused to a mixed school under a mistress only, if it is the only school in a village; since it would not be fit for boys over eight or nine years of age, and such an age for leaving school could not be approved. If the head-teacher of a school was competent but not certificated, a year's grace, for which grant would be given, would be allowed, in which he would have an opportunity of getting his certificate. Failing this he must be registered, and their lordships might at any time require that a certificated teacher should be appointed, or no further grant would be given.

The children were not to be classified according to age; though it was to be expected that the older ones, who had been longest at school and would soon be leaving, ought to be the more advanced. Hence all above nine years of age were to be grouped in two divisions: those under, and those over, eleven years. On the day of inspection such of these as the managers claimed grant for were to be presented to the inspector, and he was to record how many in the first division were able (*a*) to read simple narratives with intelligence; (*b*) to work from dictation a sum in simple subtraction, multiplication, or division correctly; (*c*) to write on a slate from dictation, with correct spelling, a simple sentence twice read to them, first consecutively, and then by one word at a time. In the second division how many were able (*a*) to read books of general information fluently; (*b*) to work from dictation a sum in one of the four first compound rules of arithmetic correctly; (*c*) to write on paper from dictation, in a neat hand and with correct spelling, two or three simple sentences twice read to them, first consecutively, and then by a few words at a time; (*d*) to point out the parts of speech in the same sentence (orally); (*e*) to answer questions in the tables of weights and measures (orally); and (*f*) answer a few elementary questions in geography (orally), and on other subjects of useful information—the questions to be adapted to the course of study pursued in the school.

Such was the first syllabus of subjects and work drawn up for public elementary schools. At the present day some twenty pages of a blue-book are required to set forth the subjects and the work required in them, which must or may be taken in a public elementary school. The comparison clearly shows how far we have progressed, at least in the way of quantity.

To still further increase the supply of trained teachers, and to raise their qualifications, the committee resolved, Aug. 20, 1853, that as many Queen's scholarships should be given as the total number of places in training colleges (1143 men, 788 women); and that such of these as passed a satisfactory examination at the end of their first year of training should have their scholarships renewed for a second year. An augmentation of the salaries of lecturers in training colleges was to be made, if they passed an examination. Drawing was to be one of the subjects in the examination for students; and assistant teachers who had acquitted themselves satisfactorily for three years were to be allowed, without further examination, a Queen's scholarship of twenty-five pounds. No certificate of merit was to be issued to students in training unless they passed their examinations successfully, and until they had obtained two satisfactory reports whilst in charge of the same school; and grants to training colleges were to be made for those students only who had completed a second year's residence. All uncertificated teachers over thirty-five years of age were to be required to pass an examination in religious knowledge, English history, geography, arithmetic (including vulgar and decimal fractions), English grammar and composition, and the theory and practice of teaching. This examination was to ascertain if they had "sound, if humble attainments", and were qualified to be on a list of registered, as distinguished from certificated, teachers.

The same year an attempt was made to secure the insertion, in the trust deeds of Church schools, of a conscience clause. This demand was strongly resisted by most of the church party on the ground that whilst they might excuse the children of nonconformist parents from the dogmatic religious teaching in their schools, they could not allow that this should become a legal right. After much controversy between the National Society and the Education Department a compromise was arranged, by which the insertion of such a clause was still pressed by the Department, but it did not go so far as to refuse grants to those schools whose managers declined to admit the clause in their trust deeds. Churchmen seem to have regarded this as another attempt to injure their schools and their church, by rooting out definite church doctrine. How this fear could be justified, unless they regarded the schools as happy hunting-grounds for proselytes, it is difficult to understand. Not until 1864 did the Department definitely insist upon its rights to refuse grants for buildings if a conscience clause was not inserted in the trust deeds.

Early in the following year the case of infants' schools was provided for, and it was resolved that training colleges should receive grants of fifteen or ten pounds—according as the student obtained a first or second class in the examination—for every student who had received a separate and complete course of training for an infants' school during one year. The examination was to be the same as that for registered teachers, together with a practical test in teaching and managing an infant school, and an oral examination if the inspector thought fit. Those who were successful would receive grants in aid of their salaries; and those in the first class might have pupil-teachers under them, but not so those in the second class. No school was to be regarded as an infant school in which there were scholars over seven years of age, or in which the instruction was not specially and exclusively adapted to children under that age.

Several further changes were introduced in 1855. Perhaps the most valuable of these was the rule that all schools which received the government grants, for other than building purposes, must be in charge of a certificated or registered teacher. This would go a long way towards securing the standard of efficiency which was then looked upon as a reasonable one. A year's grace was to be allowed for unqualified teachers, in schools already receiving grant, to prepare for and take the examination for a certificate of merit, or for being entered on the list of registered teachers. Registered teachers might have pupil-teachers apprenticed to them if, in their examination, they passed in either Euclid (first three books), algebra, or practical mathematics. An official certificate form was drawn up, on which the teacher's attainments in each of the subjects of examination were indicated, and spaces provided for the entering of a brief summary of the annual report on his school. Also an official "scholar's certificate" was issued, which was to be awarded to those pupils who, being over twelve years of age, had attended the same school continuously for three years (at least 176 days in each year); had reached the standard of knowledge fixed for a stipendiary monitor; were regular and punctual; were clean in person and neat in dress; and had maintained a uniformly good character. These things were indicated on the certificate, and also the level of attainment in each subject of school work.

The capitation grant was extended to night-schools, under the following circumstances:—The Marquis of Salisbury had a day-school on his estate at Hatfield, and also a night-school, at which boys employed on the estate, and superintended by a skilled labourer, were obliged to attend, as a condition of employment. A second master was employed, who was to teach for half a day in the day-school and also in the night-school. The committee were asked if he could sit for a certificate, and, if successful, receive grant in aid of his salary; and whether capitation grant would be allowed for those attending the evening school. The reply to each question was, yes; but no grant would be given until the teacher was certificated, and no boy might be reckoned for grant in both schools. This appears to have stimulated the instituting of such schools, for in the following year we find them noticed in the inspectors' reports. One inspector remarks that they were constantly gaining ground in the country, and in some places more real practical work was done in them than in the day-schools. On the whole, however, their growth was slow.

The Education Department, which is but the Committee of Council under a new name and with extended powers, came into official existence on February 25, 1856. The lords of the Privy Council petitioned Her Majesty to order that the education establishments then attached to different departments, viz., the Committee of the Council, and the Science and Art Department, be united under one direction, and be called the Education Department. This was to be under the Lord President of the Council, who was to be assisted by another member of the Privy Council, to be known as the Vice-president. The latter was to act under the former, and for him in his absence. All the existing rules and regulations in both departments were to be observed as hitherto. The additional duties taken on were: to report on such questions concerning education as were referred to the Department by the Charity Commissioners for England and Wales; and to inspect certain schools connected with the Admiralty and War Office, and report on them to those departments.

In this year there was a still further opening of the doors of the training colleges to those who were inclined to qualify themselves more thoroughly for their work. A pupil-teacher might spend his fifth year in a training-college if he had been successful in his examination, and whilst there receive the usual rate of payment as a pupil-teacher, as well as the scholarship of twenty-five, or twenty, pounds. Next, Queen's scholars were to be allowed a second year of training in all cases where the authorities of the college applied for such extension. Any persons over eighteen years of age, who were selected and presented by the authorities of the several training colleges on their own responsibility, might take the scholarship examination. But such persons, if successful, might not be admitted to any college in a proportion greater than one in ten, as compared with those who had been pupil-teachers. Assistant teachers of three years' standing were to be admitted as before. Resident students in normal colleges—not having been pupil-teachers—over twenty years of age, who passed the first year's examination, might become Queen's scholars. Certificated teachers in charge of schools, who had not resided in a training college for more than one year already, might receive another year's training. Teachers in night-schools might become Queen's scholars.

To encourage teachers to qualify in drawing, pupil-teachers were allowed to attend classes at any drawing school in connection with the Science and Art Department, on payment of half the ordinary fees. Those teachers who qualified in each of the following: freehand, linear geometry, linear perspective, model and object drawing, were to receive a memorandum of full competency to give instruction in drawing, and an addition to their annual augmentation grants of two pounds for the first, and one pound for each of the other subjects. These payments were to be increased if pupil-teachers taught by the holders of the "D" certificate were successful in their drawing examinations.

The conditions regulating the training of mistresses for infants' schools were also modified, on the lines followed with regard to masters and mistresses for the schools for older scholars. Queen's scholarships of the second class were offered to pupil-teachers who had satisfactorily completed their apprenticeship in an infants' school, and to any persons over eighteen years of age, approved by an inspector, and able to read easy narrative, write simple sentences from dictation, and work easy sums correctly in the four first rules (simple and compound). Any Queen's scholar in a women's training college might take the course for infants' teachers, and private students in the colleges were also at liberty to do so. A special examination for such students, and teachers who had continued in charge of infants' schools from any time before April 29, 1854, was to be held about Michaelmas in each year.

Probably the beginning of the principle of payment by results, under the Education Department, was suggested—certainly approved—by "my lords" in a letter dated January 22, 1857, informing an inquirer that teachers have no claim whatever upon the capitation grants, but "at the same time my lords would not disapprove of an arrangement whereby the teacher was given some interest in obtaining the capitation grant, *e.g.* a percentage upon it in addition to the salary otherwise assured to him.

Any such plan, however, both in principle and detail, rests exclusively upon the discretion of the managers."

The progressive spirit seems to have taken a firm hold upon the Department, under the new name. So enlightened a step as the establishment of an educational museum was decided upon, and it was to be opened in the spring of the following year. This was to exhibit, under a proper classification, all important books, diagrams, illustrations, and apparatus connected with education, already in use, or which might be published from time to time, either at home or abroad. All producers of such things were to have the privilege, subject to certain regulations, of exhibiting their productions, duly labelled with descriptive notes and the retail prices. The museum was to be open free to the public on Mondays, Tuesdays, and Saturdays.

It is worth while to record that on March 20, 1857, Rev. Benjamin James Binns, B.A., principal of the Caernarvon training college, was appointed to be one of Her Majesty's assistant inspectors of schools. This is the first appointment of an inspector who appears to have had some specific training for his work. And in this case it was probably a very second-hand one, for he doubtless went to the training college as technically unprepared as the other inspectors went to the schools. At the same time it must be observed that the men appointed to the work were, as a rule, men of distinguished attainments, sometimes brilliant scholarship, high intellectual culture, often with exceptional gifts, and, in many cases, of broad and generous sympathies. The fact that they were so has been the salvation of the situation. Otherwise it would indeed have been a case of the blind leading the blind. Actually, it was a case of blundering intelligence leading blundering ignorance. The inspectors brought powerful, well-trained, and, in some cases, original powers to bear upon the problem which had to be faced, and often succeeded in re-discovering the more elementary and obvious principles of organization and teaching methods, whilst those who studied the writings of the great educationists and educators did something towards leading teachers back to the great foundation principles discovered and demonstrated by Rousseau, Pestalozzi, Froebel, and others.

On reading through the various reports by the inspectors one can find almost every principle of method which is now commonly regarded as sound by the best authorities, either adversely criticised or condemned; most unsound principles recommended or approved; and also many sound principles hinted, expressed, or applauded. For example, one speaks of the Catechism as "itself an excellent intellectual exercise"; whilst another says it is "like every other formula, liable to become matter of mechanical repetition unassociated with any intelligent and practical interpretation". Another excuses parents who neglect to educate their children on the ground that the education within their reach is not adapted to their wants:—"I think they are partially right in this opinion, as too little time is often given to needlework in girls' schools, and to certain industrial pursuits in most poor schools". In one case the teaching of grammar, through the study of the sentence, is spoken of as far more intellectual than the old method—through parsing—and as furnishing far more scope for mental training. This is met by the suggestion that "as to analysis, it seems premature to teach children how to break up sentences before they are well able to put them together". Of the proper size of classes there is divergence of opinion, as is shown by the following extracts:—"As a rule, that school is best in which there are the fewest classes. Nor does it appear that in any elementary school, however large, there are ever more than four really distinct grades of scholars, nor that any necessity exists for more than four classes. If we would provide qualified teachers for all the subdivisions, the gain might still, I think, be questioned." On the other hand, "while the system of collective and simultaneous lessons has conduced greatly to the general development of intelligence in children, the benefits are in very many, perhaps in the majority of instances, counterbalanced by the inaccuracy of the knowledge thus acquired, and by the artificial character of the results.

A Semi-state System.   139

... At the training colleges which I have visited this year the collective lessons are generally given to a small number of children in the same stage of intellectual development, and are therefore free from the objectionable tendencies which I have described." One other contrast, and conflict, is worth noting. "The practice of simultaneous reading is the most usual, and excellent results sometimes attend it"—when not too much time is taken in asking questions on the subject-matter. "The purely simultaneous method—the purer the more fallacious", refers to the same topic.

Such a curious complex, and conflict, of opinions would appear entirely absurd, except for the frank admissions made by the inspectors themselves that they regarded the whole matter as in the stage of experimental beginnings, and themselves as beginners in experiment. Yet, even in this there was an implied paradox, for they saw and urged the necessity and value of training pupil-teachers, assistants, and heads. But no hint appears of the desirability of inspectors going through a course of two or three years' training, and passing qualifying examinations. It was as though one should advance the theory that solicitors and barristers needed training for the law, but judges could do without such training.

Another instance of opposing views is seen in the following references in reports to the pupil-teacher system: "They often conduct lessons in reading, arithmetic, and writing from copies and dictation, better than many adult teachers of ordinary ability. . . . Many of them can teach and examine a large class in grammar, geography, and English history, and the subject-matter of books of general information, with less waste of time and greater facility in illustration than the generality of untrained teachers." Upon which one is inclined to ask why not a system of schools taught by pupil-teachers—with a drill-sergeant thrown in for discipline—and supervised by pupil-teacher inspectors (examiners)? It would be much cheaper, and, according to this theory, probably more effective. But let us reconsider the matter. "Educationally viewed, it is a low and unsatisfactory expedient. Intellectually the general education must suffer. Children only thirteen years of age are called from their proper work, learning, and apprenticed to teach. The time which should be spent in their own intellectual culture and equipment is spent on others, and thus their own range of improvement must be narrowed. The taught also must suffer. . . . They often attain great expertness in the outer forms of questioning, but it is the expertness of jugglery, the tossing backwards and forwards of the same truths, the shaking into many kaleidoscopic combinations of the same well-known facts. But as for awakening thought, stimulating and directing inquiry, and evolving exercised energies of intellect, it is never dreamed of nor attempted. . . . For hours daily the finest mechanism we know on earth—the human spirit, with all its intellectual and moral energies and capabilities—is left to be handled or tossed about by inexperienced teachers." Which truth has been rediscovered, in 1897, by a Departmental Committee appointed to inquire into the pupil-teacher system.

Chapter VII.

A Semi-state System—*Continued.*

The work of organization, from a political point of view, continued to advance. There gradually appeared clearer and more equitable ideas as to the rights and duties of a citizen in matters concerning education. The conviction that local rates, representative management (popular control), and universal provision of schools, are right principles, seemed to take possession of the public mind, and the carrying them out in practice was advocated by a royal commission. There was also a demand made for a proper responsible head of the central authority, who should be directly answerable to the people's representatives in the House of Commons. All this was wholesome, and was still combined with a

A Semi-state System. 141

determination that the religious basis of education should be maintained.

But the internal work of the schools received a blow from which it is only just beginning to recover. The elements of machinery and the mechanical were raised to their highest powers, the elements of reason and right development crushed to their lowest. The good angel of humane and rational education, Sir J. Kay-Shuttleworth, was succeeded by the evil genius of beggarly elements and payment by results, Mr. Robert Lowe. The be-all and end-all of the schools was to be the imparting of a certain minimum of skill in reading, writing, and arithmetic. If this was done, a money equivalent was to be given for work accomplished. If this was not done, what was there which deserved payment? The minds of scholars were to fit to a fixed measurement by rule and compass, or they were not fit for grants. Such were to be the simple rules and practices of the new system. What wonder that they blighted and withered teachers, scholars, and system!

Of the course of parliamentary action concerning education from 1847 to 1862 it may be said that it included, for the most part, merely repetitions of the struggles between what were called religious and secular systems of education. Though how a system which mainly concerned itself with a direct storing of the memory with religious dogmas and formulæ in a necessarily more or less unintelligent and undigested form, and was meanwhile content to allow the mental powers to remain comparatively undeveloped and dormant, thus delaying the time when the individual could read, mark, learn and inwardly digest religious doctrines; how such a system could be said to be truly religious it is not easy to see. Whilst on the other hand the so-called secularists—with but few exceptions—desired nothing more than that the mental powers should be so cultivated that they might be turned to religious instruction with the greatest advantage. As Mr. Cobden declared in the Commons, secular instruction only meant the learning of ordinary subjects; and this would neither prevent nor pervert religious instruction.

The reading of the Bible, and definite moral training, were always insisted upon in the secular system.

A squabble arose as to the use of the Authorized Version of the Bible in schools. It was claimed by the Church party that no other version could be allowed. This meant that, since the reading of the Bible was a compulsory condition for receiving grant, the Catholic schools were to be excluded from government aid for their schools. Well might Lord Brougham protest that he could not help expressing the sorrow he felt that, not in 1447 or 1547, but in the year 1847, they should find, as appeared from what was going on elsewhere, the great question of education mixed up with all the embroilment of sectarian violence and bigotry.

In 1850 Mr. Fox introduced a bill to provide for education. He would have inspectors to ascertain if there was any deficiency in any part of their districts, after taking account of all public and private schools. If there was, then the inhabitants of the district were to be invited to provide for this by a local rate. This rate could be used to pay teachers according to the number and success of their scholars; or to establish free schools, open to any child from seven to thirteen years of age, all of whom were to receive the same kind of training, and no religious dogmas were to be taught. Deserving scholars at these schools were to receive a present of books when leaving, and one of these was to be a Bible. Teachers of such schools were to be appointed, paid, and dismissed by the local school committee. In any cases where the local inhabitants declined to do their duty, the Committee of Council was to step in and make proper provision. The minimum salaries paid to teachers were to be sufficient in amount to ensure some considerable degree of respectability in their social position, for on them depended the success of the whole scheme. Honourable rivalry between teachers should be stimulated by the publication and distribution of annual reports (from the Committee of Council) for the encouragement of the meritorious, and the shaming of the indifferent out of their culpable neglect of duty. By education he meant the complete training and drawing forth of the mind. This could only be accomplished by the highly-gifted teacher, or the affectionate pastor or parent. Instruction, or the mere attainment of knowledge, was a lower task, which was to be accomplished by the agency of the school, and the efforts of the schoolmaster.

During his speech he read a remarkable passage from a manifesto of the working-men of London. It was as follows:—" We cannot consent that our children should be apportioned amongst the religious sects—that their plastic minds and nascent judgments should be subjected to an external pressure which would give them a permanent bias towards peculiar notions. This appears to us to be the very way to foment and cherish those theological distinctions which already so unhappily divide mankind. Religion is intended to prepare men for heaven, where the society of the blessed will be united in peace and love. Why should it be made on earth the pretext for cutting up the community into sections, and separating them from one another by unpronounceable shibboleths? We have noticed that they all agree as to its urgent and imperative necessity; each party has vied with the others in eloquent description of the frightful condition of the working-classes. We have been called 'a multitude of untutored savages', and the places where we dwell have been designated as 'great and terrible wildernesses'. We have sat still, expecting that the religious denominations, in holy charity and pity for our sufferings, would for once lay by their peculiarities, which they themselves confess are not essential to salvation, and agree upon some plan by which the resources of the State might be employed to rescue us from our awful condition. But we have waited in vain; the controversy has waxed hotter and more furious; our little ones have been forgotten in the fray, and their golden moments have been allowed to run irrecoverably to waste."

With respect to the importance of qualified teachers, Mr. Fox mentioned the interesting circumstance that in the Isle of Man they had, on paper, the most perfect system of education to be found in the world; for every parish had its school, the ratepayers had a share in its management, and every parent was made to send his child to school. Yet the children there were in a more forlorn condition than any in the kingdom, owing to the want of proper and efficient teachers.

One member of the House asked what sort of schoolmasters would place themselves under the control of a committee chosen every year by all the ratepayers in the parish? He could not conceive a situation more objectionable to a respectable man. A ludicrous enough objection in the light of present-day experience; and yet such objections were, and are, constantly urged against changes of any considerable extent. Sir R. Inglis, the most consistent upholder of the high-and-dry church theory of education, declared that religion is the only true education, and it should be that or nothing. Other systems simply meant infidelity and scepticism. To which Mr. Fox replied, that he did not believe that a knowledge of the mountains or the stars taught infidelity, or the study of the waves and wind heresy. The bill was thrown out by 287 votes against 58.

Great excitement was aroused during this year by an attack, on the part of the Church, upon the management clauses—inserted in the trust deeds of schools, as a condition of receiving grant—requiring that there should be a committee of management in each case, on which laymen were to serve; and also that whilst all questions concerning the religious and moral instruction given in the schools were to be, in the last resort, settled by the bishop of the diocese, yet the decision as to what was, or was not, a religious or moral question was to rest with the Committee of Council. So keen was the feeling amongst clergymen that this was meant to gradually transfer the school entirely to State management, that a large number refused to accept any grant on the conditions laid down. Finally some modifications were made, and peace thereby restored.

The following year Mr. Fox brought forward, in the House of Commons, a motion to the effect "that it is expedient to promote the education of the people, in

A Semi-state System.   145

England and Wales, by the establishment of free schools for secular instruction, to be supported by local rates, and managed by committees elected specially for that purpose by the ratepayers". In introducing the resolution he very slyly pointed out that the fifty-ninth canon required the clergy to examine and instruct youths and ignorant persons for a half-hour or more every Sunday and holy-day before evening prayer, in the ten commandments, the articles, the Lord's prayer, and the Catechism. All fathers, mothers, masters, and mistresses were to cause their children, servants, and apprentices to attend at such times. If any minister neglected his duty he was to be sharply reproved for the first offence —on information being sent to the bishop—suspended for a second, and excommunicated for a third. Parents and masters who were neglectful of their duties were to be suspended for one month, and if then still in default to be excommunicated. If these requirements were fulfilled, said Mr. Fox, religious instruction would be sufficiently provided for.

Religious and secular instruction, he said, were kept distinct in all other schools. It was only when education was given to the poor, when it was to be administered as a sort of charity, that religion was inculcated— not for the sake of its own benignant influences, but for the sake of keeping the poor in order and tranquillity. But Providence never intended the Bible for a schoolbook. It is worth while noting that this theory of the vital need of dogmatic religious instruction for other people's children, and not for their own, on the part of the clergy and others, has been recently criticised with great force and point by Sir Joshua Fitch.

The management clauses were again discussed, in the House of Lords, in 1852. The debate is chiefly interesting because of the challenge of the actions of the Committee of Council as being, in many cases, altogether independent of the sanction of Parliament. The Earl of Derby asserted that, unless he was much mistaken, many of the most important alterations and decisions which had been made by the committee on education, had been made during the recess of Parliament, and consequently when the vote for education had been already passed. Lord Lansdowne, then president of the council, denied this at the time, saying that no change of system had been thus introduced, but only such steps had been taken as were necessary to carry out the spirit of the various minutes, according to the interpretation put upon them during the discussions in Parliament. But he had afterwards to admit that the Earl of Derby was in the right.

Lord John Russell again, in 1853, made an unsuccessful attempt to get a bill through the House of Commons. This was called the Borough Bill, and was designed to provide schools for incorporated towns, and towns with a population of five thousand. If a two-thirds majority of the town council agreed, they might levy a rate so as to provide aid at the rate of twopence a week for every scholar, on account of whom fourpence or fivepence was raised from other sources. A committee, consisting partly of town councillors and partly of other persons with a special knowledge of schools, was to distribute the money furnished by the rate to such schools as might receive aid from the Committee of Council. In some cases a grant for each child attending a school under a certificated teacher was to be given. All schools were to have a " conscience clause ".

Mr. Cobden said that whilst very considerable progress had been made during the last eighteen years, it had been done, if he might so express it, clandestinely. It had been smuggled, so to say, by the Committee of Council, because there was a constant apprehension of bringing the subject forward in that house, as it was thought that discussion on the subject would be fatal to education. As to the religious bogey, he did not believe that there could be got together one hundred decent and respectable men in any part of the country, to discuss the subject of education, into whose heads it would ever enter to do anything inimical to the cause of religion. He held that the religious question was a mighty bugbear, a bubble which would burst the moment they touched it with their fingers. Mr. Dunn, the secretary of the British and Foreign Schools Society, had told him that though he had heard a great deal of talk about the religious difficulty, he had never in the whole of his experience met with it in practice. If they were to have a national system of education they must have local rates for the purpose, or there would be nothing worthy of the name. At least three and a half millions a year would have to be raised, and England was well able to bear the burden. He suggested that there should be a permissive bill for corporate towns, and other localities. He would support any scheme whatsoever, so long as it was a truly national one.

Kneller Hall came into existence in the following year, as a training college, entirely under the control of the government, for those who intended to become teachers in prisons and workhouses. It is chiefly interesting from the fact that its principal was Rev. F. Temple, afterwards one of the inspectors, and to-day the Archbishop of Canterbury, whilst another member of the staff was Mr. F. T. Palgrave, afterwards an examiner in the education office, and later the professor of poetry at Oxford. The college was not a success, and was closed in 1855.

Sir J. Pakington, one of the most zealous and untiring champions of popular education, brought forward a bill in 1855 for establishing schools by the aid of local rates. All such schools were to be free, and to have a conscience clause. The local areas were to be corporate towns and poor-law unions, and the rating was to be parochial—not exceeding sixpence in the pound. The members of the local education board must be rated at not less than thirty pounds per annum, and elected by the ratepayers. Magistrates were to be *ex officio* members of the boards. Sir John said that his purpose was to place on the statute-book a law which should proclaim that no man need be ignorant, even as it already declared, on one of its noblest pages, that no man need be destitute. The bill was withdrawn, after considerable discussion.

Next year a bill for the appointment of a Vice-President of the Council was introduced into the House of Lords. Lord Monteagle seized the opportunity to express his conviction that the Committee of Council was in constitution and principle one of the worst modes of administration. The members were ill assorted; some could not attend for want of time; others had not the knowledge or opportunity of understanding the functions that nominally devolved upon them; and, as the result, the real power was in the hands of subordinate persons. However, the bill received the approval of both houses.

Lord John Russell remained faithful to his zeal for education, and submitted twelve resolutions to the Commons, the purpose of which was to accomplish improvement chiefly through existing agencies. The number of inspectors was to be largely increased, and they were to investigate, and report upon, any deficiency in the supply of schools in their district. Localities were to have the option of imposing a rate upon themselves, where other means were insufficient. If they failed to do this the quarter-sessions might levy a rate, and in case of their default the Committee of Council was to take the matter in hand. Religious instruction was to be given in all schools, but there was to be a conscience clause. Employers of children between nine and eleven years of age were to furnish half-yearly certificates of the attendance of the children at school, and to pay their fees. This bill was allowed to drop.

Public interest and activity were very keen from 1846 to 1856. Dr. Hook, vicar of Leeds, startled the Church party by putting forward a very broad and generous suggestion for a system of schools supported by the rates, under local management, and giving only secular instruction, but making provision for religious teaching by clergymen and ministers at certain hours. The scheme was, in fact, based upon the Irish system. As he shrewdly observed, a State system could only establish a pretence of religious education; because if the State supplied the funds for the school it was bound to regard the just claims of dissenters, who paid taxes as well as churchmen. He added, "I have no objection to let the State train the children to receive the religious education we are prepared to give". The idea that "the State is to supply the funds, and the bishops and clergy to expend those funds as they think fit [is] a monstrous notion in a free State where there is full toleration". If the Church desired to keep the whole of the education of the people, or nearly so, in her own hands, she must supply all the funds, and on these terms she might do so. But the Church had not sufficient piety to make a sacrifice which might require "the Bishops with the Clergy of England to tax themselves fifty per cent, aye, if need should be, a hundred per cent, and become beggars, rather than permit the education of the people to pass out of their hands".

In July, 1847, was formed the Lancashire Public School Association—afterwards, in 1850, called the National Public School Association—which was at first designed to establish a general system of secular schools in the county of Lancaster; but, later, "to promote the establishment by law in England and Wales of a system of free schools, which, supported by local rates and managed by local committees specially elected for that purpose by the ratepayers, shall impart secular instruction only, leaving to parents, guardians, and religious teachers the inculcation of religion, to afford opportunities for which it is proposed that the schools shall be closed at stated hours in each week". Messrs. Cobden, Fox, Milner Gibson, W. E. Forster, and Roebuck were some of the most distinguished supporters of the association. It established several good and successful schools on the principles it advocated, and exercised a very great influence both in the country and in parliament. It was, indeed, the principles of this association which were largely realized in the Elementary Education Act of 1870. To oppose its influence and work, the Manchester and Salford Committee on Education was formed, and started under the auspices of Sir James Kay-Shuttleworth, who was a convinced and determined advocate of the management of schools by religious communions.

It is almost amusing to notice how the Committee of Council managed to introduce into the actual working of the system of schools most of the principles and regulations advocated by the more advanced thinkers of the time, discussed and rejected in parliament, and resented and resisted by the Church party. The appointment of inspectors; the actual establishment of Kneller Hall; the introduction of the principle of popular control, in a very limited sense, by the insistence on the insertion of a clause in the trust deeds for the appointment of a committee of managers; the maintenance of the rights of religious freedom, by the gradual introduction of a conscience clause; the securing of public control, indirectly, by insisting on certain regulations as to secular and religious instruction, and by the final decision, through a special triumvirate, as to what was or what was not religious instruction; and the almost complete command —except only as to initiation—of the establishment and maintenance of schools by public money, through the part payment of teachers, the supply of books and apparatus, and the giving of annual grants: these were all measures which realized, in part and indirectly, the aims and desires of the best friends of primary instruction for the children of the poor. The force of public opinion must have been very weighty and strong to allow of these things being done in the teeth, so to say, of an adverse parliament, and of the Church party, who perceived and strenuously resisted the tendency and purpose which, they declared, underlay them. After all, the desire for the instruction of the people must have been, perhaps unconsciously, stronger in the minds of the governing classes as a whole than the desire for religious supremacy; or the actions of the Committee of Council would have been met with overwhelming opposition. Indeed it was only by the very perfection of the genius of compromise and graceful concessions that the committee escaped with its life on several occasions.

After vainly endeavouring, in 1857, to get the Commons to affirm the principles of religious freedom and toleration, local contributions for a national system, and local management and control in popular education, Sir J. Pakington was, in the following year, successful in obtaining a Royal Commission to inquire into the present state of popular education in England, and to consider and report what measures, if any, were required for the extension of sound and cheap elementary instruction to all classes of the people. He urged that the poorest and most ignorant places, which were at present unprovided with schools, and would remain so under existing conditions, were the very spots where schools of the highest order ought to be maintained at all costs. Their poverty entirely prevented them from supplying their needs, even if they wished to do so, whilst their ignorance kept them from the desire to improve. During the discussion on the matter, Sir Charles Adderley, Vice-President of the Council, speaking for the Government, asserted that they must be content with a low age and short attendance from the pupils in the country schools. Any attempt to keep the children of the labouring classes under intellectual culture after the very earliest age at which they could earn their living would be as arbitrary and improper as it would be to keep the boys of Eton and Harrow at spade labour.

The Commissioners completed their work and issued a report at the end of three years. The results of their labours may be briefly summarized, for present purposes, under four heads: the schools, the scholars, the teaching, the suggestions. With regard to the schools it was found that there was no large district entirely destitute of schools, and requiring to be supplied with them on a large scale. The means of education were diffused pretty generally and equally over the face of the whole country. There was, on the whole, a recognition, by the great mass of the people, of the value of the schools and a willingness to make use of them. This is shown by the fact that almost all the schools contained children whose parents held different religious convictions from those of the promoters of the school. Thus Jews and Roman Catholics were commonly found in Church schools, and Church children in Unitarian schools. From which it was very reasonably inferred that parents valued schools most because of the secular instruction, whilst managers regarded them as most valuable from the point of view of religious instruction.

Of the two and a half millions of children who, it was estimated, ought to be at school, only slightly more than one and a half millions were in public schools of any sort—including private adventure, dame, and charity schools—and of these less than one-half were under inspection. The attendance of pupils was very irregular and intermittent, being distributed over about four years in the case of children between six and twelve years of age. About one-third attended less than one hundred days, twenty-three per cent attended one hundred and fifty days, and forty-one per cent attended one hundred and seventy-six days—the smallest number qualifying for the capitation grant. Only ten per cent attended the same school from three to four years. This state of things was regarded as leaving great room for improvement, but compulsion was not recommended, because the demand for child labour was increasing, and independence was of more importance than education.

The teaching, discipline, and knowledge in inspected schools were found to be very much better than in other schools. But inspection was not thought to be a very reliable test of the work done in a school, since it was judged too much by what the highest class did. Even in the best schools three out of every four children left before reaching the highest class, and therefore with only such a pretence of knowledge as was to be gained in the lower classes. They got little more than a trick of mechanically pronouncing the letters, and the words which they read conveyed hardly any ideas to their minds. They left school, they went to work, and in the course of a year they knew nothing at all. The schools were educating one in eight of the class of children for which they were intended.

Before the introduction of the regulations of the revised code a school was examined, by way of experiment. Under the old conditions the inspector said it was in a very fair state of efficiency, and the master had done his duty during the past year. The results of the examinations were: of twenty children in the lowest group (seven to nine years of age), six passed in reading, none in writing, and none in arithmetic; of fourteen children in the middle group (nine to fourteen years of age), three passed in reading, three in writing, and none in arithmetic; of ten in the highest group, none passed

A Semi-state System.

in reading, none in writing, and three in arithmetic. On referring back to what was expected of children in each group, we can form an estimate of what was considered a reasonably satisfactory result, in schools much superior to those not under inspection. If this was the state of the green tree, what must have been the condition of the dry!

Another example of the results is worth giving, because it shows what came of the efforts to instil religious dogma in the minds of the children through teaching the Catechism. It must be remembered that it was a common complaint against Church schools that they gave, directly or indirectly, far too much time to religious instruction—churchmen, naturally enough, regarded this as their chief glory. The following is a written answer, by a child of average intelligence in an inspected school in 1855, to the question: What is thy duty towards God? "My duty toads God is to bleed in Him, to fering and to loaf withold your arts, withold my mine, withold my sold, and with my servth, to whirchip and give thanks, to put my old trash in Him, to call upon Him, to onner His old name and His world, and to save Him truly all the days of my life's end." In answer to another question, the duty towards one's neighbour is written out on the same lines of originality and obscurity.

It was thought that whilst inspection stimulated the work of the teachers, it also led to their cultivating the power of memory rather than the powers of reason, and to dwelling on details rather than on general principles and results. The different standards adopted by different inspectors was an inconvenience. Teachers also confined their efforts too much to the highest class, to the neglect of the lower, who ought to have gained a far more satisfactory amount of knowledge in reading, writing, and arithmetic. Nevertheless a good type of education had been set up, by the success of the best pupils, and it only remained to extend this to a larger body of schools and scholars. Above all, the moral and religious influence of the schools had been great—even civilizing a whole neighbourhood—and this, the most important function of the school, was the best performed.

But more than eight hundred thousand children were attending schools which were, for the most part, notoriously inefficient. Dame schools and private-adventure schools, in which no person was too old, poor, ignorant, feeble, sickly, or totally unqualified to be thought, by themselves or others, unfit for teaching, had nearly one-half of the scholars. The teachers in these schools were drawn from the ranks of domestic servants out of place; discharged barmaids; vendors of toys and lollipops; keepers of small eating-houses, mangles, and lodging-houses; needlewomen; milliners; consumptive patients in an advanced stage; cripples almost bedridden; intemperates; out-of-work persons of various callings; outdoor paupers; and persons of seventy or even eighty years of age. The schools were held in cellars, bedrooms, kitchens, shops, workshops, and other wholly unsuitable places, in which the ordinary domestic and industrial work were carried on at the same time as the school-work. Only a few of the private-adventure schools were in the hands of educated persons, and these, as a rule, had not received any previous training for, or had experience in, their work.

The suggestions which the Commissioners offered for a plan to secure the greater extension and efficiency of popular education were as follows:—First, it was assumed that there ought to be no interference in the religious training already given by the different denominations, though a conscience clause might be necessary, nor with the direct management of schools by the local promoters. They recommended that aid to schools should be given by means of two grants—one out of the general taxation, dependent on attendance and fulfilment of the conditions hitherto required under inspection, and one from the county rates, according to the results of an examination in reading, writing, and arithmetic conducted by examiners appointed by the county or borough board of education, the government inspector having the right to be present. The former was calculated on the average attendance, and should be not less than 5s. 6d. nor more than 6s.

A Semi-state System.

per child in schools containing less than sixty children; and not less than 4*s*. 6*d*. nor more than 5*s*. for larger schools, according to the report of the inspector as to the discipline, efficiency, and character of the school. There was to be an additional grant of 2*s*. 6*d*. per child under the instruction of a properly qualified pupil-teacher or assistant, at the rate of thirty children for each pupil-teacher, and sixty for each assistant. The county rate was to be given for every child who had attended 140 days during the year, and passed the examination in the three R's (with plain needlework for girls). It was to range from 21*s*. to 22*s*. 6*d*. But the combined grants from the central and local authorities were not to exceed the fees and subscriptions, or 15*s*. per child on the average attendance. These grants were to be paid directly to the managers, who were therefrom to provide the whole of the salaries for all the teachers in the schools.

The county and borough boards of education were to be appointed by the quarter-sessions and the town councils respectively. Each borough board was to consist of not more than six members, of whom not more than two should be ministers of religion. The county boards were to consist of six, who were in the commission of the peace, or chairman or vice-chairman of boards of guardians, and these were to elect six others. The number of ministers of religion on a county board was not to exceed four. The government inspector for the district was, *ex officio*, to be a member of each county and borough board in his district. The boards were elected for three years, but at the end of each year one-third was to retire. The examiners appointed by such boards were to be certificated masters of at least seven years' standing. It may be said that the aim of the grant from the central authority was to secure greater extension of education, that of the local authorities to obtain greater thoroughness and effectiveness of teaching.

It remains to be said that the returns of the Commissioners were shown by Mr. Lowe to be inaccurate to such an extent, that "it would be paying too great a compliment to these figures to base any calculation on them"; and the working of the Education Act of 1870 has still further exposed their unsoundness. When this act came into force it was found that there was not school accommodation for more than half of those who ought to be at school. This is hardly a matter for surprise, since the returns were mostly supplied by clergymen and others little qualified for the work, and concerned to show a favourable state of things. The reasoning of the Commissioners was but little better than their facts; for they argued that because compulsory school attendance had existed in Prussia since the Reformation, and public opinion there was so strong, and parental neglect so rare, that compulsion had become superfluous, therefore it could be no precedent for England. One would have thought that a law which had the delightful effect of making itself superfluous, was, above all others, the most desirable, since it was practically ideal in its success.

The report was attacked on all sides. The different denominations complained that they were misrepresented; Lord Shaftesbury said that the reports on ragged schools were inaccurate; the inspectors affirmed that the results of the teaching in schools were better than was represented; and statistical societies contended that the figures were from sources which had been shown, over and over again, to be unreliable. However, taken in the rough, the report gave a good general idea of the condition of matters, and was a sufficient ground for Mr. Lowe, then Vice-president of the Council, to base a sweeping alteration in the existing code. He rejected the suggestion of local rates without giving the ratepayers the right of directly electing their education boards; but accepted the suggestions that grants should be paid only to managers, and that they should be partly dependent upon the success of individual scholars in fulfilling certain fixed tests, after having attended school a certain number of times. Upon these conditions he based most of the changes in the revised code.

When moving the education estimates for 1861 Mr. Lowe made a long and brilliantly lucid and critical speech upon the report, and the action which the authorities intended to take. He justified the system of payment by results on this ground, amongst others, that it would give the teachers a much stronger motive for exertion than they then had. If the children did not pass the examination, the teacher would fall into disgrace with his managers; while, if they did pass, he would naturally be highly esteemed, and would have an opportunity of rising in his profession. He would also be able to judge, by the success of his pupils in the examination, how far his methods had been successful. The children themselves would be kept in a state of emulation in learning. Managers and teachers would be concerned to secure regular attendance on the part of the children. Thus both improvement in school attendance and teaching would result. As to the objection that education would be degraded, he pointed out that what was fixed was a minimum of education, not a maximum. It was proposed not to give any grant for the attendance of children at school unless they could read, write, and cipher, but this did not say that they should do no more. Of the whole he said: I cannot promise you that this new code will be either economical or efficient, but I can promise you that it shall be either one or the other; if it is not efficient, it shall be cheap; and if it is not cheap, it shall be efficient. Which was an attractive antithesis, but proved to be a question-begging and fallacious statement.

As has been too often the case in the history of elementary education, the recoil from error has been itself an error. Without doubt the previous administration of the grants had been, in many ways, loose and wasteful. So long as the money was spent in ways which were not in direct violation of the regulations and involved no obvious or scandalous abuse, no real inquiry into the true results produced was made. The principal effects of the grants seem to have been the following. Managers were relieved from begging letters, bazaars, amateur gambling, and all such desperate means of raising money. Archdeacon Denison writes: "As I go about now, and hear Churchmen talking about their schools as connected with the Council, I hear commonly of little else than the number of pounds they get by way of grant; this seems to be the test of a good school".

Schools were stocked with as many pupil-teachers as they could possibly secure; pupil-teachers gladly accepted what were, comparatively speaking, exceptionally good salaries, combined with unusual educational advantages; and unsuccessful workers, ambitious young men and women, eagerly left their occupations to take up with so promising a career as that of teachers, who were practically government servants. Thus managers secured parish rooms and lay helpers; pupil-teachers got a good training for clerkships, and entrance to the ministry; and teachers obtained positions of higher social standing, and comparative luxury. A few teachers were real enthusiasts, and capable, and used the freedom and resources given them to do work which is hardly surpassed by the best work of the best schools of to-day. Those who knew such schools may be found still to speak of them with enthusiasm, and to lament that the good old times are gone. But the inquiries of the commission showed a general inefficiency which admitted of no question, and revealed strong and startling evidence of incapacity not to be refuted.

Whilst, however, the total absence of proper examination is a bad thing—for examination, rightly used, is a real part of true education—examination as the be-all and end-all of teaching is equally vicious, and it was this which the new regulations brought about. Not only was it bad for teaching, but it was bad for morals. The money motive can never be a very exalted one; and where daily bread, professional reputation, and possible wealth—in the case of what is known as school farming, *i.e.* allowing the teacher to be responsible for the whole or a certain part of the expenses, and then to take all the surplus income—were at stake, it was inevitable that by far the greater number should be forced into mere money-grubbing. Children were no longer human beings to be made strong and perfect in their humanity, but money-making machines out of which the last penny must be squeezed. If they could by any trick or compulsion be made to hold, and display, sufficient memory matter to satisfy the inspector, then all was well.

A tremendous agitation against the proposals took

A Semi-state System. 159

place, both in the country and in parliament. One member of the Commons said that, judging by the letters, pamphlets, and other communications which had poured in upon them from all quarters, no topic had, for some time past, excited so much attention as the revised code of education. Numerously-signed petitions against the proposals were presented in both houses of parliament; whilst only one petition in its favour, signed by a solitary schoolmaster, was produced. As a result, the original proposal to make the whole of the grant depend upon the results of the examination was modified, as was also the intention to insist upon classification by age; and it was promised that the Department would guarantee the salaries of pupil-teachers during the period of change from one system to the other. Sir J. P. Kay-Shuttleworth was one of the most pronounced opponents of the revised code, and in a letter to Earl Granville writes: " to make such a change [without the consent of the great controlling bodies and religious communions] would be ever to be remembered with shame ".

The internal life of the school under the system of annual grants has been sufficiently revealed in the foregoing account of the external influences at work. To sum up the position briefly, it may be said that many more teachers, much better qualified for the routine and mechanical parts of school work, had been provided. The conditions and means for their work had been very considerably improved, and they themselves made more secure and comfortable in their professional and social standing. All this had been done at a large cost, and the final result had been but a poor beggarly array of pupils reasonably well taught, a large number of neglected scholars who were attending school, and a disastrously large number of neglected children as yet outside the school influence. The best forms of bad school methods were still continued, and whilst there was so little of good instruction, there was still less of true education.

True education could hardly make any real advance so long as the training colleges did not give any training in the science of education; and it is fair to say that teachers were taught the tricks of teaching rather than the principles of education. Of course they in turn taught children the tricks of learning rather than the right use of the mental powers. After all, the school will be as the teacher; and if we desire good schools we must have learned and capable teachers. The students were required, according to the certificate syllabus, to learn school management—not education. This, therefore, was the subject taught, and learnt. Richards' *Manual of School Method*, Short's *Hints on School-keeping*, and Bell's *Manual of the National System*, were typical of the books studied. Better things were occasionally done, but there was little encouragement for those who did them, the questions set in the examinations being intensely "practical".

Even so able a man as Rev. F. Temple, in a report—exceptional, at that time, for its breadth and grasp—on training colleges, makes a point of excluding psychology from the study of education. He writes: "I do not think it would be advisable to encourage a study of mental and moral philosophy. . . . Mental science is in general too abstract, too far removed from all practical applications, to be of much real value to a normal master [much less, therefore, to the student, would seem to be the argument]. It belongs to a region of study into which it would be quite hopeless for him to attempt to take his pupils; its very phraseology implies an amount of collateral knowledge far beyond their reach, if not beyond his own. I have already remarked that lectures on method are almost always of little value when the lecturer attempts to include the teaching of psychology. . . . It is of far more importance to a school-master that he should have that knowledge and that cultivation of faculties which it is his duty to communicate to children, than that he should know how to communicate them; the power of teaching he may gain by practice and experience." In this he was but agreeing with the opinion of a principal of training college to whose opinion he attached very great weight. Such a conjunction is not yet obsolete. What wonder then that the students were crammed with rule-of-thumb methods, supposed to be proved by odds and ends of quotations from works on the mental sciences, to which they had no other relation.

Not even the best books on method were used. One of the very best books on rational method, viz. Craig's *Philosophy of Training* (1847), belongs to this period. David Stow's *The Training System of Education* (1840) was, in many respects, an admirable book. Wilderspin's *Early Discipline* and *Infant Education* were books much more informing and illuminating than the generally wretched compilations on school management. It need hardly be said that none of the great works mentioned in previous chapters were the usual text-books in training colleges.

It must have been the veriest irony of fate which led to the publication of *Education* by Herbert Spencer in the year 1861. The philosopher appealed to men's reason with a work which has taken its place amongst the world's treasures, whilst the practical statesman (Mr. Lowe) appealed to their commercial instincts, on the great question of education, and the latter prevailed. Comment is obviously superfluous. And thinking men were not taken by surprise with Spencer's work, for it had appeared, substantially, as essays published in the years 1854, 1858, and 1859. Herein he had set forth the great central truths concerning the nature of intellectual, moral, and physical education, and exposed the errors of contemporary methods, in a way that the wayfaring man, though a fool, might not err therein. But men were much too busy with fighting about education to take the trouble to understand it.

Chapter VIII.

Codes and Cram.

All that is mechanical and mean in our national system of education reaches its very acme at this stage of its history. People complained that far too much money was being given to the clergy, for which no adequate return was made; and that pupil-teachers were receiving, at the tax-payer's cost, a better education than the children of well-to-do tradesmen. This plea for economy was accepted by the Education Department, and there was an avowed intention to reduce the grants. The system of the shop is the last appeal now. One can almost see the vice-president (Mr. Lowe) standing on one side of the scale slowly dropping in the pounds, shillings, and pence, whilst an inspector stands on the other side slowly dropping in the passes in reading, writing, and arithmetic; for thus the national duty towards the rationalizing of the people was measured. And yet this was, in a way, the best that could happen, for the excess of an evil is the surest, and often the only, condition for ensuring its removal. So now the evils which unadulterated commercialism in education brought upon children, teachers, and managers, raised such a spirit of criticism and resentment that reforms no longer needed pressing, but rather restraining.

This dissatisfaction largely helped to make possible the act of 1870. It found expression in both houses of parliament in attempts to take the initiative in educational matters out of the hands of the Committee of Council, and to proceed by bills which should express the will of the people's representatives and be placed on the statute-book of the realm; and also to give local authorities a direct responsibility for, and share in the administration of, national education. These ideas were, to a considerable extent, realized in 1870. But the vicious principle of payment by results, which took nearly thirty years to reach its intensest form as to details, has taken more than thirty years to abolish with regard to details.

The public mind may be said to have been possessed by a fever of education from 1856 to 1862. Bills and resolutions had been showered upon the House of Commons, public meetings and conferences were held—one in Willis's Rooms being presided over by the Prince

Codes and Cram. 163

Consort — and Mr. Keith Johnston, the geographer, issued a diagram giving a comparative view of the percentage of the population receiving instruction in the different countries of Europe, in which England stood tenth on the list. The outcome of all this had been the Royal Commission, the result of which was the Revised Code—so called because all the regulations previously scattered through the different minutes had already, in 1860, been published in the form of a Code, arranged in chapters according to subjects.

The Revised Code, issued May 9, 1862, re-stated all the conditions previously laid down for the administering of the grant, so far as these were retained—the grants for books and apparatus were discontinued in the previous year, according to the advice given in the report of the commission—and set forth the new regulations. Among other things, declarations were made in more definite form than hitherto on several points, *e.g.* "the object of the grant is to promote the education of children belonging to the classes who support themselves by manual labour"; and, "the children attend from the homes of their parents, and charge is taken of them during the school hours only". It was laid down that "schools may meet three times daily; viz. in the morning, afternoon, and evening"; but "schools which do not meet more than once daily cannot receive grants". An attendance consisted of at least two hours secular instruction during the morning or afternoon, and one and a half hours in the evening. The grant was given under two heads: first, the sum of four shillings per scholar according to the average yearly attendance in the day-school, and two shillings and sixpence for each in the night-school; second, for every scholar who attended more than 200 morning or afternoon meetings, the sum of eight shillings for each scholar, in a day-school, over six years of age. This was subject to a deduction of one-third for failure to satisfy the inspector in reading, writing, and arithmetic, respectively. For each child under six years of age, six shillings and sixpence was to be paid, if the inspector was satisfied that such children were instructed suitably to their age, and in a manner not to interfere with the instruction of the older children.

For every scholar who attended at an evening school more than twenty-four times the sum of five shillings was to be paid, subject to forfeits of one-third of this for each case of failure in reading, writing, and arithmetic. Each scholar for whom these grants were claimed must be examined according to one of the standards set down on the opposite page, and must not be presented for examination a second time according to the same or a lower standard.

No grant would be given to a school unless the principal teacher was certificated; the school premises were satisfactory; the registers were kept with sufficient accuracy to warrant confidence in the returns; the girls were taught needlework; the inspector's report showed no objection of a gross kind; and three persons were appointed to sign the receipt for the grant. Certain reductions of the grant were to be made for faults of teachers and managers. And it was definitely ruled that "lay persons alone can be recognized as teachers in elementary schools". Endowed schools might receive grants provided they educated the children of the poor, and that the endowment was not over thirty shillings per scholar per annum, according to the average number of scholars in attendance throughout the year. The last paragraph in the code stated that no revision or material alteration of any of its articles could be legally acted upon until the same shall have been submitted to parliament, and laid on the table of both houses for at least one calendar month.

In the following year one or two modifications appear. To meet the case of small rural schools whose managers were unable to raise sufficient funds to pay a certificated teacher, the code provided that any acting teacher over twenty-two years of age, who had obtained two favourable reports upon the school in which he or she had been employed, and was presented by the managers for an examination confined to elementary subjects, might obtain a certificate, qualifying for small schools. Also, all pupil-teachers who had successfully completed

Codes and Cram.

Standard.	Reading.	Writing.	Arithmetic.
I.	Narrative in monosyllables.	Form on black-board or slate, from dictation, letters, capital and small, manuscript.	Form on black-board or slate, from dictation, figures up to 20; name at sight figures up to 20; add and subtract figures up to 10, orally, from examples on blackboard.
II.	One of the narratives next in order after monosyllables in an elementary reading book used in the school.	Copy in a manuscript character a line of print.	A sum in simple addition or subtraction, and the multiplication table.
III.	A short paragraph from an elementary reading book used in the school.	A sentence from the same paragraph, slowly read once, and then dictated in single words.	A sum in any simple rule as far as short division (inclusive).
IV.	A short paragraph from a more advanced reading book used in the school.	A sentence slowly dictated once by a few words at a time, from the same book, but not from the paragraph read.	A sum in compound rules (money).
V.	A few lines of poetry from a reading book used in the first class of the school.	A sentence slowly dictated once, by a few words at a time, from a reading book used in the first class of the school.	A sum in compound rules (common weights and measures).
VI.	A short ordinary paragraph in a newspaper, or other modern narrative.	Another short ordinary paragraph in a newspaper or other modern narrative, slowly dictated once by a few words at a time.	A sum in practice or bills of parcels.

their apprenticeships, and were specially recommended by an inspector, might, without further examination, be provisionally certificated for immediate service. Thus was another means found of lowering the standard of education, instead of raising the grant to pay for more efficient teachers.

This principle of legislating down to local poverty has continued to be an element of weakness ever since; and in worse form later, for any person over eighteen years, without practical experience, training, or knowledge—so long as they are not too incapable before a class, in the presence of an inspector—was, later on, recognized as a teacher. And these are employed, as a rule, in infants' schools, and lower standards, where the very greatest knowledge, best skill, and ripest experience are required; for in them are those helpless little ones who want the most helpful teachers.

A very wise and weighty note is given in the instructions to inspectors as to the syllabus of work in the subjects for examination. It is remarked that the article "does not prescribe that, *if thus much is done, a grant shall be paid, but, unless thus much is done, no grant shall be paid*". All the emphasis that italics could give was placed upon the point. The code was to be taken as an irreducible minimum. If only this had been more fully realized and acted upon, far more progress would have been made than has been made up to the present time. But teachers and managers, as a rule, looked upon satisfying the inspector in these matters as the maximum of their endeavours. There was, of course, the strongest possible inducement to do this under a system which practically said: Whatever else you do, if you don't do this satisfactorily, there will be no grant for you. On the principle of a bird in hand being worth two in the bush, it was better, financially, to make sure of only a little knowledge, for this brought all the grant. To make every boy rote-perfect in the three subjects was better, pecuniarily, than to have nine-tenths of them with an intelligent mastery of ten times as much in ten times as many subjects.

This lowering motive soon began to take effect, and

we find the inspectors' reports full of the evidence of it. "Grammar, geography, and history having almost entirely dropped out of the course of instruction, religious instruction is now the only subject left to the inspector by which he can test the intelligence of his children", writes one. Another remarks that "the tendency of the new code is to cause the managers and teachers to regard simply the pecuniary grants, and all that does not tend to produce an increased result as to these is hardly taken into account. . . . The expression on a child's failure to pass any subject is not regret at his ignorance so much as indignation at his stupidity and consequent loss." "Grammar, geography, history, and other subjects are now, as might be expected, comparatively neglected for the more 'profitable' elementary R's, nor has the inspector time to lay great stress upon them"—or, apparently, to express a passing regret.

The money-making spirit soon obtained a concession from the Department, viz. that those children who, owing to illness or other special cause, were unable to advance a standard, might be placed upon an "Exceptions Schedule", and examined in a lower standard than would otherwise be required.

The very large amount of extra work which these requirements brought upon the already overworked inspectors led to the appointment of Inspectors' Assistants (now called Sub-inspectors), as occasion might require, to help in the work of examination. They were not to be over thirty years of age; to have been pupil-teachers; to be trained and certificated; to be recommended by the inspector under whom they were to examine; and to hold a certificate from the Civil Service Commissioners. Twelve such officers were appointed during the year 1863. In connection with their work, a somewhat double-edged remark was made to the inspectors under whom they were to work, viz. "It is only by your thoroughly comprehending the limited and subsidiary character of the assistant's duty that you will repel the imputation of setting a young man to judge his elders, and often his superiors, in the art of school-keeping". Some of the inspectors already appointed had come straight from the universities, and certainly none of them had done much school-keeping.

To help weak schools to come up to the new requirements an arrangement for improving small rural schools was made in 1865. By this, any number of schools, not being less than two or more than six, in thinly-populated districts, might be united under the superintendence of a trained certificated master or mistress. He, or she, was to be in addition to a resident teacher —who need not be certificated—for each school. The certificated teacher was to spend two clear hours at least in each week at each school during its ordinary time of meeting. The scholars in all the schools were to be collected for examination by an inspector. Under such conditions the usual grants might be obtained for small rural schools which had not a permanent certificated teacher. Grants were also to be given for the scholars at evening schools subject to an examination by printed papers, conducted by two of the managers— or one manager and at least one other responsible person.

But, on the other hand, one effect of the alterations was directly to weaken the mechanical power in the schools, for a very great diminution in the number of pupil-teachers took place under the revised code. This was due to the fact that managers had now to pay their pupil-teachers out of the annual grant. They were therefore concerned to have as few as the code permitted. One inspector says: "It is almost amusing to see the different kind of feeling which prevails about the number of scholars returned as in average attendance". Formerly it was desired to prove it as high as possible, so as to get as many government-paid pupil-teachers as were allowed, now it was made to appear as low as possible, so as to avoid having to pay a single unnecessary pupil-teacher. Also parents were much less attracted now that the government had handed over the pupil-teachers to the managers. The numbers decreased from nearly sixteen thousand to just over eleven thousand. Assistant teachers, however, increased from 449 to 912.

So demoralizing and degrading was the money motive that children were brought to the examinations with throats bandaged and skins peeling from scarlet-fever. An inspector says that after, as he thought, having completed an examination, a manager came to him, and asked "if I would examine five children who were waiting in the class-room, as it was unsafe to introduce them into the school-room, and I subsequently found the mother of one of these children crying outside the door from anxiety respecting her little boy, who had been brought out of his sick-room in order to be present at the inspection".

Notwithstanding such heroic efforts as these the grants decreased, under the new system, by no less than fifty-three thousand pounds for the year 1863, and over sixty-six thousand in the following year. There was somewhat of a recovery the next year, the decrease being nearly nineteen thousand pounds. Nevertheless "my lords" are able to say in their annual report that "the system of examination under the revised code is administratively feasible, has secured greater attention to the lower classes and to the less proficient children in schools, and has led to more uniform progress in reading, writing, and arithmetic. It has improved discipline and attendance . . . [though it] has tended, at least temporarily, to discourage attention to the higher branches of elementary instruction— geography, grammar, and history. There are, however, signs of recovery; and those schools do best in elementary subjects where the higher are not neglected."

The very serious decrease of the amount of the grants soon led to action to remedy it. Mr. Corry, the Vice-President of the council, introduced a minute in 1867 for the purpose of securing additional aid for small schools; the presentation of more scholars in standards better suited to their ages; the study of other than the three R's; and an increase in the number of pupil-teachers. Extra grants, consisting of an additional $1s.$ $4d.$ for each pass in the three R's up to a sum not exceeding £8, were to be given if the staff exceeded the required minimum at a certain rate; one-fifth of the passes were obtained in a standard higher than the fourth; and one subject (called a "specific") at least, other than the three R's, was taught. Besides this, ten pounds, or five pounds, were paid to a school for each of its pupil-teachers who took a first or second class in the Queen's scholarship examination, and an additional eight or five pounds according as they took a first or second class in the certificate examination, after residence in a training college. Under this minute was established a seventh standard, to consist of those who were being taught in one or more subjects of secular instruction beyond those for the sixth standard. If they passed in the sixth-standard work, and also in the extra subjects, a grant of eight shillings—subject to the usual deductions for failure in any subject—was given. The same pupils might be examined twice in this standard. When these conditions came into force they soon caused an increase in the grants, and it was estimated that in two or three years' time from sixty to seventy thousand pounds extra would be required for this purpose alone.

So far as many of the results of the revised code were concerned, up to the year before the Education Act, Mr. Lowe had every reason to be proud of his handiwork. In seven years nearly fifteen hundred new schools were opened, and over three hundred thousand more scholars were attending school very much more regularly and for longer periods in England and Wales. Twice as many certificated teachers were at work in the schools, and the work which they did was at least more effective in that it was distributed over the whole school, and made to do something for each pupil, instead of being confined to the very few and select bright ones who managed to reach the top class. Within the limits set by the code, and by the ideal which most people then had of education for the poor, viz. an elementary knowledge of the three R's, Mr. Lowe had more than redeemed his promises, for the work was, as compared with that previously done, both more effective and cheaper by nearly half a million pounds. The author of the revised code is far too often exclusively reviled by critics as the author of payment by results, and no regard is paid to the fact that he certainly made the best of a bad business. He was a strong man, a clear thinker, and a determined and inflexible ruler, with a well-thought-out plan designed to secure definite returns for large outlay. And he was successful. The results which he demanded and obtained were at any rate better than the absence of results in respect of three-fourths of the pupils, as had been previously the case. If for nothing else, Mr. Lowe deserves our thanks for having perpetrated a blunder, which has been one more step to our blundering out of blunders.

True, the principle was in some respects entirely vicious, and in many ways adverse to true education. But then Mr. Lowe did not believe in a science of education, and is said to have bluntly remarked to an inspector who called on him: "I know what you've come about—the science of education. There is none." Which is conclusive if not convincing. He believed in instruction, and consistently enough said: we pay for instruction; if the child has been properly instructed, he will know the things we require; if he does not know them, the work has not been properly done, and no one has a right to expect to be paid for unfinished work. He had stronger ground, had he but known it; for every ordinary child is capable of being educated up to an average standard, and had the pupils been intelligently taught they could have done the little expected from them with the greatest possible ease. Education without results, which can be tested by a reasonably-conducted examination, is a contradiction in terms. If a teacher should, after giving a lesson, proceed to question his pupils, and find that only two or three out of twenty can give him correct answers, then he has miserably failed in his efforts to educate his class. How much more will this be true of a year's work! The fatal flaw in the system was, that no proper provision was made for securing those conditions under which alone good work could be properly done, viz. a sufficient supply of capable teachers, regular attendance by the pupils, and good apparatus, premises, &c. In fact it was a case of making bricks without straw. The government said: Make bricks, and we will give you money to buy straw.

That the revised code led to cram is proved to demonstration. By cram is meant the imparting of the maximum of the forms of knowledge with the minimum of meaning. For example, a young child might learn the whole of the hundred and nineteenth Psalm, so that he could say it or write it from memory, and yet not have an intelligent idea of the meaning of a single verse. Or again, he might do addition and subtraction sums involving millions, and yet not know whether he should add or subtract in the case of a practical question involving numbers under twenty. Such are cases of cram; almost purely mechanical tricks with certain materials. Mr. Matthew Arnold reports: "The mode of teaching in the primary schools has fallen off in intelligence, spirit, and inventiveness. It could not well be otherwise. In a country where everyone is prone to rely too much on mechanical processes, and too little on intelligence, a change in the Education Department's regulations, which, by making two-thirds of the government grant depend upon a mechanical examination, inevitably gives a mechanical turn to the school teaching, a mechanical turn to the inspection, is and must be trying to the life of a school." One cannot, however, but object to this suggestion, for the implied theory that the intelligent is superior to the mechanical should lead to the conclusion that if the intelligence had been well trained the mechanical would have been easily secured. 'If education be looked after, instruction will look after itself to a very large extent', ought to be the accepted maxim.

Another inspector writes: "In dictating to the fourth standard, I have occasionally altered the words of the book slightly. In such cases I have often found the original words substituted for my own by one or more children, which of course showed that the book had been conned over and over again till it was known by rote." Of arithmetic it is reported that "the tendency to a mechanical and unintelligent type of instruction is even more apparent. Just what he expects to have to do, propounded in exactly the way in which he expects to have it propounded, a boy . . . generally does extremely well. But vary the form of the proposition in the slightest degree, or state it in terms slightly different from those which his teacher has adopted, and he is altogether thrown out and puzzled."

Nevertheless the raising of the requirements with regard to the forms of knowledge, and the very great increase in the numbers of scholars who successfully proved to demonstration that they had acquired what was demanded, was an advance by no means to be despised. Besides this, the children were being subjected to a discipline of moral and social training which was still more valuable; as well as being, in many cases, kept from the physical ruin caused by early industrial labour. Teachers also received a somewhat more advanced training in general knowledge; but their professional training was not in the same world as the ideas in Professor Laurie's *Primary Instruction* (1867) or Mr. Quick's *Essays on Educational Reformers* (1868), two excellent books, which would have given a wide, deep, and true insight into principles.

Whilst the above results had been obtained by the Department, the parliament had proceeded with its usual futilities. From 1862 to 1869 parliamentary action had been as vigorous as hitherto, and as vain. By Mr. Adderley there was brought forward, and carried, a motion "that grants from the Treasury to schools for the working-classes should not, in every case, be reduced by the whole amount of all endowments". He urged that the government had no right to penalize a district because of the benevolence of a dead patron. All citizens had equal claims on public money, without regard to private benefactions. Besides this, it was inequitable in other ways. For example, two parishes had a thousand pounds left them. In one case the money was spent on building a teacher's house, in the other it was invested and the interest used for current expenses. The consequence was, that the latter lost so much money every year, whilst the former lost none. Mr. Lowe replied that endowments almost always led to bad management, and that living donors could exercise active superintendence, direction, and authority. Again, endowment relieved the rich, whilst the poor still paid their share in the general taxes.

In 1865 Sir J. Pakington moved for a select committee to inquire into the constitution of the Committee of Council on Education, and the system under which the business of the office was conducted. This motion arose out of a resolution which had been passed concerning the way in which the inspectors' reports were dealt with, before being presented to the Commons.

This had practically involved a question of Mr. Lowe's good faith and veracity, and had led to his resignation. The discussion on the above motion was chiefly remarkable for its very open criticism of the Department. Sir J. Pakington argued that a minister of education was required. The members of the committee all had other duties to perform, and had neither time nor leisure for its work. The committee had introduced important rules, such as the insistence on the conscience clause, without consulting parliament. Quite recently they had introduced a plan for combining rural schools under a travelling certificated teacher at the suggestion, and on the evidence, of a private lady—Miss Burdett Coutts. What was to be thought of a Department which had been slumbering in inactivity for the last twenty-six years, leaving large districts of England to take care of themselves.

Lord Robert Cecil (now Marquis of Salisbury) severely criticised the committee. He said: the Vice-president has told the House that the Department possesses a *quasi* legislative power. No one could have expressed more clearly and aptly the precise nature of the objections his friends had to the constitution of that Department. They did not like a *quasi* legislative power—an *imperium in imperio*. There was one legislative power in the kingdom, and that was the Parliament of Great Britain and Ireland; and any power which interfered with that was dangerous to the State, and perilous to the liberties of the subject. And see how that *quasi* legislative power worked. The Vice-president had introduced, in his time, many important changes in the educational code. He did not conceal the importance of those changes. He told them that he had destroyed the vested interests of ten thousand teachers, and turned adrift fifteen thousand managers. He could not recapitulate the enormous changes which the Vice-president, with feelings of self-complacency, recounted. Was it, then, any presumption in the House of Commons that they should wish to have some share in such changes, and to determine whether they were right or wrong? There was, no doubt, a form gone through when these changes were made. The minutes were laid upon the table; and if any honourable member could get a Tuesday within a month, or if he was not "counted out", or beaten by an accidental division, it was possible, not to reverse a particular minute, but he might induce the Committee of Council to lay upon the table another minute differing by illusory alteration from that of which he had complained. That was the extent of the power of the House of Commons over the minutes of the council.

Parliament was, soon after, again asked to make a real effort to control education. "The Education of the Poor Bill", backed by Mr. Bruce, Mr. W. E. Forster, and Mr. Algernon Egerton, was introduced in 1867. It was to be permissive, and was to give to borough and other districts the power to levy rates for building and maintaining new schools, and for supporting existing ones. Committees were to be chosen from the town council, or elected (in other districts) by the ratepayers from those persons rated at not less than ten pounds; they were to consist of six, nine, or twelve members, and to have control of the income provided by the rate. They were to inquire as to whether there was any deficiency in the supply of schools in the district; and, if there was, and the inhabitants did not remedy it, the committee should. The schools might be free, or receive aid if the fees did not exceed ninepence per week. Any school which conformed with the rules of the revised code might enter into union with those under the local committee, which was to have no control over the constitution, discipline, or instruction of such schools, except that they could insist upon a conscience clause as a condition of receiving their aid. The committee was to appoint a clerk, treasurer, and inspector. The duty of the inspector was to inspect, once in every six months, those schools already under the Education Department, and to examine all schools not receiving government grant. The Committee of Council were to have power, after making due inquiry, to compel a district to apply the act. The bill came to nothing.

Higher ground still was taken, when in the same year occurred what may be called Lord John Russell's conversion. Hitherto he had been one of the strongest opponents of the so-called secular system. But now he was prepared to move, " that in the opinion of this House the education of the working-classes in England and Wales ought to be extended and improved. Every child has a moral right to the blessings of education, and it is the duty of the State to guard and maintain that right. . . . The diffusion of knowledge ought not to be hindered by religious differences; nor should the early employment of the young in labour be allowed to deprive them of education. . . . The appointment of a Minister of Education by the Crown, with a seat in the Cabinet, would . . . be conducive to the public interest." He said that while he would be sorry if it were found necessary to exclude religious teaching in schools, at the same time he could not help thinking that secular schools would not at all diminish the amount of religion in the country. Of course the resolutions were negatived.

Lord John Russell, like Lord Brougham, was invariably unsuccessful in his many efforts on behalf of popular education. They both seem to have lost the confidence of their friends and the good-will of their opponents in trying to succeed by endeavouring to please both sides. But his last effort was entirely worthy of himself and his devotion to the cause, for it placed the subject on a far higher level than it had ever been placed hitherto. It was almost Prussian in its principles.

But even this was rivalled in 1868 by the Duke of Marlborough, Lord President of the Council, who brought forward, in the House of Lords, a bill on behalf of the government. This proposed that a Minister of Education should be appointed; the code incorporated into an act of parliament; and the compulsory adoption of a conscience clause where only one school existed in a district. He urged that the revised code was, it might be said without exaggeration, a mass of the greatest confusion; changes in the code were made by a spurious mode of legislation, which he thought extremely objectionable; and grants were changed by the whim or caprice of a minister of the Crown. It was not proposed to establish any compulsory system of rating; but the Department would be charged with the duty of collecting information, which might be useful for future action. The bill met with some opposition, and was therefore withdrawn.

Next year, Mr. Melly and Mr. Dixon obtained a promise that an inquiry should be made into the educational conditions of Birmingham, Leeds, Liverpool, and Manchester. This report was drawn up by Mr. J. G. Fitch and Mr. D. R. Fearon, and showed what a very great amount was still undone in the way of providing schools, getting scholars to attend them, and giving a really profitable amount of instruction in the three R's to every child. About one-third of those who ought to be in school were in average attendance, whilst accommodation was provided for less than a half. More than one-third of the scholars inspected were in the standard appropriate to a child of six, and less than one-fifth in the three higher standards.

The expiring effort, before the Education Act, was the "Education of Children Bill", introduced into the House of Lords by the Marquess Townshend. This was to provide for compulsory secular education. Wherever there were free schools parents must send their children for, at least, twelve hours' instruction each week. The bill was rejected on the ground that the government had its own proposals to submit.

Meantime popular feeling in favour of national education was increasing, and popular efforts were becoming more vigorous and effective. Strange indeed would it have been if those who had made such personal sacrifices of religious convictions, and comparatively large financial payments from meagre wages, had not insisted upon better provision for national education, when the political power to enforce their desires was placed in their hands. The newly-enfranchised workers soon found political champions more than willing to do battle for them. In 1867 the Birmingham Education Aid Society was formed, under the presidency of Mr. George Dixon. It undertook an investigation of the condition of matters in the town, and found that many parents were unable to pay the school fees; that the supply of schools was insufficient; and that compulsion was necessary to secure regular attendance. Two years later this society was transformed into the Education League, with Mr. Dixon as chairman, Mr. Joseph Chamberlain as vice-chairman, and Mr. Jesse Collings as honorary secretary.

The League soon numbered among its numerous members earnest and enlightened men of all shades of religious and political convictions, and of prominent position and great ability. It was liberally supplied with money by its members, and soon exercised a very wide and powerful influence. Mr. Chamberlain was the head of the executive committee and the acting chairman of the League, and as such "was chiefly responsible in originating and conducting its policy in the country", says the secretary, Mr. Francis Adams, in his very valuable *History of the Elementary School Contest in England*. Numerous branch committees were formed in various towns; many public meetings were held all over the country; a very large number of pamphlets, &c., were distributed; and a monthly paper was published, which had a wide circulation.

The action of this society was met by the formation of The National Education Union, in 1869, which included amongst its members the whole bench of bishops, and numerous dukes, marquesses, earls, viscounts, lords, and members of parliament. Its avowed object was "to counteract the work of the Birmingham League and others advocating secular training only, and the secularization of our national institutions". Thus the question-begging epithet of "secularist" was again used as

Codes and Cram. 179

a stimulus to men's prejudices and bigotry. No more religious men than those who belonged to the League were to be found amongst the members of the Union; and the former did not, as a body, desire that religion should be excluded from the schools, though they did desire, as a matter of practical expediency, that religions should.

Before concluding our remarks on this period a word must be added with respect to the teaching of science and art. So early as 1835 what were called "Schools of Design" were established by the government, under the Board of Trade, for the purpose of extending a knowledge of art and design among the people, especially the manufacturing population. But these had, practically, no point of contact with the Elementary Schools, until in 1852 a separate department, called "The Department of Practical Art", was set up, under the Board of Trade, and made it one of its functions to promote general elementary instruction in art as a branch of national education among all classes of the community, with a view of laying the foundation for correct judgment, both in the consumer and the producer of manufactures.

Whereas, previously, only supplies of books on drawing were given to the masters of schools of design to be distributed at their discretion amongst elementary schools, now a grant of half the cost of certain sets of art examples was to be given to any school which would undertake to be responsible for their custody; and a training master was appointed to give instruction in the use of them to the teachers of such schools.

In 1857 the control and direction of science and art teaching were taken over by the Committee of Council, and the officials and offices for the work were located at South Kensington. Under the new management the rule of paying grants of 3*s*. or 2*s*. for individual successes began, and the establishing and conducting of "Schools of Art" was thrown upon private individuals in the localities which desired to have them.

The "Department of Science" was formed a year later than that for art, on the recommendation of the Board of Trade. It was intended to bring under one management the control of the science, trade, and navigation schools which already existed. It was also arranged that collections of illustrations, models, &c., relating to science and art should be formed in London; and a high-class science school, where students might complete their training, should be connected therewith. But it was not till 1859 that the Science Department had anything to do with elementary schools. Indeed, the declared object of the Science and Art Departments was to give higher education than that offered in elementary schools. However, in the year mentioned, teachers were offered the opportunity to pass examinations in science to prove their fitness to teach. If they obtained certificates of competency they might obtain augmentations to their salaries, according as the science inspector reported as to the success of their teaching of science in their schools. Prizes, medals, and certificates were given to successful students. In 1861 the first of the well-known May examinations in science and art was held. In 1862 the principle of payment by results was adopted.

There can be no doubt that the influence of the Science and Art Department has been, despite its limitations and mistakes, of inestimable advantage to the more fortunate elementary schools. It has introduced a more extensive and higher range of subjects to those schools able and willing to take advantage of its offers. In 1865, when the code was working the three R's to death, no less than 23 science subjects (including higher mathematics), besides the various drawing subjects, were being encouraged by the Science and Art Department. Besides this, a series of scholarships was established by which the brighter students might, and did, work their way to the great public schools, science and art colleges, and universities. That its system led to cram rather than education is a reproach which it shares with others. It was not necessary to know science to pass its examinations, but only to remember accurately the contents of certain text-books. Men and women (teachers), boys and girls, who had probably never seen a scientific experiment or studied nature, got prizes, medals, and first-class advanced certificates.

Chapter IX.

The Partial Reign of Law.

At last something like a real school organism, as we may call it, comes into existence; born out of due time, and after much severe travail. No longer is a fortuitous conglomeration of school atoms to be allowed to take the place of an organized, living, and growing system. The nation rises to a sense of its duty, and will no longer tolerate that, in consequence of sheer neglect, boys and girls of fourteen and fifteen years of age form a scourge and pestilence in large manufacturing towns; cohabit like men and women; have their own public-houses, solely supported by their custom and reserved for their uses; and spend their time between thieving for each other, and enjoying the proceeds in wild revels. No more shall damp cellars, crowded with miserable children, presided over by an ignorant and incompetent "dame", maybe lying in bed ill of a fever, be charitably supposed to discharge the functions of a school. The nation will provide for the national want, and wherever there is need, whether there be demand or no, there shall perforce be supply.

And yet, though this great step was taken, the still more important matter of watching over and developing the internal life of the schools was left to the "government within the government", *i.e.* the Education Department. Thus a department which is in theory, and often declares itself, an administrative department, continued to retain, what it had always hitherto exercised, a legislative and executive power with respect to the most vital and essential parts of the national system of schools, viz. its internal organization and work. So true is it that one half of the govermental world does not know how the other half lives.

With the introduction of the Elementary Education Act of 1870 the interest in education is centred chiefly in parliamentary action. Now the nation determines to try its own hand, so to say, with its system of schools. Not that it is by any means of one mind, as a nation, but that the national interest is, for once, predominant, as against the sectarian interest. When one reflects that the so-called National Schools were but a part of the denominational system of the Established Church, acting through the so-called National Society, one realizes how far the nation, as such, was from any system of truly national education. And until we can so far remember our national needs as to forget our sectarian interests, it would appear that we are not likely to possess a system worthy of our people, and equal to our requirements.

With an overwhelming majority, and pledged up to the hilt for reform, the Liberal Government at once took in hand the question of education. Mr. W. E. Forster, an advanced member of the Liberal party, a puritan, and the introducer of previous bills remarkable for their uncompromising thoroughness, was chosen to take charge of their bill. He introduced it in a speech worthy of the occasion, full of appeals to high and worthy motives, and marked by the most sympathetic attitude towards his subject, and consideration for his opponents.

There were, he said, on the school register only about two-fifths of the children between the ages of six and ten years, and one-third of those between ten and twelve, out of the total of those who ought to be attending schools. Taken in connection with the very irregular attendance, during the short periods they attended at all, this showed a lamentable condition of things; for there must be a million and a half of children who remained untouched by the influence of the schools. Those who went to school were but imperfectly educated; there was much absolute ignorance; and what might be good schools became bad schools, because their pupils attended them for only two or three days in a week, or only a few weeks in a year. The result of the State leaving the initiative to volunteers was, that when State help had been most wanted, State help had been least given; and where State power should be most felt,

The Partial Reign of Law. 183

it was not felt at all. Notwithstanding the large sums of money voted by parliament, there was a vast number of children badly taught, or utterly untaught, because there were too few schools, of which too many were bad schools. There was a large number of parents in the country who could not, or would not, send their children to school.

Hence came a demand from all parts of the country for a complete system of national education. He believed that the country demanded that they should at least do two things, namely, cover the country with good schools, and get the parents to send their children to them. In solving this problem there must be, consistently with the attainment of their object, the least possible expenditure of public money; the utmost endeavour not to injure existing and effective schools; and the most careful absence of all encouragement to parents to neglect their children. The object was to complete the existing system of voluntary schools, by filling up the gaps. Two main principles must, therefore, be realized, viz. legal enactment that there should be effective schools everywhere throughout the kingdom; and compulsory provision of such schools, if, and where, needed—but not unless proved to be needed.

The bill proposed that the country should be divided into districts, and power should be taken to collect returns which would show what, in each district, was the number of schools, of scholars, and of children requiring education. Also, inspectors and other officers would be sent to test the quality of the schools, and find out what sort of education was given in them. For his part, he believed that, in the vast majority of districts, the supply would be found insufficient, inefficient, and unsuitable—because of exclusive conditions as to religious instruction. Wherever such deficiencies existed, one year was to be allowed, in which they might be made good by voluntary efforts. Failing this, the Education Department was to put into force the compulsory clauses of the bill, and public elementary schools were to be established.

A public elementary school must keep up to the

standard of efficiency in secular instruction fixed by
parliament from time to time; be open at all times to
inspection by government officials, in secular subjects
only; and have a conscience clause. It was to be supported partly by grants from the public taxes and partly
from the local rates; and managed by a board chosen
by the Town Council, or Select Vestry, or Vestry.
School fees were to be paid—or the middle classes would
also insist upon free education for their children—and
this would, roughly, provide one-third of the cost of
supporting the schools. The local rate ought not to
exceed threepence in the pound, and should it do so,
extra grants would be given from the public taxes. But
free schools might be established in very poor neighbourhoods, subject to the approval of the Education
Department.

School boards might provide new schools or assist
existing schools, provided that, in the latter case, they
helped all schools equally. They were to have power
to make bye-laws to compel the attendance of all children between the ages of five and thirteen years. In
case of the absence of children without reasonable excuse—such as sickness, attendance at some other efficient school, or the fact that there was no public school
within a mile—parents were to be liable to a fine of five
shillings. In country districts the School Board district
was not to be the same as the Union district, since this
might cause the schools to be associated with the idea
of pauperism. Subject to the conscience clause, school
boards might choose whatever system of religious instruction they pleased.

In measures of constructive legislation, he urged, the
purpose—the end aimed at—matters much, and the
precise method matters comparatively little. What is
the purpose in this bill? Briefly this, to bring elementary education within the reach of every English home,
aye, within the reach of those children who have no
homes. For upon the speedy provision of elementary
education depends our industrial prosperity, and the
safe working of our constitutional systems. Upon the
speedy provision of education depends also our national

power. Civilized communities throughout the world are massing themselves together, each mass being measured by its force; and if we are to hold our position among men of our own race, or among the nations of the world, we must make up for the smallness of our numbers by increasing the intellectual force of the individual.

After all, therefore, it was compromise rather than convictions which determined the action of the government. In spite of the disasters of the past over the religious question, the subject was left to be fought about at school board elections, than which, surely, no better method could be devised for arousing sectarian jealousies, religious bigotry, party hatred and clamour, and generally envy, hatred, malice, and all uncharitableness. This was very keenly resented by the Dissenters in the House, and Mr. Dixon moved an amendment to the effect that no measure would be satisfactory which left the question of religious instruction, in schools supported by the public funds and rates, to be determined by the local authorities. Mr. Forster declared that this was a hostile amendment; to which Mr. Vernon Harcourt frankly replied that it was meant to be a hostile amendment—irreconcilably hostile to the principle of denominational education at the will of the dominant sect. Promise of modification was made, after a long discussion, and the amendment was withdrawn.

Almost as strongly does the element of compromise, if not surrender, appear in the year's grace for voluntary efforts, the permissive compulsion, the retention of fees, and the election by vestries. Each and all of these were directly opposed to the convictions of the Liberal party as a whole; had been declared against by popular meetings throughout the country; were strongly resisted in parliament; and were only retained, if at all, by the votes of the Conservatives and the official Liberals. It was a time of severe disappointment and almost political despair on the part of the Nonconformists and all ardent supporters of national education. Public meetings were held, and petitions in favour of more thorough and decisive action were signed by large numbers of persons.

The following amendments were made during the committee stages of the bill. School boards were to be elected by the ratepayers; "in all schools established by means of local rates no catechism or religious formulary which was distinctive of any particular denomination should be taught" (the famous Cowper-Temple clause); religious instruction was to be given either at the beginning or end of a school meeting, so that children could be conveniently withdrawn; inspectors should not examine the religious teaching in any school; school boards were not to be allowed to give assistance out of the rates to voluntary schools, but, instead, the grant to denominational schools was to be raised, so that it should be equal to half their expenditure; no building grants were to be given with regard to any application made after December 31, 1870; and school boards were to be established on the application of the inhabitants of a district, subject to the approval of the Education Department, and after due inquiry and a six months' interval, to allow voluntary effort to supply any deficiency. It was decided that members of school boards were to be elected by the system of cumulative voting, and to serve for three years. London was to have a school board forthwith, and was to be empowered to pay its chairman. The act received the royal assent on August 9, 1870.

One of the most striking immediate results of the passing of the act was the comparatively enormous increase of applications for building grants. The Church party was called upon to make full use of the grace allowed them, and manfully responded to the call. No less than 3111 applications were made—of which, however, 1332 were afterwards withdrawn—in less than five months, the usual rate having been 150 a year. It must be remembered that this would involve very considerable voluntary subscriptions to meet the sums given by the government. In ten years, *i.e.* by 1880, the Church party had provided accommodation for nearly a million additional scholars in their schools. Besides this, they organized a system of Diocesan inspectors, to supervise the religious instruction in their schools.

The Partial Reign of Law.   187

The triumphs of the act were, however, by no means small. Ten years before it was passed, the justice and possibility of a conscience clause were generally denied, now such a clause had to be universally adopted; whilst the idea of separating religious from secular instruction, even in point of time, would have been held as a godless and desperate design against the Church. How much more, therefore, was represented by the acceptance of a system of schools in which no dogmatic religious teaching was to be given! The contention that the work of educating the people belonged solely to the Church was practically defeated, and the long struggle between the ecclesiastical and the political authority resulted in another great gain for the latter. At last there is on the statute-book of the realm a law to secure the education of the people. Though ten millions of pounds had already been spent for this purpose, yet there had been no legal right on the part of the private citizen to claim for his children what the country was all the time paying so much to provide. The people were paying large sums, through the public taxes, for education, and leaving it to school managers to say whether, after all, their children might enjoy real advantage from the money, on what conditions, and to what extent—for the rights of admitting and of dismissing were entirely in the hands of managers. Now no child could be refused admission so long as the school received grants and was not already full, and the child continued to observe the reasonable requirements as to discipline and the payment of the fee. The principle of free education was very fully admitted with respect to certain children. Free schools might be established; school fees might be paid for children attending voluntary schools; and industrial schools might be established, or partly maintained, in which children could be clothed and taught without charge.

For the carrying out of the act the Education Department had to do an immense amount of work. Regulations had to be drawn up for school board elections; applications for the establishing of school boards considered; requests for building grants for voluntary schools dealt with; school board bye-laws approved; arrangements for the transfer of schools from voluntary management to school boards devised; and returns as to the school supply in the various districts obtained and acted upon. For the last-named purpose "inspectors of returns" were appointed—one for each district. To obtain these returns a form was sent to local authorities asking for information as to population, rateable value, number of ratepayers, and the number of schools in the district. Another form was sent to the managers, or teachers of schools, requesting information concerning the general character of the school; details of the school premises; the qualifications and experience of the teacher; the times during which the school was open; the number and ages of the scholars; the fees paid; the number of children receiving education in each subject taught; and whether the school was endowed.

Besides all this a New Code had to be drawn up to meet the altered conditions of things. In this some very important changes appeared. A much broader and more generous view was taken of what constituted an elementary school, viz. one in which elementary education is the principal part of the education there given, and the fee does not exceed ninepence a week for each scholar. It is worth noticing that the instruction is not to be wholly confined to elementary work, as some are nowadays too much inclined to insist was the intention of the act. Again, the limitation that children must attend from the homes of their parents, and were to be taken charge of during the school hours only, was altogether removed, so as to admit industrial schools and the like. The clauses requiring schools to be under denominational management, or to have daily reading from the Authorized Version of the Scriptures, as a condition of receiving grant, were omitted. Thus purely secular schools came, for the first time, within the sphere of grants.

Payment by results was retained as the guiding principle in awarding the grants, but a more liberal rate of payment was introduced. The sum of six shillings, instead of four, was to be paid on each unit of average

The Partial Reign of Law. 189

attendance; four shillings for every pass in the three R's; eight shillings for each infant in average attendance, or ten if they had a separate room to themselves; and a grant of three shillings for every pass by pupils in Standards IV.–VI. in not more than two "specific subjects". The specific subjects were: geography, history, algebra, geometry, natural philosophy, physical geography, natural sciences, political economy, English grammar and literature, Latin grammar, French grammar, German grammar—each of the three last to include pronunciation and translation of sentences—or any properly graduated scheme of work approved by an inspector. Before a scholar could be presented for examination he must have attended 250 times during the school year, or 150 in the case of half-timers. Each attendance was to embrace not less than two hours' secular instruction. The requirements in the three R's were raised, so that each standard under the new code took the work of the next above it under the revised code, whilst the sixth standard was to read with fluency and expression; to write a short theme or letter, or an easy paraphrase; and to work sums in proportion, and vulgar or decimal fractions. After the 31st of March, 1873, no day scholar above nine years of age, and no evening scholar above thirteen was to be examined in Standard I.; and after the like date in the following year any day scholar above nine, or evening scholar above fourteen, was not to be examined in Standard II.

To meet the extra demand for teachers a new clause was inserted to the effect that, during the three years ending 31st December, 1873, certificates of the third class—not entitling to the charge of pupils—might be granted, without examination, upon the report of an inspector, to acting teachers who were over thirty-five years of age; had been teachers in elementary schools for at least ten years; and had certificates of good character from the managers of their school. The inspector must report of them that they were efficient teachers; that they had been teaching not less than thirty children during the preceding half-year; and that at least twenty of the passes of these pupils in the three

R's were made in the second or some higher standard. For the same period the rule that two years' residence at a training college were essential for the gaining of a certificate was suspended in the case of students appointed teachers of elementary schools. And inspectors were informed that where the infants were fewer than sixty in number, a provisionally certificated ex-pupil-teacher might have charge of them. Thus was there a general weakening of the qualifications of teachers to secure the strengthening of the schools. The provision for infants was a specially unfortunate one, for if any children require a teacher with the greatest possible skill, knowledge, and experience, they are the little ones. No less than twelve hundred certificates without examination, and a thousand provisional certificates enabling ex-pupil teachers to take charge of small schools, were issued by August 31, 1873.

The duties of inspectors under the new state of affairs are set forth in the 1870-71 report (blue-book), in which appear "Instructions on the Administration of the New Code (1871)", now more familiarly known as "Instructions to Inspectors". Therein inspectors are admonished to pay "visits of surprise" to schools, so that they may be the better able to learn more of their general condition, and have the opportunity for signing time-tables and certificates, and examining registers and log-books. They were informed that the interval allowed for recreation must not exceed half an hour during a school meeting of two and a half hours and upwards, or a quarter of an hour in a shorter meeting for children under seven. For those over seven, a quarter of an hour in a meeting of three hours, or from five to ten minutes in a shorter meeting, was not to be exceeded. A school meeting might be held on Saturday morning for drill, or music, or both. But not more than one hour at a time should be given to drill. It was suggested that the local Volunteers' drill-sergeant might be engaged to teach drill. English grammar and literature were to be separate subjects, for "specifics"; and either, or both, of them might be taken up under the fourth schedule.

Very full instructions were given as to the conducting

of an examination. Careful directions were given, despite the proverb, for doing two things at once: "while listening to the reading the arithmetic and writing can be marked on the schedule". It was pointed out that the paraphrase in Standard VI., unless it was a superior school, might easily become a turning of good English into indifferent English—a mild term—and therefore a "letter" was to be the usual exercise. If the children were dull, a subject might be suggested to them; or a story read, to be reproduced in their own words; or a school picture put before them, for them to describe. The examination in "specifics" was invariably to be a written one—except, of course, in reading or repetition of English literature. A somewhat suggestive instruction was that if maps and drawings were shown, they were to be initialed and dated by the inspector, so that they might not be produced a second time. The first class in infants' schools were to be strictly examined, and if every fourth child was called out (or some convenient proportion)—the beginning of examination by sample—such children ought to be able to pass in at least as much as individual children did in Standard I. of the Revised Code.

The "stringing up" policy was soon applied to the new order of things, and the work of advancing the requirements went steadily ahead. Some alterations were made in the standards of examination for 1872, so that the requirements in the three R's were slightly raised. Several circulars were issued to inspectors, from which it appears that an unreasonable number of children were withdrawn from examination; and, as this suggested that they might not have been properly prepared during the year, the inspectors were desired to make special inquiries as to such absentees. In another circular, on the examination in arithmetic, it is laid down that dictated numbers should not exceed four figures in Standard I., or five in Standard II. This, strangely enough, because "it is doubtful whether large numbers which never occur in the range of their daily experience suggest any idea to the children of our public elementary schools, they belong to the statistician and the astronomer". To how many children, between seven and nine years of age, would thousands, and tens of thousands, be a matter of "daily experience"? No teacher, assistant, or pupil-teacher, no manager or visitor, was to be allowed to go near the classes while the children were taking down or working the sums given by the inspector, as "their anxiety might lead them to suggest corrections or point to errors, which is akin to prompting".

According to a new clause in the code, schools which failed to satisfy the inspector in singing were to have their grants reduced by one shilling for each scholar in average attendance. Six simple songs were to be known "by ear" in infants' schools, and twelve vocal pieces of whatever kind, "by ear", in schools for older scholars; and if two of these were sung fairly in tune, and the words plainly articulated, the inspectors were informed that this might be passed as satisfying the code for the present. Inspectors were called sharply to account for recommending the removal of galleries, and were told of the many advantages of such structures. Those whose experience had been heretofore limited to one kind of school organization were told that they should endeavour to make themselves acquainted with the best methods which had been adopted in other schools—in which the gallery system was used. In any case, "if satisfactory 'results' be obtained, no adverse criticism should be made on method". Which rather reminds one of the paternal advice; "Get money, my son; get it honestly, if you can; but anyhow, get money". The same principle was urged in a circular respecting time-tables, wherein inspectors were informed that they "can point out any serious objection to a time-table which is presented . . . for signature, leaving the managers to decide whether they consider any alteration necessary", for "the efficiency of their arrangements will be tested by the results produced at the annual examination of their school". Which seems like saying: Get results, even though you get them by methods against which there is "serious objection" on the part of the inspector.

Some slight but significant changes in the payment

of the capitation grant were made in 1874 and 1875. In the former year the grant of six shillings, which had been given simply on the average attendance, was modified, so that five shillings were thus given, whilst one shilling was made dependent upon the teaching of singing being a part of the ordinary instruction. The following year the conditions were: four shillings on the average attendance, one shilling for singing, and one shilling if the inspector reports that the discipline and organization are satisfactory. "To meet the requirements respecting discipline, the managers and teachers were expected to satisfy the inspector that all reasonable care was taken, in the ordinary management of the school, to bring up the children in habits of punctuality, of good manners and language, of cleanliness and neatness, and also to impress upon the children the importance of cheerful obedience to duty, of consideration and respect for others, and of honour and truthfulness in word and act"; which, one may suggest, is a splendid charter of purely ethical teaching, if it were demonstrated and taught as other subjects in the school curriculum are.

A still more important change was made in the payments for passes. For passes in the three R's, three shillings, instead of four, were to be paid, but this was to be compensated for by a payment of four shillings for each scholar, over seven years of age, in average attendance, if *the classes* from which the children were examined in Standards II.–VI. passed a creditable examination in any two of the following subjects: grammar, history, elementary geography, and plain needlework. Hence these subjects have since been called "class subjects". The examination was to be oral or written at the discretion of the inspector. But no grant was to be given if less than 75 per cent of the passes attainable in the three R's by the scholars presented in specifics had been obtained.

Two other additional grants were given. One was an apology for special help to those remote and thinly-populated districts in which it was difficult to obtain sufficient voluntary subscriptions to support a reasonably

efficient school. The sum of £10 (or £15) was to be
given, subject to a favourable report from the inspector,
if the population within two miles, by road, of the
school was less than 300 (or 200) souls, and there was
no other public elementary school, with sufficient accommodation for such population, within three miles of the
school. The other grant was to encourage a more
careful teaching of pupil-teachers. The sum of £2 or
£3 was to be paid for each pupil-teacher who passed
fairly, or well, the examination at the end of each year
of apprenticeship. Two years later it was ordered that
this grant should be divided between the teacher and
pupil-teachers in such proportion as the managers might
determine.

Some further modifications were made in the syllabus
of instruction in the three R's. Now that grammar was
a class subject, repetition was made a part of reading in
Standards IV.–VI. Copy-books had to be shown in
Standards II.–IV., and Standard V. had to reproduce
on paper a short story read out twice. No class subject
was to be taken in Standard I. This was all towards
the levelling up of the requirements.

In 1877 the matter of school-staff received attention.
Not more than three pupil-teachers were to be allowed
in any school, in respect of each certificated teacher
serving in it. The age for admission as a pupil-teacher
was to be fourteen, and the length of engagement was
to be four years. When the average attendance in a
school exceeded two hundred, a second adult, certificated or assistant—an ex-pupil-teacher, or any one who
had passed the Queen's scholarship examination—was
to be required. Stipendiary monitors were allowed
under certain conditions. This was a levelling up in
some respects, since it necessitated the employment of
more adult teachers.

Their lordships declare, in a circular of general instructions to inspectors, dated 16th January, 1878, that
it has now become evident that, by the operation of
recent legislation, the great majority of the labouring
classes will be virtually compelled to send their children
to public elementary schools. It becomes, therefore,

they go on to say, more than ever a duty to do all in their power to secure that both the most suitable and the most useful instruction, and such as is mostly desired by parents, or the character and habits of the population seem specially to require—utilitarianism determined by ignorance, one may suggest—is furnished for the children, and that their moral training is fully provided for during the years which they will be compelled to spend in public elementary schools. In the large changes made in the code during the last two years, they urge, the object throughout has been, over and above the acquisition by every child of the bare rudiments of education, to promote the development of the general intelligence of the scholars, rather than to seek to burden their memories with subjects which, considering the early age at which the majority of children leave school, would not be likely to be of use to them; and also to encourage such training in school in matters affecting their daily life, as may help to improve and raise the character of their homes, so that all children, before they leave school, shall at least have acquired the power of writing with facility, of using simple rules of arithmetic without difficulty, and of reading without exertion and with pleasure to themselves.

This is another of those fundamental fallacies which have underlain the whole superstructure of elementary education. Reading, writing, and arithmetic are but arbitrary systems for the formal symbolical expression of knowledge. It is knowledge itself—which can only come from the proper experiences acting upon the mind—which is the first and essential part of education, *i.e.* consciously cultivated mental growth in the direction of increased power, capacity, and skill. Not mechanical forms of expression, but real mental content of ideas, should be first acquired. Experiences, ideas, expressions, make up the true order of development. It is like trying to teach a child to walk on its head before it can walk on its feet, if we endeavour to thrust knowledge upon it through what are in themselves but empty signs. And it is only in proportion as the child brings real experience and knowledge, which, fortunately, it cannot avoid doing, that anything valuable can result from the process of teaching through the three R's, in the traditional way, during the early years.

Some very wholesome advice is given to the inspectors in this same circular. They are to be very tender towards the schools under the new conditions, especially in the case of new schools, and where many rough and untaught children have been recently introduced by means of compulsion. Above all, it is incumbent on an inspector to show by his manner in examining and dealing with the classes and with the individual scholars that the main object of his visit to a school is to elicit what the children know, and not to prove their ignorance. That object is entirely defeated if by a harsh, impatient, or indistinct manner of questioning the scholars he frightens or confuses them, or if he puzzles them by fanciful and unreasonable questions. Inspectors are expected to take a leading part, as so many distinguished members of their body have done, in developing and raising the character of our elementary schools, so that the country may derive the greatest possible benefit from them.

Towards this very desirable end we get a characteristic contribution in the next year's blue-book. Therein Matthew Arnold sits in the seat of the scorner, and condemns the scientific teacher of pedagogy. With polished phrases of superfine sarcasm he asks: How is a sensible teacher likely to effect most practical good in the way of cultivating the intelligence of school-children? "Is it by betaking himself to the scientific teachers of pedagogy, by feeding on generalities... by learning that we are to 'disuse rule-teaching and adopt teaching by principles', that we are to teach things 'in the concrete instead of in the abstract', that we are to walk worthy of the doctrine long ago enunciated by Pestalozzi that 'alike in its order and its methods education must conform to the natural process of mental evolution!'" The teacher "can quite well work on the old lines without busying himself with the new and (so-called) scientific theories of education. It is not true that he must of necessity begin geography, for instance, with the geography of the child's own parish if he is to interest the child in geography. He will find he can interest him in it quite well by beginning with the old-fashioned four quarters of the globe, and coming round to the child's own parish by way of Africa and Zululand. But the great thing is to give the power of reading ... perhaps the best among the gifts which it is the business of our elementary schools to bestow." Thus Arnold the poet opposes himself against Herbart the psychologist, Locke and Spencer the philosophers, Pestalozzi the father of practical educators, and all the great thinkers of all time who had dealt with the subject of education. How easy it is to condemn the trained knowledge of others out of the depth of one's own lack of trained knowledge! And yet some think Arnold a true educationist because he was a true poet.

Out of his own mouth shall he be judged. He writes: "good poetry is formative; it has, too, the precious power of acting by itself and in a way managed by nature, not through the instrumentality of that somewhat terrible character, the scientific educator. I believe that even the rhythm and diction of good poetry are capable of exercising some formative effect, even though the sense be imperfectly understood. But of course the good of poetry is not really got unless the sense of the words is known. . . Gray's *Elegy* and extracts from Shakespeare should be chosen in preference to the poetry of Scott and Mrs. Hemans, and very much of the poetry in our present school reading-books should be entirely rejected." Two pages before this he writes: "Turgot used to say that if one taught children nothing but what was true, and if one talked to them of nothing but what they could comprehend, there would be hardly any minds with unsound judgment. We shall not arrive just yet at such a consummation; but to simplify our teaching, to present to our children's minds what they can comprehend, to abstain from pressing upon them what they cannot, is the right way towards it."

Two years before, his report contains the following passage: "A stir of life is certainly more and more visible again in our schools. Scholars and teachers alike show it, and I have good hopes for the future. In what is properly to be called culture, in feeling, taste, and perception, the advance is least; and this is, perhaps, inevitable. Even second-year students will show, in this respect, an astonishing crudeness. 'Doctor, can you fulfil the duties of your profession in curing a woman who is distracted?'; or again, 'Can you wait upon the lunatic?'—these are paraphrases of Shakespeare's '*Canst thou not minister to a mind diseased?*' 'The witches who are under the control of Hecate, and who love the darkness because their designs are best accomplished then, have assembled at their meeting-place with no other protection than a wolf for their sentinel, and by whose roar they know when their enemy Tarquin is coming near them.' It seems almost incredible that a youth who has been two years in a training college, and for the last of the two has studied *Macbeth*, should, at his examination, produce such a travesty of the well-known passage in that play beginning, '*Now witchcraft celebrates*'. Yet such travesties are far too common, and all signs of positive feeling and taste for what is poetically true and beautiful are far too rare." And yet these Philistines had been under the formative influences of learning good poetry, with meanings, as pupils in the standards, as pupil-teachers in the various years, and as students in training colleges, some ten years in all; and they would be those who would teach the children "good poetry" and "the sense of the words". Truly Arnold was a poet!

Still another change was made in the payment for class subjects in 1878. Only two shillings were to be paid for passes in these, and the four-shillings grant was to be given for passes in specific subjects. Two years later the class subjects were increased in number, natural history, physical geography, natural philosophy, history, social economy, &c., being included, so that managers should have greater freedom in selecting subjects of instruction, and in organizing the teaching of the scholars in connection with their everyday life and the common objects around them—according to Sir J. Lubbock's suggestions in parliament. But it was pointed out that little good would result from such opportunities "under the system hitherto too often pursued, of teaching 'class subjects' through *lectures*, assisted by home lessons taken from short skeleton manuals, laboriously learnt by heart, and then easily forgotten".

An endeavour to secure advance with regard to the teachers was made by the insertion in the training colleges' syllabus for 1880 of Locke's *Thoughts on Education* as a subject of study, under the head of "school management". This is because students have been found to use such technical phrases as "to cultivate perception", "to strengthen the conceptive faculty", "inductive process", &c.; whilst "it was evident that these phrases were very imperfectly comprehended by a large majority of the students, and copied frequently from general schemes of lessons drawn up by lecturers on method. Lectures on the art of education have been necessarily vague from the largeness of the subject, and from the want of a text-book suited to the class of learners; most of the existing text-books, being pitched for a higher class of learners, involve the employment of the technical phraseology and disputed points of mental science." The complaint of the misuse of such phrases is almost as much justified at the present time, whilst the "practical" method, which shirks the responsibility of rightly understanding and wisely applying them, is just as much favoured. It was claimed that in Locke "the topics discussed are of a practical nature, and largely applicable to the conduct of elementary schools; and the lecturer is not fettered by any particular psychological system." Exactly; so our manufacturers have remained unfettered by any scientific system in their factories, while their German rivals have laboratories and expert scientists as permanent parts of their factories, and are thereby outstripping us in the world's race for wealth. So will they excel us in their schools, as long as we hold that it is the business of our teachers to force knowledge into scholars' minds, and not to be fettered by any scientific knowledge of the nature of those minds.

Parliamentary action from 1870 to 1880 was also doing

something to help forward the general movement. The teaching of military drill and gymnastics in all schools, and the desirability of general provision for blind and deaf-mute children being made, were brought forward by questions, but no further steps were taken. Sir John Lubbock twice introduced a resolution: "to give more encouragement to the teaching of history, geography, elementary social economy, and other so-called extra subjects in elementary schools". He argued, most soundly, that where these subjects were well taught the three R's were best done. Dean Dawes, he said, writing about the famous King's Somborne School, remarks: "Here, where so many other things are taught besides reading, the children are found in advance, in reading, of all other schools, in the majority of which scarcely anything else is taught. . . . And this is always the case, and a fact which seems to point to the expediency, if not the necessity, of teaching children something else besides reading, that we may be able to teach them to read." He drew attention to the books for class subjects adopted by the two largest educational societies, and drawn up to meet the requirements of the new code. They were full of ambiguities and errors. In the pages devoted to geography, Iceland was said to be in America. In the botanical portion, sap was said to be, "according to some eminent authorities, not exactly black, as it appears, but of a dark-blue colour". The seed of the sweet-pea was described as not much larger than a small pin's head, and yet as containing " compactly folded up, a large, branchy, flowering plant". Seals, whales, shrimps, and prawns were said to be fish. In the part devoted to insects, they were told that these were of great use, and, as an illustration, that "the fly keeps the warm air pure and wholesome by its swift zigzag flight". Elsewhere air was said to be purer in the morning than during the rest of the day.

One aim of the elementary school, he held, should be to provide that any child of remarkable ability should be able to avail himself of the faculties with which he was endowed; that genius, in whatever rank of life, might be rendered available for the common benefit. He had

The Partial Reign of Law.

no wish to lengthen the hours of study in elementary schools. He had taught a good deal in them himself, and the hours seemed quite long enough. Indeed, the fault of their system seemed to be that they loaded the brain instead of educating the mind; they taxed the memory instead of cultivating the intellect; and, in fact, had too much instruction and too little education. It was the special work of the class subjects to remedy this; therefore every class should do such subjects, as most would miss their higher influences, since so many left by the time they were twelve years old.

But such enlightened and sound views, so cheering and encouraging to the initiated, could not pass without challenge, and Sir Charles Adderley—a former Vice-president—retorted that the object of education was to qualify men mentally and morally to take their part in life in the situation in which they found themselves. Which seems to require a small army of Fagins to supply the needs of the children of the criminal classes.

Further progress was made in 1876 by a bill introduced by Lord Sandon, the Vice-president. It laid down the principle that every parent was bound to cause his child to receive efficient elementary instruction in reading, writing, and arithmetic, under the penalties set forth in the Act. To this end no child could be employed at all if under ten years of age; whilst between the ages of ten and fourteen a child could only be employed as a half-timer, *i.e.* it must attend school half the times during which the school was opened, each week, if it had passed in one of the standards, as fixed by the local authority, or had made a certain number of attendances each year during the previous five years. The bill also provided that in places where there was no school board the Town Council, Board of Guardians, or Urban Sanitary Authority might appoint a School Attendance Committee, which was to exercise the same powers in enforcing school attendance as the school boards. This committee could appoint a local committee; report infringements of the conscience class; and, on a requisition from the ratepayers, make bye-laws. But they might not establish or manage schools. The powers for carrying out their work were greatly increased. School boards and attendance committees might ask for an "attendance order" from a magistrate with respect to offenders. The order was to state at what school the child was to attend, and the number of times it must be present. This plan proved of great advantage, in that the non-observance of such an order constituted a very definite offence, for which the punishment was likely to be certain and immediate.

The penalty for employing a child contrary to the act was a fine not exceeding forty shillings. Parents who neglected to send their children to school were liable to a fine not exceeding, with costs, five shillings. If a parent had used all reasonable efforts to get the child to school but had failed, then the child might be committed to an industrial school. Any parent, not being a pauper, who was unable by reason of poverty to pay the school fees required, might demand from the guardians of the parish that they should pay—the whole, or part—for him; and he was not thereby to be deprived of any franchise, right, or privilege, or be subject to any disability or disqualification. The twenty-fifth clause of the Act of 1870 was repealed.

Where the circumstances of any class of population in any school district were, in the opinion of a secretary of state, such that schools providing industrial training, elementary education, and one or more meals a day, but not lodging, were needed for the proper control and training of the children, certified day industrial schools might be established by a school board. Children who proved unmanageable, with regard to the ordinary day-schools, might be sent to a day industrial school; and the parent ordered to contribute a certain amount, not exceeding two shillings per week, towards the cost—if unable to pay, he might apply to the guardians of the parish, as in the case of ordinary school fees.

Perhaps the most significant clause in the act was the one which established the seventeen-shillings-and-sixpence limit. Hitherto no grant averaging over fifteen shillings per head was paid unless it was met by an equal amount, per head, of voluntary subscriptions.

The change was a great boon to voluntary schools, being equal to a special grant of half a crown per unit of average attendance for most schools. The payment of school fees by the guardians would also benefit Church schools chiefly, and to a considerable extent in some cases. Lord Sandon declared that the object of the bill was to make it possible to maintain schools by the aid of the government grant and the school fees. By forcing the children into the schools, providing for the payment of their fees, and giving higher grants, this end was wholly, or almost entirely, achieved in very many cases.

It is not surprising, therefore, to find that Dissenters resented and resisted this as much as they had the twenty-fifth clause in the Act of 1870. They argued that it was but an indirect way of giving help from the rates to support denominational schools. Thus the Manchester School Board, which for several years had no schools under its control, was entirely engaged, under the Act of 1870, in putting into force its bye-laws to compel attendance at school, and in paying the fees of many of those who attended at denominational schools. That the Act of 1876 was open to accusations of partiality is confirmed by Dean Gregory, who writes in his book on *Elementary Education*: "In 1876 when a Conservative Government was in power, and Lord Sandon (the staunch friend of voluntary schools) was Vice-president of the Education Department, a measure of relief was passed through Parliament which was intended to lighten the strain upon school managers, and which has materially assisted many schools". Which reminds one very strongly of the plea of "the intolerable strain", and the Voluntary Schools Act of 1897; and also of a comparison once made by Mr. Lowe. In reply to the claim, urged by Sir J. Pakington, that ragged schools should receive special aid, Mr. Lowe said that the plea amounted to this: Take the inferior type of schools; give them bounties, foster them, throw the weight into the balance; as far as public money is concerned show that they are your favourites, while at the same time you profess that your object is to raise the standard of education in the country. It was just as though the government were advised to set up a shop for the sale of pure articles of consumption, and at the same time to establish by its side another shop for the sale of adulterated goods, largely subsidizing the latter in order that it might compete the better with the shop where everything was unadulterated and pure. Having created a good thing, they would then foster an inferior one, and give it larger grants of public money, so that it might compete more successfully with its rival. If such a plan were followed, it would drag down the whole system of education in this country.

In 1877 the pupil-teacher system was severely criticized by Mr. B. Samuelson, who moved for a select committee to inquire into the system of apprenticeship of pupil-teachers in elementary schools, and into the constitution of training colleges for elementary teachers. He declared that pupil-teachers were ignorant, and that the London and other school boards were very dissatisfied with them as teachers. They were overworked alike in imparting instruction to youthful scholars, and in attending to the claims of their own education. As to the training colleges, it seemed to him a mistake to train teachers in cloistered institutions. It would be much better to connect the training colleges to universities, as in Scotland, and so make them less exclusively boarding-houses. Inducements might well be offered to university graduates to take up work in elementary schools. Lord Sandon objected that if pupil-teachers were not made use of, the expense for adult teachers would be enormous, and that very large classes would have to be formed. Mr. Forster suggested that training halls might be set up in large towns where lectures should be given to youths from sixteen to eighteen years of age, who desired to become teachers. These should teach only a few hours each day in schools, spending the rest of their time in the training hall. They were to be called student teachers. Unfortunately no committee was appointed, and the only good that seems to have come indirectly from the debate was the subsequent establishment of what are called pupil-teacher centres, in which Mr. Forster's suggestion is carried out. This has, to a small extent, relieved the heavy burden laid upon these victims of a cheap and mistaken system; but in the great majority of cases they continue to be the slaves of the schools and lead lives which are the completest contradiction to every sound principle of true education and right living.

During the following year Mr. Rathbone drew attention to the very inadequate amount of special training given to inspectors previous to their being entrusted with the inspection of schools; and early in 1879 moved "that in the opinion of the House, arrangements ought to be at once made to provide that in future, before being appointed to an independent post, newly-appointed inspectors should have one year's training under an experienced inspector, unless they have been previously engaged in the education of children for a sufficient time to make this unnecessary". He argued that young men, however able, fresh from college, who might perhaps have had very little to do with children, nothing to do with elementary education since their own childhood, and knew nothing about the capabilities of children, must almost certainly fail to properly discharge their important and difficult duties. Was it not a monstrous absurdity that whereas in England we consider a much longer apprenticeship than one year necessary to make a man a good cobbler, a good joiner, a good merchant, or lawyer, we should expect men to do satisfactorily, without any previous technical training, such highly-skilled and technical work as the inspection of elementary schools? And would it not be well that some of the best of the elementary teachers should be made inspectors?

Mr. Mundella strongly supported the suggestion of promoting schoolmasters to the posts of inspectors. There were over a hundred assistant inspectors who were duly qualified for the office of inspectors, not alone by education and standing, but by long experience as teachers in elementary schools. Some of these had been among the ablest schoolmasters in the country, had taken high honours at the universities, and practically did all the work of the inspectors, except writing the reports. Lord George Hamilton, then vice-president, objected to the motion on the ground of the extra expense—£2000 per year—which it would involve; and said that at present newly-appointed inspectors received both instruction and probation, before being put in sole charge, the minimum period being a fortnight, while in many cases it was more. The House, however, approved and passed the motion.

On the whole, from 1870 to 1880 was an eventful period in the history of our primary schools. The first beginnings of a truly national system, as opposed to denominational systems, were made, and very considerable progress made, on the lines laid down. Over three thousand board schools (departments: boys', girls', infants') were established, providing accommodation for a million children; whilst nearly a thousand voluntary schools (departments) were established, providing accommodation for nearly one and a half million children. The total number of children whose names were on the school registers increased by nearly three millions—in round numbers, from one to nearly three and three quarter millions—and the average attendance increased nearly one and a half million—being over two and a half millions. The amount of grant had gone up from just over one million to seven and a half millions (including grants from the Science and Art Department).

How much, and yet how little, had been accomplished! Little, because, of the 1,760,040 children examined in the standards, in 1879, more than three-fourths were presented for examination in the three lowest standards, and only about one in every fifty in the sixth standard. Of those presented, about eighty-eight per cent passed in reading, eighty in writing, seventy-four in arithmetic, and sixty-two in all three subjects. Grant was paid on sixty per cent of those in average attendance, for class subjects. In specific subjects 119,429 were examined, of whom 81,381 passed.

Of seventy-two thousand teachers at work in the schools less than thirty thousand were certificated, and many of these had not been through a training-college course; whilst the remaining forty-two thousand were nearly all pupil-teachers, the exceptions being over two thousand "article 68". Those who were trained in the colleges received a more advanced course of instruction in general knowledge than formerly, and a slightly better one in professional knowledge.

The Science and Art Department continued to cause good work to be done, in spite of its methods and the fact that it was officered by military men. Although thousands of men who had advanced certificates in sciences about which they had no real knowledge, and duly imparted this knowledge to hundreds of thousands of small pupils; yet there were also good men and real scientists doing excellent work under the Department. A good story was once told by a vice-principal of a London training college about two military men sent to superintend an examination at the college. One of the college lecturers was told off to assist them. He first went to the senior man and asked if he could help him in any way. "No, thanks!" was the reply. "But if you wouldn't mind helping in the other room, I should be much obliged. Major X. is a capital fellow, but [touching his forehead]—India—touch of sunstroke. You know!" The lecturer then went to the major, who likewise declined his help, but said: "Give an eye to the other room as much as you can. Colonel Y. is a splendid fellow; but he is getting old and past this kind of thing. I can manage all right, thanks!"

Chapter X.

The Partial Reign of Law—*Continued*.

In spite of the theory, constantly restated, that the Department has only to judge of results for the purpose of proportioning the grants, and leaves methods and means to managers and teachers, we have seen how the codes, instructions to inspectors, and circulars, have more and more laid down in precise detail not only what has to be done, but also the way in which it should or might be done. Sometimes certain methods are definitely prescribed, and where they are simply suggested as being good, this expression of opinion has always amounted to a practical imperative, since the inspectors have had to act upon these suggestions as instructions, and teachers have usually been only too eager to accept them as authoritative rulings. And on the whole this necessity of initiative which was forced upon the Department by the want of knowledge and zeal amongst managers, and the diversities of opinions amongst inspectors and teachers, has worked for good. It has secured, in most cases, a reasonable uniformity with regard to a reasonable minimum of requirements; and this has been made progressive.

This contradiction in theory and practice is well shown in a circular, issued in 1880, on schemes for teaching class subjects; which circular obviously owes its origin to the faulty methods then in use. Therein it is laid down that such subjects are to be taught through reading books, which are to contain a sufficiently full and well-defined amount of matter, providing for a year's work. A special set of reading books must be provided for each subject, and be confined solely to that subject; have an attractive style; and deal with topics suitable to children. But inspectors are cautioned that they are not authorized to originate, or suggest, any schemes; their duty being confined to approving or rejecting those submitted to them. How they could do the latter without at least implicitly doing the former it is somewhat hard to understand.

But on another point, viz. the utilizing of women teachers for the lower standards in boys' schools, a very halting and undecided circular was sent out during the same year. This seems to suggest every possible objection to the plan, and then informs managers that they may ask to be allowed to try the experiment entirely on their own responsibility. As a matter of fact, the plan has since proved an unqualified success. After this effort some measure of self-assurance again appears,

The Partial Reign of Law. 209

and circulars on the encouragement of thrift, and the establishing of higher-grade schools, convey very definite information and excellent suggestions.

But the finest effort in initiative was due to Mr. Mundella, who, as vice-president, made a serious and praiseworthy effort to secure further progress. He, in 1881, invited school boards and persons interested in education to send in memorials pointing out in what directions they considered improvements to be necessary. From the material thus supplied certain general ideas were selected, and between twenty and thirty of the principal inspectors were asked to write papers on these, criticising them in the freest possible manner, and making any suggestions they wished. Then a draft report was drawn up, and this was dealt with by a committee consisting of three of the senior officials in the Education Department, three inspectors, and the vice-president. They drew up a scheme of amendments to the code, which was then reconsidered by the committee, enlarged by the addition of the Lord-President and other inspectors. Their aim was to arrive at sound educational principles, such as would produce the best results and the most thoroughly good education. A half-way house between inspectors' assistants and inspectors was made by the introduction of the rank of sub-inspector, which brought higher salary, more responsible duties, higher standing, and a more tangible prospect of promotion to the highest posts. This was a wise provision for securing technical experts in the most responsible positions, though a by no means too generous recognition of the value and deserts of a most capable body of public servants.

The following were the most important changes which were made. The fixed grant per unit of average attendance was to be four shillings and sixpence, instead of four shillings. There was to be an examination grant of one penny for every unit of percentage of passes in the three R's; that is, if, for example, one hundred boys made three hundred passes (the whole number possible), they would pass at the rate of one hundred per cent, and would be paid for at the rate of one hundred pennies per head; if they made one hundred and fifty passes, this would be fifty per cent of the possible passes, and the payment fifty pence per head. This was to take the place of the three shillings for each pass in reading, writing, or arithmetic. A new grant, called a "merit grant", was introduced. Under this head a grant amounting to one, two, or three shillings per unit of average attendance was to be paid, according as the inspector, "allowing for the special circumstances of the case, reports the school to be fair, good, or excellent, in respect of (1) the organization and discipline; (2) the intelligence employed in instruction; and (3) the general quality of the work, especially in the elementary subjects". The grant for singing was to be one shilling per head if taught by note, or sixpence if taught by ear. For class subjects the grant was to be one or two shillings per head, according as the inspectors' reports on the examination declared the results to be fair or good. Thus the grants for these subjects were reduced one-half. The grant for specific subjects was to be four shillings for each scholar who passed in any subject.

Mr. Mundella claimed that these arrangements would maintain the previous amount given yearly in grants; and that the fair schools would receive about the same, the good schools a little more, and the bad schools a little less. It was also hoped that another result would be that more attention would be given to individual scholars, and to greater uniformity of work throughout a school.

It was no longer required that a child must have made 250 attendances to qualify for presentation at the examination, but only that its name had been on the register for the last 22 weeks that the school had been opened. The children in Standards I. and II. were not to be examined individually, but by "samples"; but those in the higher standards, however, were still to be examined individually in the three R's. If only one class subject was taken, it must be English; if a second, it might be geography or elementary science; but not more than two might be taken. Since it had been found that the teaching of "specific" subjects in Standard IV. had led almost entirely to cram, these subjects were not to be commenced before Standard V. To obtain greater uniformity in examinations the chief inspectors were to hold meetings, and decide on the best methods, tests, and standard of attainments.

With regard to the improvement of staff, it was laid down that a principal certificated teacher was to count for an average attendance of not more than 60, a second certificated teacher for not more than 80, and each assistant for not more than 60. This would necessitate the employment of more teachers in schools, though, unfortunately, it would often mean the employment of the weakest and most mischievous kind, viz. pupil-teachers. Further, no teacher who had not passed the second-year certificate examination was to be allowed to have charge of a pupil-teacher. And a new article was put in the code to the effect that "graduates of any university in the United Kingdom, women over eighteen years of age who have passed university examinations recognized by the Department, and persons who have passed the examination for admission to a training college, may be recognized as assistant teachers". The university examinations were such as the Oxford and Cambridge Local Examinations for Senior Students, the London University Matriculation Examination, &c. But whilst this article required a more advanced general knowledge than hitherto, it practically lowered the technical qualification to nothing at all.

The subjects of instruction in the schools were arranged in the new code under the following heads:— *elementary subjects*: reading, writing, arithmetic, which were obligatory (with needlework for girls); *class subjects*: singing, English, geography, elementary science, and history, which were optional; and *specific subjects*: algebra, Euclid and mensuration, mechanics, chemistry, physics, animal physiology, botany, principles of agriculture, Latin, French, and domestic economy, which were also optional. Ten years later horticulture, navigation, book-keeping, and Welsh were added to the specific subjects. While this list has a very generous scope, it must be remembered that the weaker schools

English National Education.

would confine themselves to the elementary subjects, with perhaps one class subject; the average schools would do two class subjects; and only the best schools would take any specific subjects, and then not more than two.

The instructions to inspectors concerning the new conditions direct that "a school of humble aim, which passes only a moderately-successful examination, may properly be designated 'Fair', if its work is conscientiously done, and is sound as far as it goes; and if the school is free from any conspicuous fault. Generally, a school may be expected to receive the mark 'Good', when both the number and the quality of the passes are satisfactory; when the scholars pass well in such class subjects as are taken up; and when the organization, discipline, tone, and general intelligence are such as to deserve commendation."

The description of an excellent school deserves to be preserved as an almost ideal expression of the aims and characteristics of such a school, from the practical point of view. It is as follows: "A thoroughly good school in favourable conditions is characterized by cheerful and yet exact discipline, maintained without harshness and without noisy demonstration of authority. Its premises are cleanly and well-ordered; its time-table provides a proper variety of mental employment and of physical exercise; its organization is such as to distribute the teaching power judiciously, and to secure for every scholar—whether he is likely to bring credit to the school by examination or not—a fair share of instruction and of attention. The teaching is animated and interesting, and yet thorough and accurate. The reading is fluent, careful, and expressive, and the children are helped by questioning and explanation to follow the meaning of what they read. Arithmetic is so taught as to enable the scholars not only to obtain correct answers to sums, but also to understand the reason of the processes employed. If higher subjects are attempted, the lessons are not confined to memory work and to the learning of technical terms, but are designed to give a clear knowledge of facts, and to train the learner in the practice of thinking and observing. Besides fulfilling these conditions, which are all expressed or implied in the code, such a school seeks by other means to be of service to the children who attend it. It provides for the upper classes a regular system of home-exercises, and arrangements for correcting them expeditiously and thoroughly. Where circumstances permit, it has also its lending library, its savings-bank, and an orderly collection of simple objects and apparatus adapted to illustrate the school lessons, and formed in part by the co-operation of the scholars themselves. Above all, its teaching and discipline are such as to exert a right influence on the manners, the conduct, and the character of the children, to awaken in them a love of reading, and such an interest in their own mental improvement as may reasonably be expected to last beyond the period of school life." No school " which falls short of that standard in any important respects, or which is not, in some of them at least, entitled to special praise", was to receive the mark " Excellent ".

Three other points in the instructions deserve notice. First: good infants' schools are not only to teach the three R's, needlework, and singing, but also to provide a regular course of simple conversational lessons on objects and on the facts of natural history, and a proper variety of physical exercises and interesting employments. And it is remarked that "it is of little service to adopt the 'gifts' and mechanical occupations of the *Kindergarten* unless they are so used as to furnish real training in accuracy of hand and eye, in intelligence, and in obedience". Second: where specific subjects are taught, inspectors are to satisfy themselves that "the teacher has given proof of his fitness to teach them, by having acquitted himself creditably at a training college or at some other public examination". Third: owing to the frequent complaints of the excessive use of corporal punishment in schools, received by their lordships, inspectors are to impress upon managers and teachers "that the more thoroughly a teacher is qualified for his position, by skill, character, and personal influence, the less necessary it is for him to resort to corporal chastisement at all".

Altogether there is, on the code for 1882, much that is good, much that makes for progress, and much to justify the compliment paid to the chief author of it, by its being popularly called "the Mundella Code". There are the usual fundamental weaknesses in it, due partly to want of scientific technical knowledge, and partly to the inherent difficulties of the state-cum-public-cum-private system of management and control. Thus, all Mr. Mundella's good intentions, great personal efforts, and official innovations only made, for the most part, an improved rearrangement of the good and bad points of the system. Soon the teachers were declaiming against the merit grants; the examination of those who had been on their registers the short time required, and in their schools a small fraction of it; the actual terrors of the percentage of passes, upon which their salaries and the holding of their positions were made to depend, by the local authorities; and the general stress, anxiety, and uncertainty which arose. Their last state was far worse, in many respects, than former ones had been.

With respect to the above a very significant clause was inserted in the code for 1884. The inspector, in considering the organization and discipline of a school, was instructed "to satisfy himself that the teacher has neither withheld scholars improperly from examination, nor unduly pressed those who are dull or delicate in preparation for it, at any time of the year; and that in classifying them for instruction regard has been paid to their health, their age, and their mental capacity, as well as to their due progress in learning". There was to be special consideration shown to the weaklings, and another clause stated that "the following, among others, will be considered reasonable excuses for either withholding a scholar or not presenting him in a higher standard: delicate health or prolonged illness; obvious dulness or defective intellect; temporary deprivation, by accident or otherwise, of the use of eye or hand. If a scholar has failed in two subjects, or twice in the same subject, he may generally be presented again in the same standard." Besides this, inspectors were instructed to report in every case in which they had reason to believe that the scholars were improperly detained beyond the prescribed time, or that it was attempted to make up for neglect or for an injudicious distribution of work throughout the year by special exertions just before the examination. But when teachers' reputations, salaries, and employment, and the amount of local rates and subscriptions, depended upon success in "passes", what were all these precautions worth? Children were both unduly pressed and kept back at the same time. As one inspector put it, thousands of years of school life were lost—so far as progress was concerned—in a single large school, in four or five years.

As an instance of what zeal without knowledge does, it is worth while noticing that there was a craze for the teaching of agriculture about this time. It was arranged that it might be taken in every standard in the schools, by pupil-teachers, by students in training, and by adult teachers (under the Science and Art Department); and "instruction in this important subject" was urged upon all. Of course the idea was that the subject was of vital importance to the national welfare. The result was that thousands of individuals "took" this subject. For the most part they were dwellers in towns, of whom probably most had never been on a farm, and knew nothing whatever of the materials and objects studied; and, assuredly they did not get any real knowledge of them from learning the contents of small books labelled *Agriculture*. Certainly not one per cent of those who passed in the subject was ever likely to go to work on a farm. So the national welfare was advanced.

In 1885 drawing and history were added to the class subjects. The former subject might be taught, as a class subject, only by teachers who had a second-grade certificate from the Science and Art Department in freehand, model, or geometrical drawing; or who had earned grants, in the year 1884, for teaching freehand, or model drawing, or practical geometry of the first grade, in an elementary school. Two years later drawing was removed from the list of class subjects. In the instructions to inspectors for this year occurs this passage relating to specific subjects: "It is not the intention of my lords to encourage a pretentious or unreal pursuit of higher studies, or to encroach in any way on the province of secondary education. The course suited to an elementary school is practically determined by the limit of 14 years of age; and may properly include whatever subject can be effectively taught within the limit." Given bright boys and good teachers, it is somewhat difficult to see how the first and second halves of this passage are to be reconciled.

Another effort resulting in extensive and valuable reform was made in 1890, under the guidance of Sir William Hart-Dyke, vice-president, and Sir George Kekewich (not then knighted), secretary, and based upon the recommendations of the Royal Commission appointed in 1886. The principal changes are summarized in the instructions to inspectors for 1890. The first object aimed at was to give greater financial stability to schools, by means of a liberal fixed grant. Instead, therefore, of a fixed grant of 4s. 6d., there was to be a "principal grant" of either 14s. or 12s. 6d., according to the report and recommendation of the inspector on the accuracy of knowledge and general intelligence of the scholars in the elementary subjects. This covered the ground of the old "fixed grant" and the "merit grant" (except as to organization and discipline), and obviously did much to secure greater certainty as to income. A separate grant was to be given for organization and discipline, and might be either 1s. 6d. or 1s., according to the inspector's recommendation. The declared object of this was to emphasize the importance of conduct and moral training as essential factors of the success and usefulness of a public elementary school. In awarding it the inspector was to consider how far the children had been trained in habits of good manners and language, cleanliness and neatness, &c., and also to satisfy himself that the teacher had not unduly pressed any of his pupils in their work. Either the lower or the higher of these grants must be given in every case, unless a school was declared inefficient after due warning and careful testing, in which case it got no grant at all. The grant for singing, needlework, class subjects, and specifics, remained unaltered.

The abolition of the merit grant, and the payment according to the percentage of passes in the three R's, undoubtedly did much to lighten the very serious strain upon both pupils and teachers. And this was still further lightened by the introduction of examination by "sample", in place of individual testing. Instead of examining each scholar in each of the three R's, one-third of a class was examined in reading only, another third in writing only, and the other third in arithmetic only. And, better still, full liberty of classification, according to the ability and attainments of the scholars, was given to managers; which, of course, practically meant the teachers. This, the very corner-stone of a true education, was at last won, after great sorrow and suffering had made it inevitable. Truly necessity is the mother of virtue, and the disasters of ignorance the dawning of knowledge.

Decidedly our system of instruction was becoming more humane. It was also becoming more rational. So far as a scheme of work may be said to be uneducative or educative, with regard to the starting-point and steps of progress which it suggests, the newest new code was distinctly an advance on its predecessors. Alternative schemes for class subjects were drawn up. In grammar the teaching might begin with the very simple analysis of very simple sentences: the rational way of learning parts of speech, by their functions. The old plan, still retained, was to begin with pointing out nouns; an impossible task, in any intelligent sense, without analysis, since the same word may be different parts of speech, according to its function in a sentence. An improved progressive scheme of lessons for elementary science was given, well arranged, except that Standards I. and II. repeated the work done in infants' school classes. A scheme of history work was also arranged, which erred only in that it required the subject to be begun in the quite unknown and largely unrealizable past, instead of in the more or less known and easily understood present. But it is difficult not to make some progress in the right, even when doing the wrong. Special schemes were drawn up for small schools, which allowed of the grouping of the standards, and thus secured the most effective use of small staffs.

One of the best of the new features was the introduction of manual training as a school subject for which grants would be paid. This is referred to, in the instructions to inspectors, in a sentence which appears to involve a mystery. It is said: "the difficulty which has hitherto prevented the recognition of manual training, as part of the ordinary course of instruction in a public elementary school, has been removed by the alteration in the terms of Art. 12 (*f*)". Now this article, hitherto, had simply set forth that drill and cookery might be taught during the hours set apart for secular instruction. What mysterious power had included these, and excluded manual instruction—or any other subject whatsoever, which the Department might select—and how it was defeated by the alteration in the terms, are matters which are too hard for us.

Another valuable innovation was the provision for the establishment of Day Training Colleges, in connection with a university, or college of university rank. Nothing better has been done for national education since its commencement. If anything will raise primary education to its highest level, the imparting of a broad and generous culture, combined with the highest scientific technical training, to the teacher, is surely the sure and certain way. The deepest learning, the widest sympathies, the closest relations with the learned professions, ought to be secured in a properly organized Day Training College. No man is too highly educated, in every sense of the term, for our primary schools; and we must have the best-educated teachers, if we are to have the best elementary schools. As the teacher, so is the school. But this admirable plan was not made so effective as it might have been; since a training course which was bound to be, in almost every instance, far more expensive than one in a residential training college, was to receive considerably less pecuniary assistance from the government. The annual grant for students in residential colleges was £50 for men, and £35 for women; in day colleges, £35 for men, and £30 for women.

Two other provisions for raising the qualifications of teachers were: pupil-teachers were not to be regarded as having successfully finished their apprenticeship, unless they passed the Queen's scholarship examination; and no teachers were to receive a certificate, or have charge of pupil-teachers, until they had passed in both the first and the second year certificate examinations.

The old spirit of commercialism is, however, still present in all this, and is shown in the severely 'practical' tone of the instruction to inspectors. In estimating the results of the instruction in the various class subjects they are to bear in mind their "practical usefulness". English grammar is to be so taught as to bring out "its important practical bearing on everything else which the child learns". Geography should demonstrate how suitable are "our distant possessions for emigration, and for honourable enterprise". The giving a grant for laundry-work is declared to be an experiment which will have to be carefully watched. The regulations for night-schools were materially altered, for the purpose of giving encouragement to more advanced and varied teaching to the pupils, and to enable managers to adapt the course of study to the industrial and other requirements of particular districts. It is to be no longer necessary that every scholar must be presented in the three R's, and greater freedom and scope is allowed in the choice of special subjects.

But the true spirit of education is gradually creeping in, and, in the instructions to inspectors for the following year, we find this admirable passage on infants' schools: "The infant school contemplates in the length, variety, and character of its lessons the training of scholars whose delicate frames require very careful treatment. It is essential, therefore, that the length of the lesson should not in any case exceed thirty minutes, and should be confined in most cases to twenty minutes; and that the lessons should be varied in length according to the section of the school, so that in the babies' room the actual work of the lesson should not be more than a quarter of an hour. Each lesson should also be followed by intervals of rest and song; the subjects of the lessons should be varied, beginning in the lowest section with familiar objects and animals, and interspersed with songs and stories appropriate to the lesson; the spontaneous and co-operative activity of the scholars should form the object and animate the spirit of the lesson." Herein is the spirit of Froebel.

At last also it seems to be recognized that a pupil-teacher should not be almost wholly a teacher, and hardly at all a pupil, but almost entirely a pupil, and very little a teacher; and a memorandum on the training and instruction of pupil-teachers was issued in 1891. It generally condemned the acquirements of, and teaching received by, pupil-teachers. Moreover, it declared that pupil-teachers were not appointed to be merely youthful assistants in the work of a school, but to receive training in the art of teaching. This latter had been almost wholly neglected, and it was laid down that the time-table of every school should provide that the head-teacher should be free, once a week at least, to listen to his pupil-teachers while they gave lessons, and afterwards to criticise their methods. There was to be a time-table of the pupil-teachers' instruction and private study, and their note-books were to be shown, with each exercise therein dated. Pupil-teacher centres were strongly recommended, and it was suggested that the younger pupil-teachers should be relieved from teaching during certain times in the day, and allowed to have the time for private study. Prize schemes, pupil-teachers' libraries, membership of the National Home Reading Union, history clubs, cricket clubs, debating and literary societies, university extension lectures, visits to places and objects of interest, and well-planned holiday excursions were all advised as means of improvement; for "the future usefulness of the teacher depends, not only on what he knows and can do, but on what he *is*—on his tastes, on his aims in life, on his general mental cultivation, and on the spirit in which he does his work."

And something was done to make it less likely that persons wholly without technical training should become responsible teachers, by some valuable changes as to the conditions for training made in 1892. Any graduate in arts or science of any university in the United Kingdom might enter for a year's training (the second-year course), if the authorities were willing to admit him. And a third year of training might be allowed to any student, on the application of the authorities of a college. This has not only resulted in a more generous education—many students, especially in day training colleges, being thus enabled to graduate before leaving college—but some students have spent a year in a training college in France or Germany. Queen's scholars now include any person eighteen years of age who has passed the Queen's Scholarship examination (almost entirely pupil-teachers) in the first or second class; certificated teachers, who have not been through a training college, and who, having been for two years in a training college, are desirous of having a third year of training; and any graduate, or one who has passed examinations qualifying for graduation, of any university in the United Kingdom. But before they can receive the government grants they must be accepted by the authorities of a training college, and actually residing and studying therein.

A generous widening of the borders of primary school work was made in the next year's code by the introduction of the Evening Continuation School code. This involved the raising of the night-schools to the dignity of a separate system. They were no longer to be mere copies of, and apologies for, day-schools, but a real addition to them. The regulations for them were revolutionized. Persons of any age might attend them; no scholar whatever was to be compelled to take the three R's; individual examination was abolished; grants were to be paid for the time devoted to each subject, and the quality of the instruction given; and inspection was to supplant examination. The method of inspection was to be as follows: The inspector was to visit, without notice, every school for which a grant was claimed, once at least. He would then observe the methods and nature of the instruction given; question the scholars on at least two different subjects; satisfy himself that the premises were suitable, and the register and time-table properly kept; and so form his estimate of the qualifications of the teachers, and the success of the work of the school. A conference was to be held with the managers and teachers, when this could be conveniently arranged.

The list of subjects for which grants would be paid included the three R's; English, geography, history, life and duties of the citizen; French, German, Welsh, Latin; Euclid, algebra, mensuration; elementary physiography, elementary physics and chemistry, science of common things, chemistry, mechanics, sound, light and heat, magnetism and electricity, human physiology, botany, agriculture, horticulture, navigation, bookkeeping, shorthand; vocal music; domestic economy, needle-work, cookery, laundry-work, dairy-work; and drawing, manual or technical instruction, suitable physical exercises, military drill, and housewifery. For this last group only a "fixed grant" was given; whilst for all the others a "variable grant" was also given. The "fixed grant" was at the rate of a shilling for every complete twelve hours of instruction in the total of all the hours for all the subjects; and the "variable grant" was at the rate of 1s. or 1s. 6d., according to the inspector's report, for every such twelve hours, provided that not less than fifteen hours' instruction had been given in each subject for which it was claimed. No scholar was to be admitted who was under fourteen years of age unless he was exempt from attendance at a day-school. The teachers might be any person, layman or clergyman—other than pupil-teachers engaged in a public elementary day-school—over eighteen years of age, and approved by an inspector. An excellent guide and help to such teachers was given by detailed schemes of work in six of the subjects, and brief outlines for the others—a feature as admirable as new in the history of code-making.

In the day-school code very few changes were made. Dairy-work was added for girls; provision was made.

for teaching the blind and deaf, and for bi-lingual work in Wales; an excellent alternative scheme for the teaching of arithmetic was drawn up; and pupil-teachers were allowed to obtain marks by attending university extension lectures. The grant for specific subjects was to be 2s. or 3s. for every scholar presented, according to the inspector's report, instead of 4s. for each individual pass.

The new spirit of education, as opposed to mere school management, again appears in a valuable circular on the instruction of infants issued this same year. Whereas, in previous instructions to inspectors, it has been observed that the "varied occupations" should be "such as will relieve the younger children, especially during the afternoon, from the strain of ordinary lessons, and train them to observe and imitate", it is now "strongly urged that sufficient attention has not been paid in the past to these principles: (1) The recognition of the child's spontaneous activity, and the stimulation of this activity in certain well-defined directions by the teachers. (2) The harmonious and complete development of the whole of a child's faculties. The teacher should pay especial regard to the love of movement, which can alone secure healthy physical conditions; to the observant use of the organs of sense, especially those of sight and touch; and to that eager desire of questioning which intelligent children exhibit. All these should be encouraged under due limitations, and should be developed simultaneously, so that each stage of development may be complete in itself. . . . Indeed, it is often found that the kindergarten occupations are treated as mere toys, or amusing pastimes, because they are attractive for children, and the intellectual character of the 'Gifts of Froebel' is disregarded, whereas the main object of these lessons is to stimulate intelligent individual effort." The circular goes on to show how the different subjects can be interwoven with one another in the infants' school, and to suggest the necessity, and practical means, of proceeding from experience to ideas, and thence to verbal expression. Altogether this is a circular which is worthy of a true Education Department.

An even better circular on the instruction of lower standards in schools for older scholars appeared during the following year. In this it is asserted that scholars in the lower standards "are too often taught by arbitrary and conventional methods, and there is little in the general course of instruction to lead them to observe or to reason. Object-lessons are in many cases discontinued . . . and hand-and-eye occupations are very rarely found, . . . and it is to be feared that, when examined, they often reproduce knowledge which has been conveyed by methods which are not truly educational. It should be borne in mind that object-lessons cannot be dispensed with if habits of observation are to be duly fostered, and they should be treated as a means for mental exercise and not merely as opportunities for imparting miscellaneous information." The realistic method of teaching; the close interconnection of subjects to make them as mutually helpful as possible (the correlation of subjects); and the value of continued hand-and-eye training, are then dealt with. The learning of spelling through systematic word-building; the cultivation of the habit of answering in complete sentences, by the children; and the employment of women teachers who have had experience in infants' schools, are strongly advised.

The beginning of a fundamental change was quietly introduced in 1894 by the substitution of the system of inspection instead of examination for infants' schools. Not less than two visits without notice were to be made during a year. A part, or the whole, of the time during one school meeting was to be given to observing the general conduct and arrangement of the school, and in hearing lessons given. All the ordinary matters relating to registration, time-table, organization, discipline, &c., were to be inquired into and reported on. Teachers were to prepare, at the beginning of the year, a full syllabus showing the work of each class in each subject, and the gradation of these. This system of inspection was extended, in the following year, to all schools for older scholars "which have reached, upon the whole, a good educational standard". Only those schools "to which it might be necessary to apply a more exact test of efficiency" were still to be examined. This was afterwards changed, by implication, to "those schools likely to fall below the level of efficiency". At least two visits, as a rule, were to be made, and the first of these was to be "to note and record the strong and weak points of the school, as to its discipline, organization, and methods of instruction". At the second visit, the inspector was to be "careful to pay special attention to the weak points noted at the former visit and to note whether the general good character of the teaching is maintained". All the usual details of school management as required by the code were to be observed and reported on. Teachers were to draw up syllabuses and keep records of the work of each class, and the exercises and notebooks of the pupils were to be dated. After a visit of inspection, there was to be a conference between inspectors, managers, and teachers, with regard to securing any necessary improvements. Any serious defects were to be entered in the log-book.

The right attitude of mind of an inspector was admirably sketched in the following terms:—"The main and primary object of your visits is not to inflict penalties for defective points, but rather through your educational suggestions and influence to remove defects in the school management and instruction. . . . It is the desire of the Department that its officers should aim at being the helpful and sympathizing friends of all concerned in the work; and that, without dictating to managers or teachers, they should throw out suggestions, whether towards greater freedom of organization or in the direction of more effective educational work, and confer with all concerned both as to the general school arrangements and as to the details of the teaching." Surely for practical purposes no better expression of the inspectorial function could be desired. Certainly the idea of estimating a school as a whole represents a wholesome advance on the system which regarded the standards as convenient units for enabling inspectors mechanically to assign grants from the Treasury. The new order of things was welcomed with almost universal and heartfelt approval by teachers, and soon received general praise from inspectors for its practical value, as shown by its effects on school work. From this time the old order had definitely to change and give place to the new.

Still another admirable circular, expounding truly educational principles of method with regard to object-lessons, was sent out in 1895. The mere imparting of miscellaneous information was condemned, and the gaining of knowledge at first hand through direct observations of and judgments about objects held up as the end to be aimed at. The pith of the whole circular is well put in the following: "To sum up the main value of Object Teaching, there are three principal uses. The first and most important is to teach the children to observe, compare, and contrast; the second is to impart information; and the third is to reinforce the other two by making the results of them the basis for instruction in Language, Drawing, Number, Modelling, and other Handwork." Appended to the circular are nineteen excellently graduated syllabuses of instruction on plant life, animal life, the sky, the air, the surface of the land, water, object-lessons for town schools, object-lessons for country schools, object-lessons in the science of common things, and measuring, weighing, and testing. One other matter deserves special notice, viz. the fact that instruction in Swedish or other drill, or suitable physical exercises, was to be a condition for receiving the higher grant for discipline and organization, for any school whose year began after the 31st August, 1895. Of the immense value of this only those can really know who have had experience in teaching before and after such a condition.

For all these great and beneficent improvements the chief praise is due to the efforts of Mr. A. H. D. Acland, vice-president at the time, and the sympathetic and able co-operation of Sir G. Kekewich, the permanent secretary. Of the work of Mr. Acland it would be difficult to speak too highly, for he has probably studied more, worked more, and suffered more, for the cause of education than any other non-educationist (in the technical sense). He took a distinguished part in organizing intermediate education in Wales; and his work for English schools, as shown in the evening continuation code and the code for day-schools, should cause his name ever to be honoured in the annals of elementary education. He is an example—like Sir U. Kay-Shuttleworth—of the good that an able non-expert can do for what should be a scientific system, as Mr. Robert Lowe (Lord Sherbrooke) is of the evil that such an one can do.

During 1897 two more circulars dealing with school-work were issued, one on varied and suitable occupations for older scholars, and the other on the method of dealing with very backward children in schools for older scholars. The former enumerates the conditions which ought to be satisfied to make an occupation suitable; gives a list of subjects suitable for Standards I., II., and III.; and then suggests how such subjects may be made to bear upon the ordinary school subjects. In connection with this subject it is interesting to notice that the Code for 1895 says that one Suitable Occupation in Standards I., II., and III. is to be compulsory for those schools whose year began after 31st August, 1895. But, when most schools had prepared for this, and many had actually begun the work, the Department discovered, owing to the representations of the teachers, that the addition of this subject would overcrowd the time-tables; it was, therefore, made an optional subject. The other circular pointed out that those children who were very backward, through irregularity, slow development, or delicate health, required separate organization for their instruction and training. It was suggested that, where the numbers justified such a course, an additional teacher should be provided; the class should have a separate class-room, and be conducted as a preparatory mixed class; and the teacher should be one specially skilled in the training of older infants.

The present year, 1898, has begun well in the issue of a report on the pupil-teacher system by a Departmental Committee. This committee, consisting of four inspectors, five training college officials, two heads of pupil-teacher centres, and one headmaster of a voluntary school, has gone very thoroughly into the whole question, and has produced a very valuable report. Perhaps the most interesting feature thereof, to a student of the history of education, is the fact that they have rediscovered a truth which the Dutch discovered just at the time that the pupil-teacher system was introduced into England. After the pupil-teacher has for more than half a century been the mainstay of our education system; has received unqualified praise from most of the education officials; and is still believed, by some, to be the most effective teacher; after all this, the Committee reports thus: "we wish to record as emphatically as possible, at the outset of this report, our conviction that the too frequent practice of committing the whole training of classes to immature and uneducated persons is economically wasteful, educationally unsatisfactory, and even dangerous to the teachers and the taught in equal measure". And yet, at the present moment about one-third of the total of teachers at work in our primary schools consists of pupil-teachers, whilst no less than one-ninth (12,838) of the total consists of those who have not even the pretensions of the pupil-teacher, viz. "Article 68's", as they are called, that is, women over eighteen years of age who manage to appear not hopelessly incompetent in giving a routine lesson before an inspector. Well may the committee say that they "apprehend grave danger from their increase, which has been continuous, and, in our view, excessive".

The chief recommendations of the Committee involve the following reforms: the age of admission to be raised from 13 to 16 (15 in country schools); the number in a school to be strictly limited to two for the principal certificated teacher, and one for each additional certificated teacher; the juniors (first and second years) not to be employed in a school for more than four meetings a week, nor to be responsible for a class; and the seniors (third and fourth years) to attend only six meetings, and not to be responsible for a class exceeding twenty-five in average attendance. It is recommended that they should receive their instruction at central classes; or they might attend wholly at a secondary school for a certain portion of the apprenticeship. As to "Article 68", it is urged that only one should be allowed for each certificated teacher in a school, that every candidate should pass an entrance and an annual examination, and no additional teacher shall be recognized under this article after the year 1900.

The code for 1898 arranges that the inspection of drawing and manual instruction shall be transferred from the Science and Art authorities to the Education Department, and that the grants shall be paid upon reports based on inspection and not upon examination. The grant for "specifics" is no longer to be 2$s.$ or 3$s.$ per head according to the results of an examination, but 1$s.$ or 6$d.$, according to the inspector's report, for every complete 24 hours of instruction in the total of hours made by all the scholars, who have not received less than 40 or more than 60 hours' instruction. Thus the last item of payment according to the results of individual examination disappears. The reduction of the number of pupils to a teacher according to his qualifications, and the issue of combined schemes of geography and history, elementary science and geography, history and English, are two other important changes.

Of the parliamentary actions concerning education, since 1880, a brief record will be a sufficient account. A motion in the House of Lords, by Lord Norton, in 1880—he made several similar motions in subsequent years—"that the present introduction of secondary instruction in the publicly-aided elementary schools requires consideration; and that the Code of Regulations of the Committee of Council on Education be referred to a Select Committee for revision and simplification", deserves notice, because it expresses the feelings, and methods of attacks, of those who have had to acknowledge the advantages and permanent value of accomplished facts, and also because of a speech made by Lord Sherbrooke (Mr. Robert Lowe). He laid down the astounding doctrine that the three R's cannot be crammed, whilst the "specific" subjects were easy to cram. There was no doubt about whether a boy could read a piece of print, get some sums right, or do some writing; but it was quite easy to remember technical names and phrases, and reproduce them more or less accurately, without in the least intelligently understanding them. For his part he would give two-thirds of the grant for reading, and one-third for writing and arithmetic. If a boy was intelligent, and could read with ease, he would soon teach himself to cipher.

Anything more absurdly wrong than these ideas it is difficult to conceive. Lord Sherbrooke, when he was Vice-president, must have read reports from inspectors setting forth how children learnt off reading-books by rote, and would "go on" at any point, without looking at the book, if a phrase were given; and how the least change in the usual method of giving out sums adopted by a teacher entirely baffled the scholars. Inspectors resorted to the plan of making children read a passage backward, so as to make sure that they really knew the words. Teachers, in giving out such a number as 907, would say: "Nine hundred—*and*—seven", thus indicating the 0; and if the inspector then gave out, say "Three hundred—*and*—twenty-eight", the children would write down 3028. Indeed Lord Sherbrooke only showed in his speech, as a warning and example for all time, how profoundly ignorant a brilliant and able man can be in a technical subject which he has not studied; and the great need there is of educating our political masters.

In the same year, 1880, an Act was passed to amend the Act of 1870, with regard to the making of bye-laws to compel attendance at school. This, which had been optional, was now to be compulsory on all School Attendance Committees, or, in case of their default, the Education Department was to make them. Earl Spencer, in introducing the bill to the House of Lords, gave some interesting statistics. During the last ten years the number of schools had risen from just over eight thousand to over seventeen; the accommodation provided, from two to four million places; the names on the school registers, from just over one and a half to over three and a half millions; and the percentage of the scholars in average attendance from sixty-seven to seventy.

Three years later Sir J. Lubbock brought forward the motion: "That, in the opinion of this House, it is desirable that there should be a separate Department of Education". He pointed out that Lord Derby had recommended this in 1856, Sir J. Pakington in 1865, whilst Mr. Disraeli's government introduced a bill to create a Secretary of State for Education in 1868. All the control of the Department was, practically, in the hands of the vice-president, although the patronage was in the hands of the lord president. Such was the importance attached to the office in France that the Minister of Education was head of the government. But nothing came of the motion, as Mr. Gladstone held that the time had not yet arrived for such a step.

Towards the end of 1883 arose a great agitation concerning the over-pressure upon children in elementary schools. Questions were frequently asked in parliament about the matter, and harrowing details of illnesses and deaths, really or presumably due to overwork in schools, were published. Finally the Department appointed Dr. Crichton Browne to investigate the matter. The doctor drew up a scathingly condemnatory report, to which an official reply was made by Dr. Fitch. The result of all this was that the authorities inserted certain clauses—previously mentioned—in the code for 1884, which did much to relieve the undoubtedly severe pressure upon certain children caused by a combination of the effect of the mechanical classification by age; the payment on individual passes; the dependence of teachers' salaries upon the children's success; and the mechanical and unintelligent methods of teaching.

Directly connected with this question was that of the publication of the instructions to inspectors at the same time as the code for which they were drawn up. Practically these instructions constituted a superior code, for they interpreted, more or less, the spirit of the conditions and requirements laid down in the code itself. Yet it was a secret document so far as the teacher was concerned, until the end of the school year, when it might be used to heavily penalize him for having failed to divine the Department's interpretations of its own regulations. This matter was agitated within and without parliament, until the code and its interpretation were issued together.

A very sensible motion, if it had only been made quite general, was introduced in the House of Commons by Mr. Kerans (Lincoln) in 1888. It was to the effect that the principle of the parliamentary grant in aid of schools (voluntary) was unjust, and that it should be given rather in proportion to the poverty of the districts than their wealth. If only such a sound principle had been acted upon from the first, much more effective work would have been done throughout the country. But then this would mean making education a State matter; and the interests of the State in education have yet to rise superior to those of the sects. In the discussion on this motion Mr. Mundella informed the house that the 17s. 6d. limit was fixed by the fact that no school had previously earned more than 15s. 9d. per head, and it was not thought that they would ever go higher. The motion was allowed to drop on the plea, by Sir W. Hart-Dyke, that it would be wise to wait for the report of the Royal Commission, which was then sitting.

This commission drew up a report (1888), which was in many ways practically helpful, and led to some desirable reforms, though it cannot be said to be a profoundly scientific or very statesmanlike production. However, its recommendations concerning better conditions for pupil-teachers; the establishment of day training colleges, and the admission of day students to residential training colleges; the appointment of women as inspectors; the giving freedom of classification of scholars to managers; the teaching of drawing, object-lessons, and manual instruction; the establishment of an ex-VII. standard; the replacing of the "individual" and "merit" grants by "fixed" and "variable" grants; the reducing of the numbers of pupils in the charge of a single teacher; the introduction of physical training; and on other matters, have, for the most part, been adopted.

As indications of its limitations, we may state that it held that the three R's were the most important subjects for a child to know; that "free education" would be a mistake; that voluntary schools should be assisted out of the rates; that school boards should put an end to the interference of board school teachers in elections; and that voluntary management is better than school board management for the internal work of the school. The commission marks a step in progress in that Mr. T. E. Heller, the secretary of the National Union of Elementary Teachers—himself an ex-teacher, and an admirable and able representative of the profession—was a member of it.

Following this report, the Earl of Meath, in 1889, endeavoured to get the House of Lords to condemn the education code as defective, inasmuch as it failed to provide adequate facilities for the physical education of children attending elementary schools. He rightly insisted that whatever over-pressure existed in the schools was largely due to a too exclusive attention to training the mind, and that it was necessary to obtain physical hardness and force—sturdy arms and steady nerves, which were as important in peace as in war. Earl Fortescue said that a manufacturer had told him that a young man who had learnt drill was worth 1s. 6d. per week more in wages, since promptness in obeying the word of command was often of immense industrial importance, and prevented many accidents. Lord Cranbrook, the Lord President of the Council, urged that it would be very expensive to introduce Swedish drill and gymnastics, since special teachers would have to be employed, and that gymnastic exercises were too severe for weak children. He added that military drill was being introduced in the schools.

The conclusion of the Royal Commission concerning free education was soon to receive a practical refutation. In 1891 Sir W. Hart-Dyke, the Vice-president, introduced a bill providing for the payment of a "fee grant" in aid of the cost of elementary education in England and Wales. He accepted the principle that compulsory education should imply gratuitous education, and proposed that a grant of ten shillings per head, for all children from five to fourteen years of age, should be authorized. He estimated the cost at two millions per year. The following year he was able to announce that during the first three or four months of the operation of the Act the increase in the attendance of children at school had been enormous. The attendance of children at school was still further improved by a bill, introduced by Mr. Acland and passed in 1893, which raised the age at which a child might qualify for leaving school for labour from ten to eleven years.

A very sweeping change in the organization of schools was attempted three years later. Sir J. Gorst introduced a bill to secure the establishment in every county and county borough of a paramount authority on education. This was to be the one channel through which the education grant was to reach the schools; it was, in fact, to be a local education department. But it was to supplement, not to supersede, existing institutions. This authority was to be the County Council, acting through a Statutory Education Committee, the composition of the latter being entirely in the hands of the former, except that a majority of its members must be members of the County Council. Power was to be given to this committee to make such modifications in the code issued by the Education Department as they might think suitable to the particular local circumstances; and they were to administer a special aid grant of 4s. for each pupil in voluntary schools or necessitous board schools. If a reasonable number of the parents of children attending a school desired separate religious instruction for them, it was to be provided.

The bill was based upon recommendations made by several education commissions, and involved principles which had already been submitted to parliament in several bills previously noticed. It was, however, mismanaged in its progress through committee, and had to be withdrawn. But the idea of giving special aid to voluntary schools and necessitous board schools—but at the rate of 5s. per scholar—was carried out by two separate bills—"The Voluntary Schools Act" and "The Necessitous School Boards Act"—which were passed in 1897. The former also provided that voluntary schools should be exempted from rates; the seventeen-and-sixpence limit abolished; and that associations of voluntary schools should be formed, who should advise the Department as to the distribution of the special-aid grant. So that, after all, the principle of setting up local authorities to share in the administration of grant was partially realized.

Since 1880 the training colleges have made great advances in the courses they give their students. The study of such books as Spencer's *Education*, Sully's *Psychology for Teachers*, Fitch's *Lectures on Teaching*, Bain's *Education as a Science*, and Quick's *Educational Reformers*, has been prescribed by the Education Department; and the syllabus of work in general knowledge has been raised well up to the standard of an ordinary university degree. Some of the day training colleges offer university courses, under university conditions, and take their students through an advanced course of professional studies. Yet there is still a predominance of the "School Management" text-book as a sufficient source of knowledge, and students at the end of two years' training show a truly lamentable ignorance of the scientific principles of their professional work.

Chapter XI.

Retrospect and Prospect.

It is a melancholy series of successes which one passes in review when taking a backward look over the history of national education. Melancholy because of the disastrously slow progress, the woeful waste of energy in sectarian struggles, and the incomplete way in which the scraps of progress were seized upon. And the conviction is forced upon one that this was not so because men did not see the truth and know the good, but because partisans were suspicious that opponents might gain party advantage. One cannot help believing that had the people as a whole been appealed to, by universal vote, the plausible pretensions of religious advocates would have been swept away, as the mist before the rising sun, and a national system of education established half a century before the Act of 1870. Only once can the people be said to have shown any signs of real opposition to popular education.

One of the most interesting features which a retrospect reveals is the manner in which the alarmist fears of opponents to change have been almost invariably shown to be groundless, if not wholly absurd. The fear that education would make more, and cleverer, rogues and rascals has been shown to be entirely groundless. On the contrary, it is admitted on all sides that crime has very largely decreased in consequence of the spread of knowledge. Of course the rogue has been made a cleverer rogue, but the number of criminals has grown less, and other people have been made more capable of guarding themselves against roguery. Another argument against education was that the masses would become discontented, and overwhelm the richer classes by brute force, and then plunder and spoil the country. As a matter of fact the working-classes have become more and more constitutional, and less and less violent and revolutionary, as they have become more educated. Although there are regrettable instances to the contrary, yet, on the whole, the self-restraint, good temper, and common-sense of the workers, have made the reputation of the English workman a very enviable one, in social, industrial, and political crises.

The supporters of the voluntary system used to insist that voluntary subscription would cease altogether, if State schools were established side by side with denominational schools. Now it is their glory, and boast, that never was so much money given by voluntary subscribers. For example, from 1811 to 1870 Churchmen spent just over six million pounds on school buildings, whilst from 1870 to 1893 they expended just over seven million pounds. Not only Churchmen and earnest Nonconformists, but probably ninety-nine per cent of the people of the country, at one time believed that if dogmatic religious instruction were not given in the schools, the nation would in a few years consist of a godless and immoral community; whilst the very existence of the national church would be endangered. It is now claimed that never was the vitality of the churches so great, their members so numerous, their work so popular, and their stability so unquestionable.

Never have those directly and personally concerned had any religious difficulty with regard to the schools except in the sense that they objected to having other people's religious views forced upon their own children. Not the religious rights of the people, but the supposed rights of the clergy over the people's religious training, have constituted the bone of contention. Parents, as a whole, have been prepared to look after their children's religious affairs in their own way, but parsons have always wanted to look after them vicariously. The clergy have, with doubtless the best of intentions, been the great barrier to thorough and general progress. Under the plea of saving the souls of the children they have sacrificed their minds and bodies. They have themselves admitted that it has proved impossible for them to keep up their schools to the level of the board schools. Mr. Ernest Gray, M.P., himself a headmaster of a Church school and a Conservative member of parliament, said only the other day, with reference to the present London Voluntary Schools Association: "Certain Church dignitaries, mistaking altogether their functions and duties, had determined to retain these schools, utterly regardless of their pernicious influence upon the children attending them, because the clergy had not been able to carry on these schools in an efficient state, or in buildings which were satisfactory. Two of these schools had been closed within the last few weeks, by the sanitary authority, to be whitewashed. . . . The medical officer posted up in the schools:—'This school must be closed to abate a public nuisance'. They had paid teachers a starvation wage, and they had not paid the wage to time. . . . The London Diocesan Board, which was now the Federation, had reduced the salaries of the teachers, and some of the schools were so dirty that he would not keep a dog in a place where he had seen young girls being taught."

One by one the great fundamental principles of a national system of schools have been slowly and painfully rescued from the bottomless pit of sectarian envy and jealousy. Meantime, hundreds of thousands of children had been, more or less, intellectually, and therefore morally, starved, stunted, and sterilized. Painfully convincing evidence of this is to be found in the appalling evidence of vice and degradation of both young and old, brought out by the inquiries of the education commissions. And even when this made all men cry out for something to be done, only a poor and inefficient machinery was brought into existence. Schools which were mainly four walls with windows, and teachers who had almost every qualification that was opposed to fitness for the work, were the means appointed to do the work which should purge the nation of a great danger and a greater reproach. Little by little, and at long intervals, were slight improvements made. Never did unwisdom make haste more slowly to seize time by the forelock, though opportunity turned its flowing locks full in her face.

Much there has been, in the way of achievement, for which we may be truly grateful, but not unduly proud. The masses of our children have been gathered into the schools, and have enjoyed the advantages of an ever-increasing and improving syllabus of instruction, at the hands of more experienced, capable, and devoted teachers. The lives of the young have been made happier, their bodies healthier and stronger, their minds more skilful and learned, and their morals higher and truer, by the influence of our schools. Many a school building is a real palace of delight to the children—especially infants' schools—where they are far more kindly treated than at home, have cleaner, bigger, and brighter rooms to live their little lives in, and are kept in a constant state of cheerfulness and profitable activity. Many a teacher is a truer mother, or father, to their pupils than the real parents. They comfort them in their little troubles, share their joys, provide games and entertainments for them during summer and winter, often find the means to clothe and feed them in hard times, and sacrifice their time and money for them in ways completely outside their professional duties. There are schools which give a real pleasure and delight to visitors capable of appreciating what is meant by excellent tone and discipline. And this is not only good for the children, it is good for their homes, and thus for the future social life of the nation.

Higher grade and organized science schools are doing a great work as "finishing schools" for those who cannot go to secondary schools, even if they obtain scholarships for that purpose. It will be a real hardship to the children of the poor if such schools cease to be available for such. If they were regarded as the "college" of the elementary school, they would fill a real place in the primary branch of a national system. On such a principle they should be largely multiplied, placed in convenient centres, and remain an essential feature of the system of primary schools. Evening schools might well be the technical schools for the workers.

Scholarship schemes have become numerous and fairly general, though much still remains to be done. The best schools—some of them in the poorest neighbourhoods—have highly distinguished themselves by their success in winning scholarships; and they supply some of the most successful pupils in some of the most successful secondary schools. But only a very limited number of scholars—chiefly from the aristocracy of the artisan class and small tradesmen—seem ever likely to take the step which leads to a secondary education, and possibly to the university. The primary system should, therefore, to a large extent, be a self-contained whole.

We must not, however, in looking back upon the past, be too self-righteous in our condemnations. It is still possible to find school buildings which would not be strange to the pupils of fifty years ago, school methods which would be perfectly familiar to them, and ideals thriving now which governed them then. To-day we have no less than forty-seven per cent of our teachers untrained, except that some of them have gone through the routine experiences of pupil-teachers. A considerable proportion of those who do the most delicate and difficult work, viz. the teaching of infants and the lower standards, are without any pretence of previous training or experience, the only qualifications required from them being that they are over eighteen years of age, respectable, and approved by the inspector. Only last year the following advertisement appeared in a Cumberland paper: "Schoolmistress wanted, for Dame School at Berrier, to teach reading, writing, and arithmetic, also knitting and sewing. Salary, £6 per year and free house. The wife of a shoemaker or working-man might suit."

Has all this no value for us, except for regret? Are we not yet wise enough to recognize our ignorance, and learn from our failures to seek first if there be any knowledge already possessed, which might save us from continuing to go forward as though stumbling through a pathless country, while, as a matter of fact, good roads have already been made through it?

It should be a truism that as the teacher so is the school. A good teacher triumphs in spite of adverse mechanical and material surroundings. How much more, therefore, will he succeed with these in his favour! What are we doing then to secure this life-giving element in our schools, without which all else is but dead? Undoubtedly capable and brilliant men and women have been attracted to the profession. Many teachers in elementary schools are graduates of London, and some of Oxford and Cambridge. One assistant-mistress in a London Board School is a Doctor of Science of London, has passed through an Oxford course, and had a most distinguished career as a student. Some of the most successful head-teachers of public and private secondary schools have been drawn from the ranks of teachers in elementary schools. Scholars, wranglers, fellows, and dons at Oxford and Cambridge are men who have been pupils and teachers in the schools of the people. Men holding high positions in Church and State have the proud distinction of having risen from such beginnings. As a body, it is probably true to say of the teachers in our public primary schools that they have no superiors, as practical teachers, in the world. And yet it is also probably not untrue to say of them that not one per cent of them are true educators. They have been trained to the last state of complete preparation to be practical teachers, they have not been taught and trained to be educators; and at present the teaching in our schools is, as a whole, but little better than the most intelligent form of cramming.

Ought not, therefore, the training of our teachers to be true educators to be the first feature of future reform? Should not the mental sciences be the main part of their training, and should these not be studied in the same way as other natural sciences? This is being done, in one or two cases, in the training colleges at present. The mental sciences must be studied not only as pure sciences, but as applied sciences. They must be applied in the school. The practising school must be the laboratory of the training college, at least up to the point at which it does not thereby suffer as a school. And this study of education as pure and applied science must be a concentrated one. To make it an incident in the struggle to get a higher literary and general education, is to invite failure with respect to it. Very little that is valuable is likely to result until the two are separated. If three years of training were made universal, the first two might be given wholly to the finishing of the general education, and the last wholly to the study of purely professional subjects. Most of those who have had experience in the matter believe that such an arrangement would be of the greatest possible advantage.

Immediately connected with this is the question whether every training college ought not to be at least affiliated to, if not locally connected with, an institution of university standing. To take young men and women from the strict limitations, and severely narrowing influences, of the pupil-teacher life, and shut them up in training colleges, where they still further accentuate and intensify their professional traits by contact with only those who have similar experiences, thoughts, habits, aims, and pursuits, is hardly the best way to develop broad and generous intellectual and social sympathies. Living and working with those who have had different trainings, are pursuing different courses of study, and have different modes of thought, has a formative and developing influence upon personal character, which only those who have experienced both, or closely studied them, can appreciate. More than half the value of residence at Oxford or Cambridge comes from this. And not only is this lost, but the conduct of training colleges must, surely, entirely cease to be of the half-school, half-barracks order. Self-dependence and the right ordering of one's own life, within reasonable limits, ought to be encouraged to the greatest possible extent. The theory of self-governance was a deadly heresy according to the traditions of fifty years ago; and it is a question if these do not still survive. Where impositions are given, fines imposed, and students addressed by their Christian names; where they march in pairs to and from church, and where to have an opinion of your own is to be in conflict with the authorities; such are not the institutions to turn out wise rulers of others. If training colleges have any of these features, they are, so far as their government is concerned, but boarding-schools for adults, and not of a generous order.

To the reproach of training colleges, it must be said, that whilst they should have been the centres from which new light and leading continually came forth, as a matter of fact they have been the last to recognize and utilize the advances which have been made and have become well established in principle and practice. With a few honourable exceptions, such things as scientific pedagogy, Herbartianism, Froebel's kindergarten, Pestalozzi's principles, and the like, are regarded in some training colleges as but terms used by theorists. Young students fresh from college, in their moments of frankness, candidly avow that School Management is all very well for examinations, but they never think of bothering about it in school. Moreover, students are not by any means fully prepared during their course of training for the work they will have to do in schools. Many subjects have to be learnt afterwards in evening classes. Another element of weakness in these institutions is the fact that vacancies in the staff are generally filled up by the ablest student of the second year at the time. The

Retrospect and Prospect. 243

result of this is the perpetuating of traditions, which become a serious hindrance to progress.

Formerly this kind of treatment was justified, at least to the minds of the authorities, by the statement that any other course would result in a moral and mental disaster to the students. But such superstitions are no longer excusable, since Day Training Colleges prove the exact opposite. At these, or, at least, at some of them, the usual liberty of university life is allowed, and nothing very dreadful from the official point of view has happened, whilst from the students' stand-point very much advantage has resulted. Of course there are the bad cases which will come to grief under any system. But if we desire as teachers those who will form and regulate rightly the early lives of their pupils, we must have those who have learned to regulate their own lives wisely and well by their own wisdom and self-control; not those who have lived under a system which does the greatest possible amount for them, and leaves them to do the least possible amount for themselves.

Another matter which seems open to amendment is the syllabus of work gone through by those who become teachers. As pupil-teachers they repeat all the work which they did, and are supposed to have done satisfactorily in the standards; and as students in training they, in their first year, repeat what they have done as pupil-teachers. Of course in each case they do something more than this, but the question remains whether it ought to be necessary to have this double repetition. If this were done away with, as it easily might by insisting that in each case the work should be thoroughly well done, then every trained teacher should be able to take a university degree as a part of his, or her, college course. Many do this already both at the Residential and Day Training Colleges. But it is to be feared that under present conditions this involves very serious pressure, if not dangerous over-pressure—a matter which seems urgently to demand investigation.

Above and beyond all there would appear to be wanting that proper use of expert technical knowledge for guiding and controlling the technical machinery. The failures in the past have been largely due to the fact that the knowledge and interests of those with influence and authority have not included special knowledge of the proper work of the school, nor a real interest in the success of the school as such. Their knowledge and interests were both connected with the church, or with the state; and it was in relation to these that they regarded the existence and work of the school as useful, or otherwise Now it may seem a strange thing to say that the school must primarily exist for itself, and only secondarily for the advantage of the churches and the state. And yet this must be the case. With liberty of conscience in religion, and freedom of thought in politics, it is an injustice to the community to endeavour to make a churchman or a nonconformist, a monarchist or a republican, through the agency of the nation's schools. Just as education (as such) seeks not to form a statesman, a carpenter, a soldier, a merchant, or any particular kind of worker, but a being so well and harmoniously developed as to be best fitted, so far as his natural powers allow, to do his very best in any particular direction whatsoever; so the school must aim to produce a moral,—surely it is unnecessary to protest that morality is entirely distinct from religions, though not religion,—intellectual, and physical being, who shall be capable of becoming the very best that is possible for him, as a member of the church, the state, and society at large.

If this be so, then the school should be directly governed, as a school, no more by the state than by the church; but by those best fitted by special knowledge to devise the means for enabling it to fulfil its proper functions. And who are these, if not those who have spent their lives in gaining the knowledge and skill necessary for conducting schools—the teachers, and trained scientific educators? This may sound like revolution; but it is not so. No substantial change of the present machinery for controlling schools is involved; but only a supplement, and limitation and definition of functions. At the present moment the London and other school boards very wisely and properly call to their aid committees of teachers to collect evidence, and draw up recommendations with regard to certain internal matters of school work. Make this statutory, and school government will be reformed and transformed, though not revolutionized. In other words, the proper function of the popularly-elected ratepayer is to look after the rates, not to devise and determine schemes of education. He who pays the piper, doubtless has thereby some right to call the tune, but absolutely no capacity is thereby imparted to him for composing the tune. Yet the law at present gives these popularly-elected ratepayers full control over the ordering of the education in their schools, within the limits laid down by the code. They are the "managers", who are empowered to do this, that, and the other in classifying scholars, selecting alternative or extra subjects, &c. And in some cases they insist on doing such things. It is even possible for a very ignorant (technically) school board clerk to rule both the board and the schools, and become the veriest despot in the internal life of the schools.

To suggest that because Mr. X is the most intelligent, able, and popular workman in a certain town, and receives a large majority of votes from his fellow-workers, he thereby becomes competent to sit in judgment on, and control the technical work of all the architects in that town; or that Squire Y, who owns three-fourths of a district, becomes capable, by a process of popular election, to supervise and have authority over the work of the bishop and clergy of the diocese, is to propose ideas that are too absurd to be even read about with patience. But do they not, in any way, apply to the case of school boards and schools, so far as the purely technical work of the latter is concerned? What then is the remedy? To make it a law that all school boards, and other public elementary schools' authorities, shall be assisted in their work by a consultative committee of experts, chosen from teachers—not limited to the district—by the teachers of the district governed by such authorities. No scheme for the internal work of the school should be put into force unless approved by this committee, subject to appeal to the central authority.

Other matters to be dealt with by the school board as at present.

Some consideration might profitably be given to the securing of reasonable uniformity in our schools. A step in this direction has lately been taken by the London School Board, by making the school year begin in July in every one of its schools. The practical gain from this will be very great, for however often a pupil may change from one district to another—and many thousands change very frequently—he can take up the class work in a new school at the point where he left off in the old. Hitherto the probability has been that a child was likely to be put back, and there has undoubtedly been a serious waste in this way. There seems to be every reason for making such a plan uniform throughout the country, and no very serious objection to it.

This is by no means the only, or the most valuable, instance of desirable and possible uniformity. Take the subject of writing as taught in our schools. The number of different styles is a positive hindrance to good work in writing. In one and the same building one may find that one style is taught in the infants' department, only to be changed to a different one when the children go to the senior departments—the styles being different in the boys' and girls' departments. It is no exaggeration to say that a child may be required, if it changes schools, to learn four or five different styles of writing in one year. Not only a great economy of time and effort, but the prevention of much bad writing would be effected by an authoritative set of copy-books. Is it not generally as mistaken to sacrifice reasonable uniformity to intense individuality, as to sacrifice individuality to unreasonable uniformity?

Similarly in other subjects, the existence of a set of authoritative books would have many and great advantages. The principal rule to be observed with regard to these would be that in such subjects as reading, arithmetic, geography, grammar, history, &c., the books should only cover the ground represented by the minimum requirements in each case. This would secure an indispensable freedom for teacher and scholar in everything beyond, whilst it gave all the advantages which reasonable uniformity offers. With such a system, combined with correspondence of school year, a child going from one extreme of the country to the other would at once fall into his right place in a school. Teachers would know exactly what they could take for granted in the new scholar, in a general sense, and the pupil would be familiar with the groundwork of the teaching in his new school.

There would be no real difficulty in compiling such series. A representative committee of teachers, chosen by the general body of teachers, acting with a committee of inspectors appointed by the Education Department, would do all that was required. The principle is working with success in our colonies and on the Continent, and would be likely to work well here. The objection that this would be likely to stereotype education is an idle one. The true basis of the best individuality is always found in a general conformity in universal elements. The best way to bring out differences to the greatest advantage is first to cultivate similarities to a reasonable extent. Make sure of the minimum and the maximum is the better able to take care of itself. More especially are these things true when we have to deal with groups, and those not small ones. It is, as a matter of fact, done at the present moment. All the schools using the reading books, arithmetic books, grammar books, &c., issued by certain publishers, have formed themselves into such groups as are suggested. The only point at issue is whether it would not be wise to make the same thing universal. The element of variety could be provided for by having alternative sets, to be used, say, every other period of three years. By this means the best materials in our best schools would be shared in by all, whilst the inferior material which is found in some schools would be entirely cleared away.

Another matter of great moment to the progress of education is the unification of authorities, and, consequently, the codification of regulations and laws. At present there is a multiplicity of authorities, and, therefore, much confusion, conflict, and overlapping. All men seem agreed that a Ministry of Education is required, and, as usual, this seems the only and sufficient objection to establishing it. A Minister of Education, assisted by an Education Council consisting wholly of experts and specialists, would be likely to secure that which we most lack at present, viz. a true organic life in the internal work of our schools, living principles which give purpose, cohesion, and system to it, and upon which all regulations and detail depend, and ought to be able to bring order out of the present chaos of grades, authorities, schemes, &c. It could deal with such a question as the training of students who were to become teachers and inspectors, and might find it worth while to establish state training colleges. The matter of a "leaving certificate" for primary schools would doubtless be considered by it. At present the work of these schools seems likely to suffer from insufficiency of examination as they have previously suffered from excess of it. From such a ministry should proceed scientifically sound and authoritative opinions and guidance, which might do much to discount the mischievous effect of irresponsible chatter. At present almost anyone who is specially unqualified for the work writes leading articles, pamphlets, or books on the subject. Any empirical blunderer who has happened upon what is to him a discovery seems to believe that nobody knows anything about education except what he has to tell. All the talk about the "new education" is only a confession of supreme ignorance about the old and true. The honest cobbler of yesterday is the school-board member of to-day, and the so-called educationist—probably "new"—of to-morrow, and every person with ordinary intelligence thinks himself thereby qualified to make experiments in education.

An Education Council would, one may venture to hope, lay it down as a sound principle of education that not reading, writing, and arithmetic, but such subjects as nature knowledge (object-lessons, science, geography, &c.); language (English, &c.); manual, physical, and moral training; are the true obligatory subjects. The

Retrospect and Prospect.   249

three R's are essential, but they are secondary. We must first have vitality and living tissue before we can build up a framework of dry bones to support our body of real knowledge. Pupils must have experiences and thoughts concerning real things before forms of expressions are either possible, necessary, or useful to them. Let writing as the recording of thought, reading as the re-expression of recorded thought, and arithmetic as the mechanical shorthand for recording and manipulating thoughts concerning quantities, take their proper places as the mechanical pegs on which we hang knowledge, and no longer pretend to be either the substance or even the sustenance of knowledge.

Just as the principle of helping those schools least which want it most still holds, so the children who need the longest periods at school escape with the shortest. Often the bright but weakly child, who badly needs the sheltering ease of the school, passes the necessary labour certificate examination and leaves at the earliest possible moment; and then maybe has to do work which overtaxes the feeble strength, under conditions which press still more severely on the sickly body. The lazy and the dull hang on till the limit of age, miserably fail in the attempt to pass the poor examination, and then get what is known as the "dunce's certificate", *i.e.* one which excuses them because of attendance at school. The blue-book for 1896–7 says: "Bradford, 1440 children, irregular in attendance, ignorant and dull, with malformed habits, who need to remain at school for a longer period than other children, find a ready escape from the salutary influence of the school by means of this certificate".

Then there is the terrible waste through irregular attendance, and it would seem that not until a special machinery is set up for dealing with this will our compulsory laws ever really compel. The last blue-book points out that though the attendance of children at schools still shows steady improvement, it is not yet entirely satisfactory, and in some districts much remains to be done in enforcing attendance. One inspector complains that some country gentlemen who are loud in their praises of law weaken the law-abiding habits of the people by the example they set in illegally hiring boys to "beat" for them when shooting. Another says that some school boards continue to be very remiss in enforcing attendance, that farmers are unwilling to keep children from the fields, and that as a result of such examples children stay away from school for no other reason than that no firm authority is exercised to check irregularity. A third writes very strongly on the matter, and says that rural local authorities may be given up as hopeless, for they are largely composed of people indifferent, if not actively hostile, to education, and interested in obtaining cheap child-labour. They pay their attendance officer a salary hardly sufficient to buy the boot-leather he consumes in his tramps through a large area —sometimes so large that a school is fortunate if it is visited once a month. Some of the blame for the miserably irregular attendance rests upon the magistrates, who treat bad cases with a mistaken, or prejudiced, leniency.

Until public opinion is educated up to the true value of education, probably the best thing to do would be—as proposed by the National Union of Teachers—to have inspectors of attendance appointed by the Education Department, whose business it should be to investigate and report upon the condition of attendance in certain districts, with special references to the causes of irregularity. The Home Office might then do something authoritative to cause magistrates to enforce the law, instead of their own private prejudices, in districts where it was shown that the compulsory regulations were not properly administered. If, besides this, it was made a rule that the age limit should be raised in the case of those who failed to make a certain number of attendances each year, there would, probably, not be much ground for reasonable complaint as to irregular attendance.

From the practical point of view, the only solution of the present difficulties appears to be the payment of a grant sufficient for carrying on the work of each school efficiently without any condition other than that the work of the school as a whole shall be thoroughly satisfactory. Then there would be a real and complete liberty for putting into practice true educational principles. There would no longer be any need for insisting on certain subjects being taught because another shilling or so, per head, of grant is earned. Teachers and inspectors could work together to secure the very best curriculum for a school with a view to purely educational ends. But the grant would have to be such that well-qualified and well-paid teachers, small classes, good and sufficient apparatus, and convenient and commodious premises could in all cases be secured. Give all the conditions and materials for doing well, and punish only those who are responsible for bad work in spite of good opportunities. Then should our primary schools be the first schools for all learners, and not merely the schools for the poor.

We have all the raw material out of which to make a splendid system of schools. There remain but two things to be done to make practically perfect our system of national education, viz. to make it national, and to make it educational.

Index.

Abbott, George, 9.
Acland, Mr. A. H. D., 226, 233.
Act, Free Education, 233.
,, Necessitous Board Schools, 234.
,, Voluntary Schools, 203, 234.
,, "1870", 181–7.
,, "1876", 201.
Adderley, Mr., 173.
Agriculture, 214–5.
Aim of schools, 19–22, 195, 200, 211–2, 215, 218–9, 243–4.
Alfred the Great, 11.
Aristotle, 23.
Arnold, Matthew, 172, 196–8.
"Article 68", 206, 228.
Ascham, Roger, 24.
Ashley, Lord, 81.
Attendance at school, 210, 249–50.
Aubrey, John, 18.

Bain, Dr., 234.
Battersea College, 103–4.
Bell, Dr., 40–1.
Benefit of Clergy, 12.
Bill, Education, "Borough", 146.
,, ,, Brougham's, 57, 75–6.
,, ,, "Parochial Schools", 54.
,, ,, Fox's, 142.
,, ,, Graham's, 81–2.
,, ,, Hume's, 83.
,, ,, Marlborough's, 176.
,, ,, "Of Children", 177.
,, ,, "Of Poor", 175.
Blake, Wm., 28.

Blomfield, Bishop, 72, 73.
Boards of Education, 155.
British and Foreign Schools Society, 38, 102.
Brougham, Lord, 55, 69.
Butler, Bishop, 33.

Canada, schools in, 50.
Certificates, teachers', 124, 126, 134, 189.
Charity schools, 28–35.
Church and State, and schools, 72–4.
Classification of scholars, 131, 216, 250.
"Class subjects", 193, 198, 211, 215.
Clergy and the schools, 102.
Cobden, 141, 146.
Code, "The Revised", 163–70.
,, "The New", 188.
,, "The Mundella", 208–13.
Colquhoun, Mr., 65.
Comenius, 25, 26.
Committee of Council, 147, 150, 174.
Compulsory attendance, 201–2, 230.
Conscience clause, the, 132.
Cram, 172.
Curriculum of schools, 131, 163, 194.

Day training colleges, 218.
Dekker, 12.
Denison, Archdeacon, 72, 157.
Dixon, Mr., 185.
Dutch schools, 93, 194.
Duty towards God, 153.

Education, true, 195, 248.
Education Department, the, 67-8, 135.
Education League, the, 178.
"Elementary subjects", 211.
Elyot, Sir Thomas, 23.
Erasmus, 23.
Evening schools, 125, 134, 221.
Ewart, Mr., 84.
Examination of schools, 158, 216, 247-8.
"Exception Schedule", 167.

Fitch, Sir J., 145, 177, 234.
Forster, Mr. W. E., 182, 204.
Fortescue, Earl, 233.
Fox, Mr., 142, 144.
Froebel, 47-8.

Giddy, Mr., 54.
Girls in Charity schools, 33.
Gladstone, Mr., 72-3.
Gorst, Sir J., 233.
Grammar schools, 15-16.
Grants to schools, 59, 80, 81, 87-90, 94, 95, 97, 115-6, 118-9, 123, 125, 128-31, 155, 157-9, 169, 188-9, 192-4, 198, 209, 216, 221-2, 228, 231.
Gray, Mr. E., 237.
Gregory, Dean, 203.

Hart-Dyke, Sir W., 215, 233.
Heller, Mr. T. E., 232.
Herbart, 27, 48.
Higher Grade schools, 238.
Holland, schools in, 49.
Home and Colonial College, 42.
Hook, Dr., 148.
Hooker, 20.
Hullah, Mr., 80, 94.
Hume, 83.

Industrial schools, 202.
Infants' schools, 133, 136, 213, 219, 222-3.
Inspectors of returns, 188.

Inspectors of schools, 91, 96, 97-8, 120-1, 137-40, 190, 196, 204-5, 209, 224-5.
Instructions to Inspectors, 121, 211, 231.
Ireland, grant for education, 55.
 ,,   schools in, 50.
Irish Board of Commissioners, 71.
Isle of Man, schools in, 144.

Jesuits, 22, 30.
Jews' schools, 125.
Johnson, Dr., 11, 46.

Kay-Shuttleworth, Sir J. P., 99-101, 159.
Kay-Shuttleworth, Sir U., 227.
Keble, 72.
Kekewich, Sir G., 215, 226.
Ken, Bishop, 28.
Kennet, Dr., 29.
Kerans, Mr., 231.
King's Somborne School, 200.
Kneller Hall, 69, 147.

Lancashire Public School Association, 149.
Lancaster, Joseph, 37-40.
Lansdowne, Lord, 84.
Latimer, R., 18.
Latin, method of teaching, 14-5.
Leach, Mr. A. F., 10.
Lecky, Prof., 27, 85.
Locke, John, 26.
Lowe, Mr. R. (Lord Sherbrooke), 156, 170-1, 203, 226, 229.
Lubbock, Sir J., 200.

Macaulay, 73.
Malthus, 45.
Management clauses, 123, 144-5, 244.
Manchester School Board, 203.
Mandeville, 31-2.
Manual training, 217.
Meath, Earl of, 232.
Merit grant, 209, 216.
Methods, in schools, 98-9, 122, 207-8, 222-6.

Index. 255

Milton, 25-6.
Ministry of Education, 174, 176, 247-8.
Monitors, system of, 107-10.
Montaigne, 24.
More, Sir Thomas, 28.
Moss, Dr., 30.
Mulcaster, 17, 24, 27.
Mundella, Mr., 205, 208.
Museum, educational, 120, 137.

National Education Union, 178.
National Society, the, 38, 42, 44.
National Union of Teachers, 250.
New England, schools in, 51.
Newton, Sir Isaac, 11.
Norton, Lord, 229.

Over-pressure in schools, 214, 230-1.
Overton, Dr., 71.

Pakington, Sir J., 147, 150, 174.
Payment by results, 136, 157, 188.
Pensions for teachers, 116, 119.
Pestalozzi, 46-7.
Petty, Sir W., 27.
Plans of schools, 92, 96.
Pounds, John, 44.
Progress, points of, 43, 52-4, 57-8, 66-7, 78, 85-6, 94-5, 101, 106, 110-4, 140, 159, 162, 173, 181, 187, 205-6, 207, 217, 235-9.
Prussia, schools in, 49.
Punishment in schools, 16.
Pupil-teacher system, the, 116-8, 125, 168, 203, 219-20, 227-8.
Pupils as teachers, 15.

Quarterly Journal of Education, 60.
"Queen's Scholars", 118, 132.
Quick, Mr., 22, 234.
Quintilian, 23.

Rabelais, 25.
Ragged schools, 128.
Rathbone, Mr., 204.

Reading, method of teaching, 13.
Reformation, schools at, 11, 20.
Registered teachers, 132.
Religious teaching, in schools, 141-142, 145, 148, 236.
Report of Commission (1888), 232.
Roebuck, Mr., 62, 83.
Roman Catholics' schools, 123.
Rose, Mr., 78.
Rousseau, 46.
Royal Commission, 150-6.
Russell, Lord John, 64, 148, 176.

Salisbury, Lord (Cecil), 134, 174.
Samson, Abbot, 12, 13.
Samuelson, Mr., 203.
School apparatus, grants for, 122.
School books, early, 200.
School staff, 133, 194, 210.
Science and Art Department, 179-80, 206-7.
Scotland, schools in, 50.
Seneca, 23.
Seventeen-and-sixpence limit, 202-3, 231.
Sick children at examination, 169.
Sinclair, Archdeacon, 77.
Small schools, 168.
Smith, Adam, 44.
Society for Promoting Christian Knowledge, 29.
"Specific subjects", 170, 189-90, 211.
Spencer, Herbert, 11, 161, 234.
Stanhope, Earl, 54-5.
Stanley, Lord, 69-70.
Sully, Dr., 234.
Sunday-schools, 36-7.

Teachers' qualifications, 18, 42-3, 103-7, 127, 136, 154, 218-9, 240-3.
Teachers' salaries, 105, 119.
Temple, Rev. F., 147, 168.
Training colleges, 102, 135, 159-61, 199, 203-4, 234, 242.

Uniformity in schools, 245-7.

Varied occupations, 226-7.
Vives Ludovicus, 24.

Ward schools, 32.
Watts, Dr., 31.
Whitbread, Mr., 54.

Wilderspin, Samuel, 41.
Working-men and education, 78-9, 143.
Writing, method of teaching, 13-4.
Wyse, Mr., 63-4, 68.

PRINTED BY BLACKIE AND SON, LIMITED.

www.ingramcontent.com/pod-product-compliance
Lightning Source LLC
Chambersburg PA
CBHW021406230426

43666CB00006B/649